ON THE PREPARATION AND DELIVERY OF SERMONS

On the Preparation and Delivery of Sermons

JOHN A. BROADUS

Fourth Edition

Revised by VERNON L. STANFIELD

1817

Published in San Francisco by Harper & Row, Publishers

NEW YORK / HAGERSTOWN / SAN FRANCISCO / LONDON

Designed by Jim Mennick

Library of Congress Cataloging in Publication Data

Broadus, John Albert, 1827–1895.
  ON THE PREPARATION AND DELIVERY OF SERMONS.

  First ed. published in 1870 under title: A treatise on the preparation and
delivery of sermons.
  Bibliography.
  Includes index.
  1. Preaching. I. Stanfield, Vernon L. II. Title.
BV4211.2.B678 1979   251   79–15005
ISBN 0–06–061112–X

84 85 10 9 8 7 6 5 4

Contents

Preface to the Fourth Edition

AS a second-year student in Southern Baptist Theological Seminary, I began a study of homiletics in the fall of 1942. The primary text used for this study was E. C. Dargan's revision of John A. Broadus, *On the Preparation and Delivery of Sermons.* The instructor for the class was J. B. Weatherspoon, the author of the third edition of *On the Preparation and Delivery of Sermons.*

In the fall of 1946, I began to teach preaching at the Southern Baptist Theological Seminary. For thirty-two years I have used *On the Preparation and Delivery of Sermons* as a text. I have not done this out of loyalty to the Broadus tradition or to my former professor, Dr. Weatherspoon. I have done so because it remains the most complete text for the study of homiletics. I have used many supplemental texts, but no other text has matched Broadus for complete basic material.

This edition of *On the Preparation and Delivery of Sermons* attempts several things: (1) to delete material that has become dated and therefore less important, (2) to add material that is more contemporary, (3) to rearrange the contents to make them conform to the regular sermon-building task, and (4) to call attention to a broad range of homiletical literature. The last has been done by extensive notes located at the end of chapters and by lists of books For Further Reading given at the end of each part. These additional books are not generally cited in the notes. The lists For Further Reading generally include contemporary books on preaching, while the notes more often cite classic works published in the last one hundred years.

I have tried to give credit were credit was due, but I am certain that bits and pieces of many books on preaching have become a part of my mental store. For any omissions of credit I apologize.

On the Preparation and Delivery of Sermons has been helpful to preachers for more than a century. My hope is that it will have a continuing usefulness in our time. Increasing enrollments presently characterize many seminaries. The churches are pleading for preachers who can preach. It is my sincere hope that the principles which have helped several generations of preachers will help the present one.

VERNON L. STANFIELD

New Orleans, Louisiana
March, 1979

Preface to the
Third Edition

THE first edition of Broadus's *Preparation and Delivery of Sermons* was published in 1870. In 1897 it was revised by Dr. E. C. Dargan, student of Dr. Broadus and his successor as professor in the Department of Homiletics at Louisville. That revision was made largely on the basis of Dr. Broadus's own notes and suggestions made in numerous conversations with the reviser. In 1926 Dr. C. S. Gardner, successor to Dr. Dargan, revised the bibliography, classifying and appraising the principal works on preaching. That the book has been in constant and increasing use since its first appearance and after three quarters of a century remains the outstanding textbook of Homiletics is full justification for its continuance.

At the request of the publishers, and with the consent and generous co-operation of Mrs. Ella Broadus Robertson, daughter of Dr. Broadus, the task of making such further revision as the passing years require is now undertaken by still another professor in the department where the book was born. He accepts the task with humble appreciation of the honor of standing in so noble a succession as Broadus, Dargan, and Gardner, and in the belief that a revised Broadus will have greater worth for the next generation of preachers than a new book. Few if any books on Homiletics have been able to achieve the comprehensiveness, the timelessness, and, withal, the simplicity of Broadus. Refusing to yield to the temptation to impose on the student his own favorite methods, he gave steadfast attention to principles and tested procedures, bringing to his aid the classical works of the centuries which bore upon the art of preaching. For that reason the book still lives and even now needs revision only in secondary matters.

In the present edition the purpose has been to retain the essential character of the work of Dr. Broadus. Teachers, however, will find numerous changes—condensations, expansions, restatements, omissions, insertions—which cannot be explained in a preface. It is hoped that they will commend themselves as being wholly in the interest of present-day students.

Perhaps the most obvious changes will be observed in the plan of the book. In former editions all the material elements of the sermon were included in Part I. This has been divided into two parts: the one, Foundations of the Sermon, including chapters on the Text, Interpretation of Texts, the Subject (a new chapter), Classification of Subjects, and the General Materials of the Sermon; the other, Functional Elements of the Sermon, including chapters on Explanation, Argument, Illustration, and Application. Between these two, Part II of earlier editions is inserted as the Formal Elements of the Sermon, in keeping with teaching practice as followed by most teachers, including Dr. Broadus himself. The remaining parts of the book follow the order of previous editions. Part V, dealing with methods of preparation and delivery presents a rearrangement of material, with an enlargement of the discussion of methods of preparation, bringing to the student the advantages of the practice of outstanding modern preachers.

Other changes are based on the observed needs of students over a period of years. The chapter on Interpretation of Texts has been somewhat reduced, but with the hope that its value will not be impaired for students who have not had separate courses in Interpretation. The chapter on Argument also has been reduced and rearranged. Literary references and footnotes have been revised by eliminating such as are of no great value to the modern student and by inserting references to selected modern authors. The excellent bibliographical work of Dr. C. S. Gardner has been retained with the addition of a supplementary book list.

The kindness of the various publishers in permitting the use of quotations from the books that have been of so great value is most gratefully acknowledged, as are also the many helpful suggestions made by my students and colleagues.

J. B. WEATHERSPOON

Southern Baptist Theological Seminary
November, 1943

Preface to the Second Edition

THE first edition of this work was published in the summer of 1870. Immediately after getting it through the press, the author went abroad for some months and did not expect to teach Homiletics again after his return. But circumstances made it necessary that he should resume his work in that department—always a favorite subject with him. The book was a great success. It became the most popular and widely-read textbook on Homiletics in this country and has passed through twenty-two editions, thousands of copies having been sold. It has been adopted in many theological seminaries of different denominations as the textbook; and in many where no textbook is used, it is highly commended for study and reference. Besides this, it has had a wide and useful circulation among the ministry in general. Two separate editions were published in England; the book was used in the mission schools in Japan, in its English form, and was translated for similar use in the Chinese missions. A translation into Portuguese for the Protestant missions in Brazil has been prepared and only waits for funds to be published.

The following several things call for a revised edition at this time: The copyright will have to be renewed in 1898, and this affords good opportunity to bring out a new edition; the original stereotype plates have become greatly worn; the correction of a few minor errors and some additions and alterations, made desirable by the author's larger experience in studying and teaching the subject, are called for; there have been great contributions to the literature of Homiletics since the work was first published, and the author always kept abreast of progress; and, most of all, the continued demand for the book after twenty-seven years of useful service requires response in the way of bringing the work up with the times.

The present writer's connection with this revision is easily explained. In the fall of 1892 I became associate professor of Homiletics with Dr. Broadus in the Southern Baptist Theological Seminary and had the privilege of teaching the subject with him up to the time of his lamented death in March, 1895. We divided the work of teaching under his direction, and as the state of his health permitted. It fell to my lot to do more and more of the work as his health declined.

During these years we had frequent conversations in regard to the revision of this volume. It was one of his cherished plans to bring out a revised edition before his death. With that end in view he had accumulated a good deal of material, mostly in the shape of notes, some in various note-books, and some written on the margins and flyleaves of the book which he had used in the classroom for a number of years. In addition to these notes there were many points which he had discussed in conversation with me in regard to changes and improvements in the work. At the opening of the session of 1894–95 he gave me an interleaved copy of the book to use in the classroom, with the request that I should note on the blank pages every suggestion which occurred to me, looking toward the proposed revision. In the latter part of February, 1895, I took him the book and talked to him about the revision; but alas! in less than three weeks he was in his grave.

As the revision seemed absolutely imperative, with the full approbation of Dr. Broadus's family, I have felt it a sacred duty and privilege to undertake the task. How well or how ill it may have been executed will appear in the following pages.

Three classes of changes have been made: (1) I have made changes which were clearly indicated in the author's notes already mentioned. These I have made without hesitation, as being certainly what he himself would have done. (2) I made some changes not particularly noted by him, but concerning which I have distinct recollections of conversation, or concerning which on other accounts I feel reasonably sure that he would have made the alterations adopted. (3) There are also some changes wherein I have had to rely upon my own judgment, believing that they would be for the better. It is right for me to say that these are comparatively few, and, further, that I have made no changes without consultation with members of the author's family, from whom valuable help and suggestions have been received.

As most of the alterations are the author's, I beg to say distinctly that whatever improvements may be noticed in the book should be ascribed to him, and the editor will cheerfully take the responsibility of any changes which may not meet the approval of the reader.

It is my earnest prayer and hope that this book, which has been so useful for twenty-seven years, shall go forth in its new form on a mission of continued and larger usefulness to those whose blessed work it is to preach the unsearchable riches of Christ.

E. C. DARGAN

Louisville, Kentucky
December, 1897

Author's Preface
to the First Edition

THIS work is designed, on the one hand, to be a textbook for classes, and on the other, to be read by such ministers, younger or older, as may wish to study the subject discussed.

As a teacher of Homiletics for ten years, the author had felt the need of a more complete textbook, since a course made up from parts of several different works would still omit certain important subjects and furnish but a meagre treatment of others, leaving the class to a great extent dependent entirely upon the lectures. The desire thus arose to prepare, whenever possible, a work which should be full in its range of topics and should also attempt to combine the thorough discussion of principles with an abundance of practical rules and suggestions. When the labor involved in teaching Homiletics and at the same time another branch of Theology became excessive and it was necessary to relinquish Homiletics—though always a favorite branch —the author determined, before the subject should fade from his mind, to undertake the work he had contemplated.[1]

The treatise is therefore a result of practical instruction, but it is not simply a printed course of lectures. The materials existing in the form of brief notes have been everywhere rewrought, the literature of the subject carefully re-examined, and the place which had been occupied by textbooks filled by an independent discussion.

Those who may think of employing the work as a textbook are requested to note that it is divided into independent Parts, which, while arranged in the order indicated by the nature of the subject, may be taken up in any other order required by the exigencies of instruction. Some would prefer to begin with Arrangement, in order that students may at once have the benefit of this in preparing sermons or sketches. Others might begin with Style, in order to give the student general exercises in composition, and possibly others would begin with Delivery. The author would himself prefer, if using the book, to take, after the Introduction, the first three chapters of Part I, and then Part II, and perhaps other portions before completing Part I. The cross references from one part to another will be found somewhat numerous. In the plan of the work, a few instances occur of departure from a strict technical distribution of the topics, for the sake of practical convenience. Thus the matters embraced under Illustration, Expository Preaching, or Imagination would strictly belong to several different parts of the work, but it is practically better to discuss all at the same time. So it is with Occasional Sermons.

It may be necessary to explain the introduction of copious chapters on the Interpretation of a Text and on Argument. The former subject is discussed in treatises on Hermeneutics. But besides the fact that not a few of those who use this book will not have previously studied Hermeneutics, those who have done so may be interested and profited by a discussion bearing more directly on the work of preaching; and such students will be able to read the chapter rapidly. Much improvement has been made during the past century in respect to pulpit interpretation, but it is a point as to which our young ministers still need to be very carefully guarded. The subject of Argument is thought by some to be out of place in a treatise on Homiletics or on Rhetoric in general. But preaching and all public speaking ought to be largely composed of argument, for even the most ignorant people constantly practise it themselves and always feel its force when properly presented; and yet in many pulpits the place of argument is mainly filled by mere assertion and exhortation, and the arguments employed are often carelessly stated, or even gravely erroneous. Treatises on Logic teach the critical inspection rather than the construction of argument, and so the latter must be discussed in works on Rhetoric, if anywhere. The well-known chapters of Whately have been here freely employed, but with very large additions and with the attempt to correct some important errors. The examples of argument given are nearly all drawn from religious truth. With these explanations it is left to instructors to use or omit these portions of the work at their pleasure.

But the great mass of young ministers, particularly in some denominations, never study Homiletics under a teacher, whether they have or have not enjoyed a college education. The attempt has been everywhere made to adapt the present work to the wants of these students, as well as to the purposes of a textbook. They will choose for themselves what portions to take up first, but such as have had no college education may be urged not to abandon the book without reading the discussion of Arrangement and Style, as well as of Interpretation, Subjects of Preaching, and Argument.

Those who have had much experience in preaching often find it interesting and useful to examine a treatise on the preparation and delivery of sermons. New topics and new methods may be suggested, things forgotten or hitherto neglected are recalled, ideas gradually formed in the course of experience are made clearer and more definite, and where the views advanced are not deemed just, renewed reflection on some questions need not be unprofitable. Moreover, the desire for high excellence in preaching may receive a fresh stimulus. Such readers will remember that many practical matters which to them have now become obvious and commonplace are precisely the points upon which a beginner most needs counsel. And while there are in the present treatise numerous divisions and subdivisions, so marked as to meet the wants of students, the attempt has been made to preserve the style from becoming broken and unreadable.

The author's chief indebtedness for help has been to Aristotle, Cicero, and Quintilian, and to Whately and Vinet. The two last (together with Ripley) had been his textbooks, and copious extracts are made from them on certain subjects. A good deal has been derived from Alexander, Shedd, Day, and Hoppin, from Coquerel and Palmer, and a great variety of other writers. Besides quotations, there are numerous references to works in which may be found some impressive statement of similar opinions, or further considerations bearing on the subject in hand. Only such references have been given as it was thought really worth while for the student to consult. At the close of the Introduction,[2] there is a list of the principal works forming the Literature of Homiletics, with brief notices of their character and value. It is believed that to give in a treatise some account of previous works on the subject, as judged from the author's point of view, is a thing appropriate and calculated to be useful. Such notices, in the case of contemporary writers, ought not to be reckoned discourteous if they frankly express disapprobation in some respects as well as praise in others. Were they somewhat more extended, these critical appreciations would be more useful. Besides this general account of the literature, essays and treatises upon particular branches of Rhetoric or Homiletics are briefly characterized in foot-notes upon the introduction of the respective topics. Two important and valuable works, McIlvaine on Elocution (New York, 1870), and Dabney's Sacred Rhetoric (Richmond, 1870), were received after the Introduction was stereotyped, but are noticed in Part IV, Chapter 2, and were made useful in that and the following chapters. Two articles published by the author in the Baptist Quarterly for January, 1869, and January, 1870, have been incorporated into the work, with the necessary rewriting; and some articles forming other portions of it have appeared in the Religious Herald and the Central Baptist. The author is grateful to his colleagues and his pastor[3] for sympathy in his undertaking and for valuable suggestions. The Index has been prepared by the Rev. John C. Long of Virginia.[4]

Special pains have been taken, at the proper points of the treatise, to give practical suggestions for extemporaneous speaking. Most works confine their instruction as regards the preparation of sermons to the case of writing out in full; and many treat of delivery as if it were in all cases to be reading or recitation. The effort has here been to keep the different methods in view and to mention, in connection with matters applicable to all alike, such as apply to one or another method in particular.

As to many of the practical questions connected with the preparation and delivery of sermons, there is much difference of opinion; and an experienced preacher in reading any treatise on the subject must find points here and there which he would prefer to see treated otherwise. He would decide whether, notwithstanding, the work is likely to be useful. In the present case, criticism, whether favorable or adverse, would be welcomed. Where the author is in error, he would greatly prefer to know it. Where the views presented are just, they may become more useful through discussion.

No one could prepare a work on this subject without feeling, and sometimes deeply feeling, the responsibility he incurred. It is a solemn thing to preach the gospel and therefore a very solemn thing to attempt instruction or even suggestion as to the means of preaching well.

July, 1870

NOTES

1. [This relinquishment was only temporary, being required by the author's state of health, though he at the time supposed it would be permanent. After one year he resumed Homiletics and taught it with enthusiasm and success to the end of his life.—D.]
2. [It was thus in the earlier editions; but in this, the Bibliography will be found at the end of the book.—D.]
3. [The Rev. Dr. Wm. D. Thomas, then the beloved pastor of the Greenville, S. C., Baptist Church, now Professor of Philosophy in Richmond College, Richmond, Va.—D.]
4. [Afterwards Professor of Church History in Crozer Theological Seminary, Upland, Pennsylvania, and since deceased.—D.]

ON THE PREPARATION AND DELIVERY OF SERMONS

Introduction

PREACHING is characteristic of Christianity. No other religion has ever made the regular and frequent assembling of groups of people, to hear religious instruction and exhortation, an integral part of divine worship. Judaism had something similar to it in the prophets, and afterwards in the readers and speakers of the synagogue; but preaching had no essential part in the worship of the temple.

In the Graeco-Roman world of the first century A.D. the preaching philosopher, employing the finely polished instrument of Greek rhetoric, was not an unfamiliar figure. But neither Jewish religion nor Greek philosophy gave to preaching the significance it has in Christianity where it is a primary function of the church. Following the successes of Christian preaching, and especially in modern times, other religions and sects have adopted preaching in a limited way. Nonetheless, it remains true that, as a basic service of the church in its history and significance, preaching is a peculiarly Christian institution.

CHAPTER 1

Christian Preaching

1. THE NATURE OF CHRISTIAN PREACHING

Since Christian preaching has such importance, it is necessary to understand its nature. What is Christian preaching?

In the New Testament, preaching is the proclamation of glad tidings. It is a person receiving a message from God and sharing that message with other people.

Preaching has been defined in various ways. Henry Ward Beecher called preaching "the art of moving men from a lower to a higher life."[1] David Smith conceived of preaching in terms of "incarnation." He said, "One man's spirit is quickened by the heavenly breath, and he breathes upon others, and thus their spirits are quickened too."[2] Perhaps the classic definition of preaching came from Phillips Brooks, "Preaching is the communication of truth by man to men." "Preaching is the bringing of truth through personality."[3] These two statements have been combined, and preaching has been defined as the communication of truth through personality.

Many later definitions have been patterned after Brooks's concepts. For example, T. H. Pattison wrote, "Preaching is the communication of divine truth with a view to persuasion."[4] Henry Sloan Coffin arrived at essentially the same concept. For him "preaching is truth through personality to constrain conscience at once."[5] A. W. Blackwood made this modification of Brooks's definition: "Preaching is divine truth voiced by a chosen personality to meet human need."[6]

Later definitions have built on these definitions. Modifications have been made in the areas of the biblical message and in the objectives of preaching. Von Allmen has declared, "God is not so much the object as the true source of Christian preaching. Preaching is thus speech by God rather than speech about God."[7] J. Daniel Baumann has stressed the primary purpose of preaching: "Preaching is the communication of biblical truth by man to men with the explicit purpose of eliciting behavioral change."[8]

Christian preaching could be defined in this way: Preaching is the proclamation of God's message by a chosen personality to meet the needs of humanity. This definition gives three basic elements in preaching: God's message, the chosen personality or preacher, and the needs of human beings.

2. THE CENTRAL PLACE OF PREACHING

However preaching may be understood, it had a central place in the life of the church. In the ministry of Jesus, preaching was central. Although greatly tempted to give primacy to other methods of approach to the world, he "came preaching." In the synagogue at Nazareth he described himself as having been divinely ordained "to preach good news to the poor . . . to proclaim release to the captives . . . to proclaim the acceptable year of the Lord" (Luke 4:18–19, RSV). And all the gospels give unforgettable pictures of the itinerant Preacher, in the synagogues, on the mountains, by the seaside, going from village to village, drawing after him almost unbelievably large crowds, and amazing the people by his words of grace and the authority of his teaching. John, writing many years afterwards, remembered vividly his Lord's preaching in the temple during one of the great feasts. Of one day he reported that "Jesus therefore cried out in the temple, teaching and saying . . ."; and of another, the last day of the feast, that he "stood and cried out,

saying, 'If any man is thirsty let him come to Me and drink' "
(John 7:28, 37).* His preaching was a cry, urgent in its compassion and masterful in its urgency.

That the oral ministry of Jesus is more often called teaching than preaching, a fact so often referred to by modern educators, is easily misunderstood and made the basis of erroneous distinctions. The general term for preaching in the New Testament is κηρύσσειν, to proclaim or herald. Another word, εὐαγγελίζεσθαι, emphasizes the nature of the proclaimed message as good news. A third word, διδάσκειν, is used to indicate the purpose of imparting to men divine truth and instructing them in righteousness. This last word is applied to other methods of instruction, but is freely used also for preaching to crowds. For example, Jesus taught (ἐδίδασκε) the Sermon on the Mount. In proclaiming the good news of the Kingdom of God, he went on to show its relation to Scripture and history, to moral purpose and social conduct, and to the destiny of humanity. In one discourse he proclaimed, evangelized and taught. The proper distinction is not between preaching and teaching, but between the evangelistic and didactic emphasis or element of preaching; and even this distinction is not absolute. Preaching in the meaning and purpose of Jesus included all elements calculated to stir the mind in all its functions and lead people to see, to feel, to evaluate, and to make moral decisions.

Thus our Lord preached. And for their mission after him, he gave his apostles the same strategy.[9] Preaching was in his announced purpose for them when he chose them. And at the end of his ministry he gave the Great Commission which, according to Mark, was a simple command to go everywhere preaching the gospel; and according to Matthew, the purpose was to be threefold: to make disciples, to lead to confession in baptism, and to instruct in Christian living according to his commands. In the book of the Acts and in the Epistles of the New Testament, as well as in the strength of the church at the end of the apostolic period, the record and influence of their preaching are found.

* Biblical quotations in this book are from the New American Standard Bible, unless otherwise indicated.

In the power of the same Spirit, they and those who came after them faced the pagan world with the message of salvation (κήρυγμα) and a theology and ethic (διδαχή) that in three centuries made Christianity the foremost religion in the Roman Empire. And in the centuries since those early triumphs of the gospel, the quality of preaching and the spirit and life of the church have advanced or declined together. If preaching, never wholly free from the pressure of world movements, has often faltered in periods of spiritual crisis, it has always led in the periods of revival. Of every age it is true that there has been no great religious movement, no restoration of scriptural truth and reanimation of genuine piety without new power in preaching. P. T. Forsyth had great insight when he declared, "With preaching Christianity stands or falls, because it is the declaration of a gospel."[10]

3. THE COMPETITION TO PREACHING

The central place of preaching as God's appointed means of spreading the good news of salvation is constantly being challenged. Some competition is outside the church, and some is within the church and even within some preachers.

For example, many other methods of communicating truth have been greatly multiplied and refined. The great increase and availability of books, magazines, and newspapers, the reach of the radio, the appeal of the motion picture, the instant availability of television, have seemed to many to depreciate preaching. They are, indeed, a challenge to intelligence, freshness, relevance, and reality in preaching; and they must be utilized for the ends of preaching, but they cannot be substituted for it. Television studios have their auditoriums, and crowds go to see the performers; the personal appearance of the film star draws a larger attendance than the film alone; the television performance has not done away with the desire of viewers to see the actor in person; the broadcasting of operas has not closed New York's Metropolitan Opera House but rather advertised it. The abundance of speech and literature does not call for a moratorium on preaching, but for fresh enthusiasm, improved skill, and spiritual power.

In *The Urgency of Preaching,* Kyle Haselden has caught the essence of God's method of communication.

> The spoken word . . . is an instrument especially suited to the promulgation of a gospel; it is the form into which an urgent message most naturally flows. For whatever tradition is worth, this was the experience of missions, prophecy, and evangelism throughout biblical history. When God would speak to men he sometimes chose a writer but much more frequently he chose a sayer: Amos, Jonah, Jeremiah, Ezekiel. In volume at least the Bible has a preference for "go, tell" over "write, send."[11]

The living voice will never be superseded as long as it is a voice and not an echo.

Then the other duties of the minister may interfere with the primacy of preaching. The Christian minister is not only a preacher; he is also a teacher, a pastor, an administrator, a counselor, a community servant, and perhaps other things. This multiplicity of duties may lead to a serious neglect of preaching. These various tasks are not unimportant, and they are not to be disdained. However, they should be given a secondary role.

When the first apostles encountered this tension between tasks, they decided, "It is not desirable for us to neglect the word of God in order to serve tables" (Acts 6:2). These first preachers requested assistance with other duties, delegated responsibility, and resolved, "We will devote ourselves to prayer and the ministry of the word" (Acts 6:4). Because the apostles gave priority to proclamation, "The word of God kept on spreading; and the number of disciples continued to increase greatly" (Acts 6:7).

Still another challenge to the centrality of preaching may come from within the minister. He may lose faith in preaching. He does not see preaching as "an event in which God acts."[12] He does not expect great life changes to take place as a result of his preaching. Many ministers have come to believe that the only commitments which will be registered publicly are those that have been made privately. The worship service is not a place for decisions, but only a place to register decisions. For such men, joyous expectation has gone out of preaching.

Yet when the word of God is proclaimed, it has its own intrinsic power, for "the word of God is living and active and sharper than any two-edged sword" (Heb. 4:12). Faith in preaching will still be rewarded, for the gospel is still the power of God for salvation.

4. THE NECESSITY FOR EFFECTIVE PREACHING

It follows that preaching is always a necessity, for preaching is inextricably linked to the life of the church. It was the proclamation of the good news that brought the church into being. Only the same proclamation can keep life in the church. The record of Christian history has been that the strength of the church is directly related to the strength of the pulpit. When the message from the pulpit has been uncertain and faltering, the church has been weak; when the pulpit has given a positive, declarative message, the church has been strong. The need for effective preaching has never been greater.

Then the very nature of the Christian faith demands effective preaching. Preaching is essential to Christianity. Christianity began with the proclamation of an event. God entered human history in Jesus Christ. Christ came to earth and "pitched his tent" among men. He died, was resurrected, and ascended to heaven. Something wonderful had happened, and men felt compelled to talk about it. Take away this witness, and Christianity dies. The essence of Christianity is preaching.[13]

Moreover, when the preacher declares these mighty acts of God in Christ, he speaks so that God may say these things himself. P. T. Forsyth maintained that preaching is "the Gospel prolonging and declaring itself."[14] Robert H. Mounce had the same insight when he asserted, "True preaching is an event— an event that effectively communicates the power and redemptive activity of God."[15] In other words, when the redemptive acts of God in Christ are proclaimed, Christ himself is present to act redemptively. Through proclamation, Christ is present to free mankind from sin.

Also, effective preaching is necessary today because of the other "gospels" being proclaimed in today's world. The Christian gospel is only one of many. A thousand voices are shouting to be heard. These voices have their messages and their promises. In the midst of confusion, the true gospel should be communicated clearly and attractively. The true message must be declared in a way to which the common man will be willing to listen. Preaching deserves the highest excellence because it remains God's chief instrument of reaching a lost world. "So faith comes by hearing, and hearing by the word of Christ" (Rom. 10:17).

NOTES

1. Henry Ward Beecher, *Lectures on Preaching,* First Series (New York: Fords, Howard, & Hulbert, 1900), p. 29.
2. David Smith, *The Art of Preaching* (London: Hodder & Stoughton, 1924), pp. 14–15.
3. Phillips Brooks, *Lectures on Preaching* (New York: E.P. Dutton & Co., 1907), p. 5.
4. T. H. Pattison, *The Making of the Sermon* (Philadelphia: American Baptist Publishing Society, 1898), p. 3.
5. H. S. Coffin, *What to Preach* (New York: George H. Doran Co., 1926), p. 157.
6. A.W. Blackwood, *The Fine Art of Preaching* (New York: Macmillan Co., 1937), p. 3.
7. J. J. Von Allmen, *Preaching and Congregations* (London: Lutterworth Press, 1962), p. 7.
8. J. Daniel Baumann, *An Introduction to Contemporary Preaching* (Grand Rapids, Mich.: Baker Book House, 1972), p. 13.
9. Mark 3:14 ff., 16:15; Matt. 18:18–20.
10. P. T. Forsyth, *Positive Preaching and the Modern Mind* (Grand Rapids, Mich.: Wm. B. Eerdmans, 1964), p. 5.
11. Kyle Haselden, *The Urgency of Preaching* (New York: Harper & Row, 1963), pp. 28–29.
12. Von Allmen, p. 7.
13. Herbert Farmer, *The Servant of the Word* (New York: Charles Scribner's Sons, 1942), pp. 18–20.
14. Forsyth, p. 5.
15. Robert H. Mounce, *The Essential Nature of New Testament Preaching* (Grand Rapids, Mich.: Wm. B. Eerdmans, 1960), p. 155.

CHAPTER 2

Homiletics

GRADUALLY, an art or science evolved to assist in the publishing of the Christian message. That science came to be called homiletics.

1. THE DEVELOPMENT OF HOMILETICS

Christian preaching began in a Jewish context. Its first preachers and audiences, its background and spiritual affinities, were Jewish. It was natural, therefore, and necessary that the manner of preaching should follow the pattern of the Old Testament prophet and the teaching rabbi. Moreover, in the hands of unscrupulous lawyers and false teachers, rhetoric had fallen into disrepute, being associated with sham and sophistry and regarded as a subtle instrument for making the worse appear the better reason. It was true, also, that among many Jews anything Hellenic was regarded as a threat to the very substance of Jewish life. Accordingly, early preaching was in Jewish style rather than that of the gentile culture. The sermon was called, as indeed it was, a homily, a familiar discourse or talk. So the adaptation of rhetoric to the ends of Christian preaching was a gradual process, depending upon conditions and needs.

Nonetheless, Greek rhetoric was a ready instrument for the proclamation of the gospel to the gentile world. By the latter part of the fourth century B.C., it had reached its highest development among the Greeks in the oratory of Demosthenes and in Aristotle's famous treatise on rhetoric. Later contributions were made by Roman orators, particularly Cicero and Quintilian. In the Graeco-Roman world into which Christianity came, rhetoric was the crown of a liberal education.

Grammatic (the study of literature) offered the student the wisdom of the past and developed his literary aptitudes; *Dialectic* trained his reasoning powers; and *Rhetoric* taught him to use his abilities, especially in the law-court and the Senate, by instructing him in the art of extemporization, appropriate expression, and moving appeal.[1]

Two influences, however, gradually drew Christian preaching toward rhetorical forms. One was the extension of the gospel to gentile populations among whom Jewish traditions and forms were not well known. Recall the criticism of Paul by some of the people at Corinth and their delight in Apollos, which David Smith says was "the first intimation to the ambassadors of Christ that, if they would win the world, they must address to it a congenial appeal."[2] The second influence was the conversion of men who were already trained in rhetoric. An increasing number of such men became preachers, and naturally they used their rhetorical gifts in the proclamation of the gospel. Add to these influences the fact of decline in Jewish Christians and Jewish preachers, and one can see how the "homily" gave way to the more elaborate sermon.

This change must be viewed as an advance. It gained a wider and more favorable hearing for the gospel. The principles of discourse were the tested ways of convincing and persuading men and in the hands of devout men like Basil, Gregory, Chrysostom, Ambrose, and Augustine became, to a degree not reached by the older Greeks, an instrument of spiritual power among cultured and uncultured people alike. These men ennobled the art by filling it with the distinctive reality of Christian faith and the Christian message and devoting it to Christian ends. Thus arose the science of homiletics, which is simply the adaptation of rhetoric to the particular ends and demands of preaching. Homiletics may be defined as the science of preparing and delivering a discourse based on Scripture.

2. THE STUDY OF HOMILETICS

It is evident that both the student for the ministry and the active pastor should give careful attention to the study of homiletics. Preaching is an art, and techniques may be improved. The preacher wants the best possible vehicle to convey his message.

The sources for the study of homiletics are abundant. Even though homiletics is often classed in the practical field, a complete and valuable literature has developed, presenting preaching from almost every point of view. The notes in this volume cite nearly two hundred separate works, many of them classic works published in the last one hundred years. Additional bibliographic references, including recent books, have been included in this edition at the end of each main part. Not only the ministerial student should study books on preaching; the active pastor should also read works on preaching to rekindle his love for preaching and to sharpen his skills.

Another source for the study of homiletics is sermons. The preacher may read printed sermons, listen to sermons on tapes, or hear sermons preached. Questions may be raised about these sermons: What are the strengths and weaknesses? Is the sermon based on Scripture? How is it introduced and concluded? These questions and others may help the preacher to add to his own technique.

Still another source of study may be the criticism of instructors and listeners. The student preaches a sermon, and both content and delivery are evaluated by a competent instructor. The video recording of a sermon has also proved helpful to both student and instructor. Strong points and weak points can be noted, then the strengths magnified and the weaknesses eliminated.

Since the experienced pastor may develop patterns or mannerisms, he should have regular evaluation of his preaching by a competent teacher of speech or preaching. He should also listen to "feedback" from his hearers. Comments of listeners are often discerning and helpful.

Several values will accrue from the study of homiletics: (1) The student will be introduced to a wide range of homiletical material. (2) The student will discover a wide variety of methods. Variety of method will enhance the preacher's ability. (3) The student should find real help on both organization and delivery.

NOTES

1. David Smith, *The Art of Preaching* (London: Hodder & Stoughton, 1924), p. 45.
2. Ibid., p. 58.

CHAPTER 3

The Preacher

ALMOST every definition of preaching includes the preacher. For example, preaching is truth through personality, or preaching is proclamation by a chosen man. The preacher is not the source of the message; it is from God. But he is the channel of the message. The message moves through his personality. He is the transmitter.

Since the ultimate goal is that the message reach the people, the preacher should be a good channel. He must never obstruct or hinder the message. The message should flow freely from its source to its destination.

What, then, are the requisites for an effective preacher? Because of his high function he must not omit any discipline of heart and mind and body and soul.

1. A SENSE OF DIVINE CALL[1]

The preacher should be a person with a call from God. Ministers are classed as professionals, but they should never be persons with just a "profession." They are people with a divine calling. Paul declared that he was "called as an apostle, set apart for the gospel of God" (Rom. 1:1). Spurgeon asserted, "I am as much called to preach as Paul was."[2] And so it has been with every true preacher. The impulse to preach comes from God.

Moreover, this call is intensely personal. It comes to people of all ages and classes in a variety of ways. Samuel was a child when he heard God's voice; the apostle John answered the call with all the enthusiasm of youth, as did Spurgeon and Alexander McLaren. However, Matthew was a mature man, and so were Augustine, John of Antioch (Chrysostom), and John Knox.

Amos was a shepherd, but Paul was a "university" man. John of Antioch, Ambrose, Canon Liddon, and Phillips Brooks had the advantage of wealth and social position; while Bunyan, Spurgeon, Joseph Parker, and D. L. Moody were from families of sturdy, working people.

To Peter and John the call came quietly; to Paul it was a great, cataclysmic experience; to F. W. Robertson the call came when other doors were closed.

Regardless of how the call comes, it must be present. "And how shall they preach unless they are sent?" (Rom. 10:15).

2. A VITAL CHRISTIAN EXPERIENCE

A second requisite for being an effective preacher is a vital Christian experience. It is assumed that the minister has first been called to discipleship. However, this assumption has not always been firmly based. Thomas Chalmers worked without vitality in his ministry until an illness brought a renewing, spiritual experience. John Wesley was ordained in 1725, but his life was marked by failure until the Aldersgate experience in 1738 when he felt his own heart "strangely warmed."

The average preacher does not lack a firsthand spiritual experience with Jesus Christ, but he may allow that experience to grow dull and cold. A preacher may keep his experience real by listening to his own sermons. He, too, must engage in public and private worship; he, too, must love and serve his fellowmen; he, too, must witness to the saving power of Christ; he, too, must give to support the church. As the minister follows the road to discipleship, then his preaching is "real." Samuel McComb uttered a profound truth when he wrote, "No eloquence of tongue, no charm of manner, no artistry of homiletics can atone for a lack or a loss of a vital inward experience of a spiritual reality."[3] Arthur S. Hoyt stressed the same truth, "The world is sensitive to the power of a spiritual life. Men open their hearts to such a preacher, listen to him, trust him, follow him."[4]

George Whitefield, who was a preacher of unusual fire and zeal, prayed regularly, "O, Lord, give me a warm heart." Such a prayer would be in order for every preacher. Nothing can substitute for a vital, growing experience.

3. CONTINUATION OF LEARNING

A third requisite for the effective preacher is an enlargement of knowledge. Just as the spirit must be cultivated, so must the mind. This requires the preacher to be a person of great self-discipline. Discipline has been defined as a process whereby one gains control of oneself. The preacher sets his own work patterns. Therefore, he must have priorities. Perhaps first on the list is time to study. Cicero wanted the orator to know everything. While this ideal is impossible to attain, the preacher should know everything that a regular study schedule will bring to his mind. Halford Luccock had a chapter entitled "To Toil Like a Miner Under a Landslide."[5] This picture suggests tremendous activity.

A schedule for study will be discussed later. Too much emphasis cannot be placed on disciplined, planned study, which is the only route to enlarged knowledge.

4. THE DEVELOPMENT OF NATURAL GIFTS

Still another requisite for the effective preacher is the development of natural gifts. All are not created equal, but every person has natural gifts, and these may be greatly improved. For example, the power to think clearly, to speak forcibly, to feel deeply are capacities which the preacher may develop.

Henry Ward Beecher, the premier orator of the American pulpit, serves as a classic example of the improvement of native gifts. As a child, he did not show promise of future greatness.

He memorized slowly and spoke with difficulty. Yet a mathematics teacher taught him to think and to work through problems to solutions. A teacher of elocution taught him to endure the drudgery of repeated drill until he could speak correctly. By constant practice and rehearsal Henry Ward Beecher became a master of platform speaking.

Each man has abilities which may be developed. But again, the way is one of discipline and application.

5. MAINTENANCE OF PHYSICAL HEALTH

Again, to be a good channel of God's message the preacher should give careful attention to his health. Good health is closely related to good disposition, optimistic outlook, clear thinking, and physical vitality.

The long hours in the study should be balanced by a careful diet and regular exercise. While exercise takes many forms, walking is available in all circumstances. A walk through the community may also fulfill a pastoral role.

Every pastor should have a day off. Since he works strenuously on Sunday, he should have a day during the week which may be used for rest, recreation, meditation, or uninterrupted study. A day's recreation will return a pastor to his parish invigorated and ready for work.

To stand before a waiting congregation is a great challenge. Physical trim will add to mental acuteness and vitality. Good health promotes effective speech.

6. COMPLETE DEPENDENCE UPON THE HOLY SPIRIT

The ultimate requisite for the effective preacher is complete dependence upon the Holy Spirit. The Holy Spirit enters into every relationship of the Christian life. Repentance, faith, and maturity are his gifts. He is also the one who calls the preacher. He guides him in Bible study, in the selection of texts, and in the choice and preparation of material. He empowers his preaching, and only the Holy Spirit can give spiritual victories. Only he can convert and consecrate.

The preacher who learns homiletical skills may forget his need for the Holy Spirit. The key reason some worship services are cold and lifeless and the sermons within those services without impact is that the Holy Spirit is not present to give warmth and life.

Yet the Holy Spirit may be the preacher's constant support. He stands beside to support and empower. Generally, he is not present because he is not sought. "If ye then, being evil, know how to give good gifts unto your children, how much more shall your Father which is in heaven give good things to them that ask him?" (Matt. 7:11, KJV). When John Calvin mounted the pulpit stairs, he prayed a prayer which every person who enters the pulpit could pray with earnestness of soul, "Come, Holy Spirit, come."

These requisites will help the preacher become a more effective channel of God's message.

NOTES

1. For an excellent discussion of this topic see J. H. Jowett, *The Preacher, His Life and Work* (New York: Harper & Brothers, 1912), Chapter 1.
2. Lewis O. Brastow, *Representative Modern Preachers* (New York: Macmillan Co., 1904), p. 402.
3. Samuel McComb, *Preaching in Theory and Practice* (New York: Oxford University Press, 1926), p. 57.
4. Arthur S. Hoyt, *The Preacher* (New York: Macmillan Co., 1909), p. 122.
5. Halford Luccock, *In the Minister's Workshop* (New York: Abingdon-Cokesbury Press, 1944), pp. 211–20.

CHAPTER 4

God's Message

PREACHING is the proclamation of God's message by a chosen personality to meet the needs of humanity. The central part of this definition of preaching is God's message. The preacher has nothing to transmit apart from the message. The needs of humanity, however great, go unmet apart from God's Word. Ideally the preacher stands in God's stead and speaks for him.

1. THE BIBLE AS SOURCE

If the preacher is to speak for God, he must of necessity go to the place where God has spoken most clearly. This means that the preacher must search the Scriptures for an authentic word from God. Karl Barth has caught this relationship in his *The Preaching of the Gospel.*

Preaching is the Word of God which he himself has spoken; but he makes use, according to his good pleasure, of the ministry of a man who speaks to his fellowmen, in God's name, by means of a passage from Scripture. Such a man fulfills the vocation to which the Church has called him, and through his ministry, the Church is obedient to the mission entrusted to her.[1]

The message which the Christian preacher proclaims is a given message. He does not have to create it. It has been revealed. Every basic idea which the Christian preacher needs has been given to him. To be sure, he must interpret, apply, and illustrate, but he does not have to invent. Indeed, he must not invent. In the Scripture he has his core message. In a real sense, preaching is giving the Bible a voice. It is letting God speak out of his Word.

This means that in the Bible the preacher will find his primary material, his "text" book. A lifetime of study will not be sufficient to master the Scriptures. If a minister carefully studies two books of the Bible a year, he has spent thirty-three years. Dr. J. B. Weatherspoon, author of the third edition of this volume, urged many generations of seminary students to study seriously one book of the Bible all the time. Dr. Weatherspoon believed that the study of two or three books of the Bible each year would provide adequate material for the next year's preaching.

2. REASONS FOR USING THE BIBLE

These claims made for the place of the Bible as the source in preaching are high claims. Yet the reasons behind these claims are strong.

(1) One reason to use the Bible is to make a sermon truly homiletical. Preachers like sermons to be homiletical. Generally, this means that the sermon is structurally sound. But homiletics is the science of preparing and delivering a discourse based on Scripture. The real essence of homiletics is not structure but Scripture. "Three points and a poem" do not constitute homiletics. That which is truly homiletical is scriptural. Preaching is not just public speech; it is not a person making a talk; it is a person sharing a message from God.

(2) Another reason for using the Bible is that the Bible gives the preacher something spiritually relevant to proclaim. Not a few ministers have had the experience of coming to Saturday night without anything to say. Their desperate prayer has been, "O, Lord, anything." The Bible always gives something to preach, and it is spiritually relevant.

Dr. Halford Luccock tells of the homiletical poverty of preachers who had thrown the Bible out of the study window:

In those days quite a number of young Apolloses, on graduating, having become men, put away such childish things as texts and Bible stories. In the pulpit they lived amid the immensities and starry galaxies. But after a while, when the little long-suffering congregation had heard their sermon on 'The March of Progress' (for progress was marching in those days) and the one on 'Science and Religion' and the one on 'Pragmatism' (for pragmatism was going big then), like the prodigal son, they began to be in want. Then they came to themselves and said, "In my father's Book are texts enough and to spare." And they said, "I will arise and go to the Bible."[2]

Exactly opposite is true of men who search the Scripture. Rather then poverty, they have homiletical wealth. J. H. Jowett made this observation years ago:

Texts will clamor for recognition, and your only problem will be to find time to give them notice. The year will seem altogether too short to deal with the waiting procession and to deal with their wealth. Yes, you will be embarrassed with your riches instead of with your poverty.[3]

(3) It follows that to use the Bible will save the preacher time in sermon preparation. He does not waste time looking for subjects or scanning sermon books. He goes to work exploring the text that he has chosen. The thorough exegesis of a passage of Scripture will provide the thought for a sermon. The preacher adds illustration and application, and a sermon is prepared. It is amazing how much time is saved because the preacher can go to work on a text Monday morning.

(4) The preacher who uses the Bible will also be growing in grace and in knowledge. As a person delves deeply into Scripture to give others spiritual food, he feeds his own soul.

Paul was fearful that after he preached to others he might be a castaway. Today "castaways" are numerous. Moral failure is rarely a sudden act. People move away from the God they claim to know. Then, when temptations come, they are vulnerable.

This is not true of the person who studies the Word and first feeds his own soul. While he prepares to share with others, he matures in Christ.

(5) Another reason for using the Bible is that the Bible adds variety to preaching. The Bible discusses a myriad of theological and ethical ideas. The Bible mirrors almost every virtue and almost every vice. Through the pages of the Bible walk all kinds of people with every kind of need. Contrary to the idea that the use of Scripture limits one's preaching, just the opposite is true. It enlarges the scope of any pastor's preaching.

(6) Then to use the Bible will allow the preacher to treat delicate topics in a tactful way. Prejudice, self-righteousness, integrity, honesty, divorce, money, and gossip are examples of such topics. To handle these topically may give the impression that the preacher is sharing his own ideas.

Little good is to be done if dealing with these hard issues should degenerate into a contest of minds between the minister and his people. If, however, in the natural course of unfolding the meaning of various passages of Scriptures from the pulpit these unpleasant questions inevitably open up simply because the Bible has something to say about them, then the offense becomes the offense of the Bible and not that of the minister.[4]

For example, an exposition of Acts 10, which deals with Peter's call to go to the home of Cornelius, would give the minister ample opportunity to discuss racial prejudice. Passages from James on gossip would allow the minister to discuss such harmful talk.

Donald G. Miller states the case humorously and pointedly.

More than once when I have been taken to task, following a sermon, by someone who disagreed with what I said, I have found it a happy device to agree with my accuser that I did not like what I said any better than he did, for it was as hard on me as it was on him and cut as sharply across my own human judgment as it had his; but I was not giving out my own ideas from the pulpit, but declaring the word of God as I understood it in the Bible. If, therefore, my critic did not agree with what I had said, and could show me that I had misinterpreted the Bible, I would readily concede the point. But if that were not the case, there was no quarrel between him and me. And if the hearer did not like what God had said through the Bible, he should take him to task for it, not me![5]

(7) Moreover, to use the Bible will help both the preacher and the congregation to remember the sermon. Many ministers make use of notes, manuscripts, and other homiletical crutches because they feel that the memory cannot be trusted. But a passage of Scripture selected, studied, and prepared in sermonic form sticks to the mind. In addition, the open Bible is before the preacher. Congregations do not seem to class the Bible as "notes." Rather the open Bible enhances the minister's image.

Then, a biblical passage will also help the people remember the message. Few experiences are more disillusioning to the minister than to question even a good listener about the content of last Sunday's sermon. But a text is often recalled, and then other materials cluster around it.

Some ministers complain of the biblical illiteracy of their people. A new pastor may talk about the ignorance of his parishioners, but a pastor who has been with a congregation three to five years cannot. If the people have no knowledge of the Bible, the weakness is in the preacher and not the congregation. He has not taught them biblical material. But when the preacher uses the Bible, the people have an association which helps them to remember the sermon.

(8) Also, to use the Bible will give the preacher a note of authority. The preacher is not sharing his own ideas. He is declaring God's message. He is herald. He has been sent by the King. He has the authority of "thus saith the Lord." The preaching of Billy Graham is topically oriented, even though he uses many biblical references. Nonetheless, throughout his sermons the reiteration of such terms as "God says," "the Bible says," and "the Bible speaks" gives a note of authority. But to use the Scripture is to allow God to speak, and that is our reason for being.

(9) Finally, to use the Bible in preaching is to please God. God

inspired men to record his Word. Then he called men to be his messengers. When an appointed one stands before his fellow-men and speaks for God from his Word, this must please God who was the initiator of it all. It has been suggested that it should be offered to him before it is shared with the people. It seems that the biblical offering would be most acceptable. For the preacher to stand in God's stead and speak for him is most pleasing to God.

The experience of Dr. W. A. Criswell, pastor of the First Baptist Church of Dallas, Texas, reinforces the value of using the Bible in preaching:

> For eighteen years I preached through the Bible. I began at the first verse in Genesis and continued through the last verse in the Revelation. Where I left off in the morning, I picked up in the evening, and thus every Sunday, morning and evening, I followed the message of the Holy Scriptures. God blessed the procedure more than I could ever have hoped.
>
> The response of the people was amazing to me. When I began the series, some of the most discerning church members said I would empty the house of the Lord. Nobody, they said, would continue to come to the services and listen to messages that waded through all those so-called dreary and empty chapters of the Bible. But God had placed it on my heart to begin preaching through the Bible.
>
> The result is a finished story. So many people began coming to God's house that after a while they could not be packed in, although the auditorium is one of the most spacious in America. We finally had to begin holding two morning services. Now, at both hours the auditorium is filled. Our people began bringing their Bibles, reading their Bibles, studying their Bibles. They began witnessing to others as never before. More and more souls were saved. The spirit of revival and refreshment became the daily order in the house of the Lord. It was the greatest experience of my life.[6]

3. METHODS OF INTERPRETATION

For the Scripture to have value for preaching and for the preacher's text to become God's message, the Bible must be interpreted correctly. To interpret and apply his text in accordance with its real meaning is one of the preacher's most sacred duties. He stands before the people for the very purpose of teaching and exhorting them out of the Word of God. He announces a particular passage of God's Word as his text with the distinctly implied understanding that from this his sermon will be drawn. But using a text and undertaking to develop and apply its teachings, he is solemnly bound to represent the text as meaning precisely what it does mean.

How can the preacher find this true meaning and thus fulfill his responsibility? The suggestions, here offered in the form of rules, are intended to aid the preacher in getting for himself the exact meaning of the passage of Scripture which he proposes to use as the text for his sermon.

(1) Study the text minutely. Notice carefully both the grammar and the rhetoric of the text. (a) Endeavor to ascertain the precise meaning of the words and phrases used in the text. Inquire whether any of them have a peculiar meaning in Scripture, and whether that peculiar meaning applies to the passage under consideration. If there are key words in the text, or words of special importance, examine, with the help of a concordance, other passages in which such word is used. This is best done in the original languages. But for those who are limited to the English language, excellent concordances, translations, and commentaries are available.

(b) Pay special attention to any figures of speech that may occur in the text. In the language of Scripture, as in all other language, the literal meaning is usually presumed. Still, much in Scripture is clearly figurative and should be so interpreted.

(2) Study the text in its immediate connection. The context of a text will of course throw light upon its meaning and is usually indispensable to understanding it. The immediate context will usually embrace from a few verses to a few chapters before and after the text; and of this context the preacher should not only have a general knowledge but should make special examination when studying his text; and he must resist the common tendency to imagine that this context begins or ends with the chapter in which the text occurs. The extent to which one

should study the context will vary in different cases, but rarely can such a study be entirely neglected.

(3) Study the text in its larger connections. These remoter relations of the text are also important to its correct interpretation. They commonly embrace the three following particulars. (a) Sometimes the logical connection will really be the entire idea to which the text belongs. There are few sentences in Hebrews or in the first eleven chapters of Romans, for instance, which can be fully understood without having in mind the entire argument of the epistle. Of course this is not so strikingly true in most of the books, but each of them has its own distinctive contents, connection, and character. Few things are to be so earnestly urged upon the student of Scripture as that he shall habitually study its books with reference to their whole connection. Then he can minutely examine any particular text with a correct knowledge of its general position and surroundings.

(b) Apart from the biblical context in which a text is found, general historical knowledge is often helpful. In the narratives which make up the larger part of Scripture, one must always observe facts of geography which would clarify the text as well as the manners and customs of the Jews and other nations who appear in the sacred story. These aids for understanding texts are seldom used as diligently as they should be. But there is also much to be learned by taking account of the opinions and state of mind of the persons addressed in a text. The relations between the speaker or writer and those whom he is addressing need to be remembered. In order to do this, also, the errors or evils which existed among them need to be ascertained. This can often be gathered from the book itself. For example, the supposed contradiction between Paul and James with regard to justification is obvious if attention had been paid to the theoretical and practical errors at which they are respectively aiming. In the case of our Lord's teachings, much may be learned from the Gospels and also from the Jewish writings and the modern works founded on them, concerning the incorrect beliefs and evil practices existing among the Jews and to which his sayings have often a very direct and specific reference. With respect to divorce, to oaths, to the Sabbath, or to the duty of paying tribute, his teachings will be imperfectly apprehended unless one understands the practical abuses and vehement controversies which existed among his hearers on those subjects. On such points the best commentaries give some information.

(c) Study the text in accordance with the general teachings of Scripture. These teachings are harmonious and can be combined into a symmetrical whole. If a passage may have two meanings, the one chosen must be in harmony with what the Bible in general plainly teaches rather than one which would make the Bible contradict itself. When trying to decide between possible grammatical meanings, an important principle to be considered is that the teachings of Scripture must be consistent.

It is necessary also that one should keep in mind the fact that revelation was progressive. Understanding grew from less to more. There is a marked advance of knowledge from Abraham to Moses, from Moses to the prophets, and from the prophets to Christ. This holds true in matters of theology and also of ethics. This fact means two things for the interpreter: first, that the teachings of the Old Testament must be interpreted in the light of the New; and, secondly, that the use of proof-texts must be made with great care. The finality of any text or portion of Scripture must be judged by the total revelation. Scriptural authority has been claimed for many erroneous ideas by failure at this point. The law of Moses, for example, recognized polygamy and made provision for divorce, which Jesus declared to be not ideal and contrary to the high purpose of God. The imprecatory prayers of certain psalms cannot be properly evaluated apart from the injunction of Jesus, "Love your enemies." Many of the ideas of Ecclesiastes and Job are but the transient groping of men struggling toward the light.

The careful examination of Scripture "references" in studying a text is also a matter of great importance. These will often help in the grammatical part of interpretation by showing how the same words and phrases are used elsewhere. Historically, such references can show the same subject presented under different circumstances or the peculiar state of things in which the text was uttered. These references will also help the preacher to form his own opinion as to the meaning of his text, without depending too much on commentaries and other aids. Moreover, the "reference" passages will very often furnish useful material for the body of the sermon by suggesting new aspects, proofs, illustrations, or applications of the subject treated. The young preacher should make it a practice to consult the references to his text. Many preachers have become "mighty in the Scriptures" by the diligent use of references.

NOTES

1. Karl Barth, *The Preaching of the Gospel* (Philadelphia: Westminster, 1963), p. 9.
2. Halford Luccock, *In the Minister's Workshop* (New York: Abingdon-Cokesbury Press, 1944), p. 149.
3. J. H. Jowett, *The Preacher, His Life and Work* (London: Hodder and Stoughton, 1912), p. 121.
4. Donald G. Miller, *Fire in Thy Mouth* (Nashville, Tenn.: Abingdon Press, 1954), p. 103.
5. Ibid., pp. 102–3.
6. W. A. Criswell, "Preaching Through the Bible," *Christianity Today* (December 9, 1966), p. 22.

For Further Reading:
Introduction

Cox, James W. *A Guide to Biblical Preaching.* Nashville, Tenn.: Abingdon Press, 1976.

Dargan, Edwin Charles. *The Art of Preaching in the Light of Its History.* Nashville, Tenn.: Sunday School Board of the Southern Baptist Convention, 1922.

Demaray, Donald E. *An Introduction to Homiletics.* Grand Rapids, Mich.: Baker Book House, 1974.

Fant, Clyde E. *Preaching for Today.* New York: Harper & Row, 1975.

Griffith, Leonard. *The Need to Preach.* London: Hodder & Stoughton, 1971.

Keck, Leander E. *The Bible in the Pulpit.* Nashville, Tenn.: Abingdon Press, 1978.

Killinger, John. *The Centrality of Preaching in the Total Task of the Ministry.* Waco, Tex.: Word Books, 1969.

Miller, Donald G. *The Way to Biblical Preaching.* Nashville, Tenn.: Abingdon Press, 1957.

Mounce, Robert H. *The Essential Nature of New Testament Preaching.* Grand Rapids, Mich.: Wm. B. Eerdmans, 1960.

Pearson, Roy. *The Preacher: His Purpose and Practice.* Philadelphia: Westminster Press, 1962.

Perry, Lloyd M. *A Manual for Biblical Preaching.* Grand Rapids, Mich.: Baker Book House, 1965.

Pitt-Watson, Ian. *Preaching: A Kind of Folly.* Philadelphia: Westminster Press, 1976.

Read, David H. C. *Sent from God.* Nashville, Tenn.: Abingdon Press, 1974.

Reid, Clyde. *The Empty Pulpit.* New York: Harper & Row, 1967.

Von Rad, Gerhard. *Biblical Interpretation in Preaching.* Translated by John E. Steely. Nashville, Tenn.: Abingdon Press, 1977.

Part I

FOUNDATIONS
OF THE SERMON

JUST as the structure of a house has foundations, the structure of the sermon has foundations. These could be called sermon beginnings or basic definitions. These beginnings are the keys which unlock logical sermon development.

CHAPTER 5

The Text

1. MEANING OF THE TERM

The word *text* is derived from the Latin *texere* ("to weave"), which figuratively came to signify to put together, to construct, and hence to compose, to express thought in continuous speech or writing. The noun *textus* thus denotes the product of weaving, the web, the fabric, and so in literary usage the fabric of one's thinking, continuous composition. The practice arose of reading the continuous narrative or discussion of some author and adding comments, chiefly explanatory, or of taking the author's own writing and making notes at the sides or bottom of the page. Thus the author's own work came to be called the "text," as distinguished from the fragmentary notes and comments of the editor or speaker. This use of the word still survives, as when we speak of the text of ancient authors or others, meaning their own original composition; and textual criticism is the science of determining what was their exact language. Early preaching was of the nature of running commentary on the connected train of thought, or text, of Scripture, which was so named to distinguish it from the preacher's comment or exposition. As the practice grew of lengthening the comments into an organized speech and of shortening the passage of Scripture used, text has come to mean the portion of Scripture chosen as the suggestion or foundation for a sermon.

2. USE OF THE TEXT

The history of the word *text,* like that of homiletics, points back to the fact, which is also well-known otherwise, that preaching was originally expository. The early Christian preachers commonly spoke on passages of considerable length, and their sermons were largely exposition. This practice was modified, and the use of a short text or a brief passage became common. In the early twentieth century, it was not uncommon to have a sermon without a text. At the present time, the expository sermon is gaining in popularity.

In this whole matter of using texts, the law is value, not custom. Let the preacher decide. The important thing is that the sermon must be Christian in content and spirit and purpose. One may take a text and still preach a sermon that misses the mark of being Christian; on the other hand, a sermon without a text and without formal Scripture reference may be thoroughly Christian. And merely to follow a cult of novelty or to copy some admired rebel against convention is quite as bad as following tradition. Let the preacher have a reason for what he does. Sometimes he may omit a text because no suitable text can be found for what he wants to say. But this should rarely occur, for as Dr. Coffin suggests,

if within the ample range of the biblical literature a preacher cannot find a text for what he wishes to say, the chances are that he is deviating from the historic faith of which he is a teacher.[1]

Occasionally he may see value in preaching without a text for the sake of variety. Or again he may deal with a number of passages, no one of which is suitable for a central text. But as a general rule, the objectives of the sermon are better realized with a well-chosen text.

3. RULES FOR THE SELECTION OF A TEXT

The proper selection of a text is a matter of major importance. The minister, or student for the ministry, should keep a notebook for lists of texts. In reading the Scriptures and books of theology, in reading collections of sermons, biographies, in casual reflection, and in the preparation of other sermons, passages will be constantly appearing upon which the preacher could base a sermon. These should be recorded at once. The preacher should discipline himself to do so until it becomes a habit. And he should by all means put down at the same time, however briefly, the proposed outline of the sermon, or any specially valuable view or illustration of it that may occur to him. Otherwise, he will find many passages in the list that will have little meaning to him because the association will have been broken, the point of view will have disappeared. At times the minister will think of plans of sermons or suggestive texts or topics in rapid succession. These ideas should be carefully preserved. Many good texts and creative ideas are forgotten, when a brief note or even some little effort to associate them with other things might have retained them.

To aid in the selection of texts, the following rules are offered.

1. The text should be clear. As a rule, its meaning should be obvious. Otherwise, the people either will be repelled by what they see no sense in, or they will have only idle curiosity concerning what the preacher will make of the text. Still, there are important exceptions. If the preacher is satisfied that he can explain an obscure passage and can show that it teaches valuable truth, he may take it. If the passage is one in which many are interested, and he is really able to make its meaning clear and bring out useful lessons, it may be very wise to use it. But remember the difficulty of making the passage instructive and useful. To explain merely for the sake of explaining is a task for which the preacher scarcely has time.[2]

2. Rarely use texts with especially eloquent language. They may seem to promise too much. And if great expectations are raised at the beginning, it is, of course, very difficult to meet them. Yet no one would say as a rule that such texts must be avoided. Many of the noblest and most impressive passages of Scripture have a natural grandeur of expression, and there would be serious loss in habitually avoiding these. Sometimes a

simpler text may present the same subject, and the more elaborate passage can be introduced elsewhere in the course of the
sermon. But when such a passage is made the text, the preacher
may prevent any undesirable effect by announcing it in a restrained manner and by giving it a simple introduction. The
pastor must carefully avoid ostentation but he must not shrink
from using any passage which may be useful to the congregation.

3. Caution should be exercised in choosing texts that will
seem odd. The quest of the unusual may sacrifice a higher value
for the small gain in initial interest. The text should indicate not
only a central concern of the message but something of its tone
also. It should have qualities of thought and emotion that can
be sustained and advanced as the sermon progresses. This does
not mean that one should be content with the much used or
standard texts, but only that in the pursuit of novelty the significance and high purpose of the text should not be violated. The
elements of surprise and shock, of humor and oddity have their
values in preaching, but they have much less value in the text
than in the midst of the sermon.[3] Dr. Austin Phelps recom-
mends the choice of novel texts as preferable to hackneyed or
standard texts because they excite interest, revive old truth,
promote variety, impress truth more deeply, and stimulate the
preacher in the composition of his sermon.[4] But novelty is not
necessarily oddity, and Dr. Phelps warns against the trivial and
anything that would violate the dignity of the text by suggesting
vulgar or ludicrous associations, or that would shock the sensibilities of the audience.

4. Do not avoid a text because it is familiar. What has made
some texts familiar to all, but the fact that they are so manifestly
good texts? It is a very mistaken desire for novelty which causes
a person to avoid such rich and fruitful passages as "God so
loved the world," and "This is a faithful saying," which Luther
used to call "little Bibles," as if including in their narrow scope
the whole Bible. The preacher who will ignore the tradition of
the pulpit as to the meaning and application of such passages
and make a personal study of them will often find much that is

new to him and his hearers, like the person who finds buried treasure where others have found nothing. Besides, the need is not for absolute novelty but for freshness. If the preacher can manage, by prayerful reflection, to present interpretations and provide illustrations of a familiar text that will give it a fresh interest to the hearers, then all the riches of the passage are made available for good. Alexander calls attention to the fact that the great sculptors and painters and the Greek tragedians took the same themes. He remarks: "Some, anxious to avoid hackneyed topics, omit the greatest, just as if we should describe Switzerland and omit the Alps."[5] In point of fact, the great preachers, all the best preachers, do preach frequently upon the great texts and the great subjects.

5. Do not habitually neglect any portion of Scripture. Some neglect the Old Testament thus losing all its rich unfolding of God's character and the methods of his Providence, all its numerous illustrations of human life and duty, and its many types and predictions of the coming Savior. Others preach on the Old Testament almost exclusively. These are either preachers who take no delight in the "doctrines of grace," in the spirituality of the gospel, or preachers devoted to fanciful allegorizing, who do not enjoy the straightforward teaching of Christ and his apostles so much as their own wild "spiritualizing" of everything in the Old Testament history, prophecies, and proverbs. The preacher should not neglect either of these great divisions of God's own Word.

The pastor should not overlook particular books. In the course of a good many years, a preacher should select texts from every portion of Scripture. He will of course choose most frequently from those books which are compatible with his peculiar mental constitution and tastes or which are rich in evangelical and practical matters.

6. Let the needs of the congregation determine the choice of texts. If preaching is to meet the needs of humanity, then texts should be chosen that meet these needs. As a minister engages in pastoral visitation, pastoral counseling, and shares with the people on social occasions, he will become aware of needs,

problems, and desires. Here the objective of the sermon will come into focus. His sermons will not be subject-centered; rather they will be person-centered. The minister will try to select texts to fulfill all of the needs of the people.

7. Let the text select the person. As a preacher gives himself to an intense study of the Bible, certain texts will take hold of his mind and heart. A text that demands preaching, that cannot be put aside, will be meaningful to the preacher and the congregation. Perhaps the easiest answer to the question, "What to preach?" is found in regular meditation on the Word of God. The man who spends time on the Scripture will discover texts demanding, "Preach me!" A text that chooses the preacher will develop easily and will bring great personal satisfaction.

NOTES

1. H. S. Coffin, *What to Preach* (New York: George H. Doran Co., 1926), p. 21.
2. Compare Austin Phelps, *Theory of Preaching* (New York: Charles Scribner's Sons, 1893), pp. 84–91, for a very sensible and more extended treatment of the comparative advantages of perspicuous and obscure texts.
3. For a good discussion of the value and use of humor in preaching, see Dr. C. R. Brown's *The Art of Preaching* (New York: Macmillan Co., 1948), pp. 135–42.
4. Phelps, pp. 95–102.
5. James W. Alexander, *Thoughts on Preaching* (Edinburgh: Ogle & Murray, and Oliver & Boyd, 1864), pp. 10–12.

CHAPTER 6

The Subject

1. THE RELATIONSHIP OF SUBJECT AND TEXT

The relation between the subject and the text should be clear and unquestioned. The best reason for the choice of a text is that it expresses or suggests ideas that are a worthy subject or support in a legitimate way a subject already chosen. Dr. A. E. Garvie's discussion of the connection between the two is worthy of study.[1] Text and subject may stand in the relation of principle and application, or general and particular truths. For example, one desires to speak on some social practice of doubtful moral character or consequences; if he is familiar enough with his Bible, he will recall Paul's words, "Whatsoever is not from faith is sin" (Rom. 14:23). Or beginning with a text such as "Whatever a man sows, this will he also reap" (Gal. 6:7), one may preach on some particular moral débâcle or triumph, either personal or social. In such instances the subject is a deduction from the text. On the other hand, the text may be a particular fact or judgment or experience, and the subject a generalization upon it or induction. For example, Luke 12:19-20 may be the text for a sermon on the futility of covetousness; so also the experience of Simon of Cyrene is a legitimate basis for the subject, "Burdens That Are Blessings." Numberless texts are particular instances of divine power, providence, love, mercy, wrath, and redemption, as many others express great principles that speak to numberless subjects relevant to life.

Garvie points out further that subject and text may have an analogical relation, suggesting, for example, that a sermon on the perils to Christian ideals relating to war may have for its basis Psalm 137, and that Matthew 18:15–17 may quite legitimately be used to discuss ways of preventing war, the method of resolving personal differences having a bearing upon the problem of group differences.

Or again the text may be related to the subject through suggestion. Horace Bushnell read the sentence "Then went in also that other disciple" (John 20:8), saw one man influencing another unconsciously, and wrote his great sermon on "Unconscious Influence." The connection of text and subject is real, though indirect.

It is legitimate also to use as a text for a sermon on some character or chapter of history a passage that reveals a central point of interest or that would serve as a starting point. The text, "And the Lord turned, and looked upon Peter" (Luke 22:61), for example, is an excellent starting point for a sermon on Peter's fall and recovery. In this whole matter the preacher needs a good imagination, good judgment, a high regard for his own integrity, and above all an intention to deal honestly with the Scriptures and with his audience.

2. THE SIGNIFICANCE OF THE SUBJECT

The sermon may or may not have a text. It must have a subject. Definitely it must be about something, some significant truth bearing upon religious life—a doctrine or ethical principle, some moral problem, personal or social, some human need such as the need to be saved, encouraged, or guided in religious living. Whether the subject or the text is first chosen will of course depend upon circumstances and the preacher's turn of mind. In considering the condition of the congregation or looking back over the sermons recently preached, the preacher will be more likely to decide upon a subject for which he must then find a text. In reading the Bible or reading over his growing list of texts, he will probably find some text which interests him, and from which he will proceed to evolve a subject. It has been thought best to discuss the text first, because the primary conception of preaching is to bring forth the teachings of some passage of Scripture. The approach does not greatly matter. The points to be insisted on are these: When the subject is first selected, then carefully look for a text which will fairly, and if possible exactly, present that subject. If the text comes first, then seek to work out from it some definite subject.

3. A DEFINITION OF THE SUBJECT

What is a definite subject? The subject is the focal idea of the sermon. The subject is the thrust of the sermon. It is exactly what the sermon is about. The subject answers the question, "What is the sermon about?" It is the specific area the sermon is to cover. Whether a sermon has two points or ten points, it must have one main point; it must be about something.

This definite subject is primarily for the preacher. It guides him in his preparation. It is the key to his organization. It also helps him choose and arrange material. Moreover, the well-chosen subject will assist the congregation. It will tell the listening people what they are to hear.

4. STATEMENT OF THE SUBJECT

It is important for the sermon to have unity.

A preacher may take a text, and say a great deal about the words, phrases, and clauses of the text, without fixing his own mind or the minds of his hearers on any one subject. There are sermons which are like a rudderless ship on a wide sea, driven hither and thither, and making for no haven.[2]

To state one central idea as the heart of the sermon is not always easy, especially in textual and expository preaching. But the achievement is worth the effort. Even when a text presents several ideas, all of which should be incorporated in the sermon, it is desirable to find for them some bond of unity, some primary idea that will serve as focus or axis. One may fix attention on one of the ideas as subject and consider the others in relation to it. The text in Hebrews 2:3 suggests three subjects: "The Great Salvation," "The Evil of Neglecting the Gospel," and "The Problem of Escape," any one of which might well be chosen, depending upon purpose and circumstance. The other two will enforce its consideration. Or it is possible to state a general idea that will include all the main points of the text, as, for instance, in dealing with such texts as 1 Peter 1:8–9. There are four verbs—love, believe, rejoice, receive. What is the text about, four things or one thing in four aspects? Let one preacher answer:

What he (the apostle) is trying to do here is something rather daring: it is nothing less than to define *the central Christian experience* in a single sentence; and you will observe that he has packed it all into four words, four short, decisive verbs. "Ye love—ye believe—ye rejoice—ye receive." That, he declares, is *what it means to be a Christian.* That, throughout the ages, has been *the high road of salvation.* [3]

The italicized words show the possibilities in expressing a unifying idea. Dr. W. L. Watkinson preached a sermon on 1 Corinthians 15:32–34, his subject being "The Personal Equation in Christian Belief." Let him tell how he arrived at it:

Our text seems to be an interruption to the great argument (concerning resurrection), and at the first glance it appears somewhat irrelevant and misplaced. Yet a little reflection shows that it is a parenthesis quite in place, and one of weightiest signification. The apostle reminds his readers that faith in the great future is not simply a question of logic, but also a question of the state of mind we bring to the consideration of the subject. He emphatically declares that it is possible for men so to live that their vision may be blurred, their sensibilities dulled, and they themselves become incapable of great ideas and hopes. [4]

Another might have stated the same idea as "Moral Barriers to Great Faith." The whole point is that the preacher can and ought to preach on one subject, clearly understood by himself and so presented to his audience.

The subject should be stated clearly. Being the focal idea of the sermon, it calls for the simplest rhetorical statement, for example, "Salvation by Grace," "The Wages of Sin," "The Assurance of Hope," "Christ—the Unfailing Light," "The Goodness and Severity of God," "Abounding Grace," "The Expulsive Power of a New Affection," "The Royalty of Service," "The Sense of What Is Vital," "The Son in the Home." Notice that there are two or more terms in each of these subjects: Salvation and Grace, Assurance and Hope, etc. They are all general terms, but by the use of prepositions, adjectives, conjunctions, or participial forms they are all brought together in some definitive relationship, which reveals particular ideas.

5. THE QUALITIES OF A GOOD SUBJECT

The preacher may be able to state his subject in a more definitive way by observing certain qualities. (1) The good subject should be clear. It should show clearly what the preacher intends to do. It should state clearly what the sermon is about. Good examples of clear titles are "The Gospel According to Christ's Enemies" and "The Christian Secret of Radiance." (2) A good subject is also specific. It takes a particular aspect of a subject and develops it. Many sermon subjects are too general. James Black related his experience:

I had a dreadful experience during my first few months as a minister, which I may use as a warning for you. Like most young men, I knew very little about the business of preaching. I had only about a dozen sermons in my possession, twelve ancient blank cartridges in my locker. Here is what I said to myself each week. "Go to, Sir! thou shalt write a sermon on Temptation." Which I did, dealing with it, in a young man's large way, as comprehensively as I could. I then found a text for it, and tagged it on like a label. And after that, I had absolutely nothing more to say about Temptation! Next week, I said, "Go to, Sir! thou shalt write a sermon on Providence." Which I did, again exhausting the subject as thoroughly as I could. And after that, I had nothing more to say about Providence! . . . And I tell you frankly, at the end of three months, I thought I had exhausted all available truth: and certainly I had exhausted myself. I remember wondering whether I could slink away decently, or whether there should be a public exposure in Presbytery.[5]

(3) A good subject should be brief. Clarity, however, should never be sacrificed for brevity. Yet a short, brief subject is better. The preacher should try to capture his focal idea in a few words. Generally the subject is a noun and its modifier. It may be a phrase, but it should be stated succinctly. (4) Then a good subject should be Christian. The preacher is a Christian preacher. The subject should be a Christian subject or should lead to Christ. The preacher is a herald of Jesus Christ.

NOTES

1. A. E. Garvie, *The Christian Preacher* (Edinburgh: T. & T. Clark, 1920), pp. 385–89.
2. Ibid., p. 420.
3. James S. Stewart, *The Gates of New Life* (New York: Charles Scribner's Sons, 1940), p. 125.
4. W. L. Watkinson, *The Shepherd of the Sea* (New York: Fleming H. Revell, n.d.), pp. 53–54.
5. James Black, *The Mystery of Preaching* (New York: Fleming H. Revell, 1924), pp. 152–53.

CHAPTER 7

The Title

1. THE FUNCTION OF THE TITLE

While the sermon must have a subject, it may also have a title. The principal function of the title is to catch attention, to attract and interest the public. In a day of church calendars, bulletin boards, and newspaper and television advertising, this function is of great importance. Dr. O. S. Davis made the observation that as the success or failure of a book is often determined by its title, "so the attractiveness of a sermon is conditioned largely by the choice of the title."[1] Occasionally the well-phrased subject may be sufficient. Generally, however, an interesting title will be more effective for public announcement.

2. THE DEFINITION OF THE TITLE

What is the title? How does the title differ from the subject? The title is what the preacher calls the sermon. It is the name he gives his sermon. It has been noted that its primary purpose is to advertise the sermon. It has no value apart from advertising the sermon. For example, when the subject is "The Christian Addict," the title may be "You Should Be an Addict." Or when the subject is "The Marks of a Worthwhile Life," the title may be "What Makes Life Worth Living?"

3. THE STATEMENT OF THE TITLE

The title may take many forms. The form it takes depends on the imagination, taste, and purpose of the preacher, and in these things preachers are not all equal. Some titles are in technical theological terms, others in untechnical words ranging from good vernacular to slang. They are in the form of questions, exclamations, prepositional phrases, contingent clauses, single words, short dogmatic statements, as well as in conventional subject form. Few writers have the ability to frame a title that gives an adequate sense of the subject in phraseology that strikes the moods, the perplexities, the tendencies, and the manner of speech of the modern person.

It is a rare gift that enables a preacher to select such titles as will be vital, interesting, timely, and also conform to the laws of good taste and dignity. With careful thought and continued practice a preacher ought to become resourceful and accurate in the phrasing of sermon titles; certainly this involves one's best possible thought and practice.[2]

4. THE QUALITIES OF A GOOD TITLE

The qualities which mark a good subject are essentially true of the title. However, certain qualities are especially necessary for the title. (1) A good title should be interesting. If it is to capture interest, this is of prime importance. However, it need not be gaudy or sensational. It may capture attention and create interest without "paying any homage to the flippancy and frivolity of the time."[3] Many sermon titles create no anticipation. To see "The Good Samaritan" on a bulletin board would not add much excitement. However, "The Story of an Ambush" might stimulate interest.

(2) A good sermon title should also be honest. It should never bear false witness. A title should not be announced and never mentioned again. Some men draw crowds by advertising sensational titles which are never discussed. When the book *Forever Amber* was popular, a pastor advertised the title, "Forever

Amber." However, he did not preach about the book, but rather about people that are like some traffic lights, not red or green, but forever amber. (3) Finally, a good sermon title should not be vulgar. It should always be in good taste. Titles such as "A Haircut in a Devil's Barbershop," "The Man Who Lost His Head at a Dance," and "The Best Town in the World by a Dam Site" are to be avoided.

Perhaps the ideal is to have a subject so attractive that an added title is not needed. Harry Emerson Fosdick preached on the theme "Six Ways to Tell Right from Wrong." This topic is both clear and interesting.

NOTES

1. O. S. Davis, *Principles of Preaching* (Chicago: University of Chicago Press, 1924), p. 199.
2. Ibid., p. 200.
3. J. H. Jowett, *The Preacher: His Life and Work* (New York: Harper & Brothers, 1912), p. 88.

CHAPTER 8

The Proposition

A MORE complete way of expressing the subject is the proposition. The proposition deserves more attention than it is often given. It is a statement of the subject as the preacher proposes to develop it. It is subject (idea) and predicate. The subject answers the question, What is the sermon about? The proposition answers the question, What is the sermon? Phelps likens the proposition to the trunk from which the body of the sermon expands, the root being the idea in the text.[1] "The discourse is the proposition unfolded, and the proposition is the discourse condensed" (Fénelon). Its form should be one complete declarative sentence, simple, clear, and cogent. It should contain no unnecessary or ambiguous words. "It should contain all that is essential to the sermon, no less and no more, and no other than the truth of the subject, stated in cumulative order."[2] It has to do with the form and substance of the message.

A few examples will make the meaning clear. In the famous sermon "Every Man's Life a Plan of God," Horace Bushnell announced the following proposition:

The truth I propose then for your consideration is this: That God has a definite life-plan for every human person, girding him, visibly or invisibly, for some exact thing which it will be the true significance and glory of his life to have accomplished.[3]

Bushnell's sermon on "Unconscious Influence" has for its proposition,

Thus it is that men are ever touching unconsciously the springs of motion in each other, (so that) one man without thought or intention or even a consciousness of the fact is ever leading some other after him.[4]

Phillips Brooks's sermon on the "Light of the World" contains two statements of the proposition, the one brief, the other more explicit:

(1) That the soul of man carries the highest possibilities within itself, and that what Christ does for it is to kindle and call forth these possibilities to actual existence.

(2) Christ when he comes finds the soul or the world really existent, really having within itself its holiest capabilities, really moving, though dimly and darkly, in spite of its hindrances, in its true directions; and what he does for it is to quicken it through and through, to sound the bugle of its true life in its ears, to make it feel the nobleness of movements which have seemed to it ignoble, the hopefulness of impulses which have seemed hopeless, to bid it be itself.[5]

The student will readily see that the briefer is the better statement.

Turning to other sermons, notice first one by Dr. G. G. Atkins. The text is Psalm 119:109; the title, "Craftsmen of the Soul"; the proposition, "In a true sense we hold our souls in our hands as an artificer the materials upon which he works, and the creative shaping of them to high uses and enduring ends is our master task."[6] From Dr. H. E. Fosdick we have the following: text, Philemon 4:22; title, "Christians in Spite of Everything"; proposition, "Christianity essentially means a spiritual victory in the face of hostile circumstance." In a volume of sermons by A. A. Cowan, a sermon on the institution of the Lord's Supper has for its texts Exodus 12:26 and Matthew 17:5; for its title, "The Banquet of Liberty"; and for the proposition, "What Jesus and his disciples celebrated in the Upper Room was a new future prepared by divine love for believing hearts and assuring them that they would be freed from all enslavements."[7] In a sermon on the "Escape from Frustration," James Reid, using Luke 5:4, 5, and 10 as his text, states his proposition as follows: "The way out of life's frustrations is found, not by resenting our limitation, but by accepting the place of frustration as the sphere of God's purpose."[8] In a sermon entitled "What Is a Christian?" A. Leonard Griffith gives the essence of his message. "It is by virtue of our relationship to Christ that we can call ourselves Christians, and from the very beginning that relationship has meant at least five things. Compare it to a star with five points of equal length and importance."[9]

The proposition is the gist of the sermon. A reading of the best sermons reveals that often the preacher repeats the comprehensive sentence more than once and every paragraph serves in some way to enforce or prove or explain or illuminate it in its deep significance. It is observed also that the proposition varies in its character; sometimes it is a thesis calling for logical argument to prove it; sometimes it is a truth to be explained, or appraised and applied. Often it is not formally stated with any such introductory words as "I propose to show," but is incidental; and sometimes it does not appear at all in the sermon. But usually the reader, or hearer, is more interested if in the introduction or early in the sermon, there is a revealing statement of the heart of the message. It may be well to conceal the steps taken and to employ the element of surprise, but it should be the process of unfolding and applying truth rather than hiding the truth that inspires the preacher. So the proposition is of value in the delivery of the sermon, adding greatly to its effectiveness.

However, it is of greater value in the preparation. To write out a proposition as one begins to compose the sermon, even though it may have to be revised more than once as one proceeds, is to give point and direction to the writing. It will serve as a sort of magnet to keep one on the main track. And not the least service is to deliver the preacher from monotony and staleness, for few people will consent to platitudes and repetitious sermons if they stare at them week after week from the written sentence. The preacher is not wasting time when he searches for a vital statement of his theme. He can get along much better with it than without it.

NOTES

1. Austin Phelps, *The Theory of Preaching* (New York: Charles Scribner's Sons, 1893), p. 308.
2. O. S. Davis, *Principles of Preaching* (Chicago: University of Chicago Press, 1924), p. 206.
3. Horace Bushnell, *Sermons for the New Life* (New York: Charles Scribner's Sons, 1907), p. 10.
4. As reprinted in Davis, p. 21.
5. Ibid., p. 43 ff.
6. G. G. Atkins, *Craftsmen of the Soul* (New York: Fleming H. Revell, 1925), Chapter 1.
7. A. A. Cowan, Crisis on the Frontier (Edinburgh: T. & T. Clark, 1945), Chapter 6.
8. James Reid, *Facing Life with Christ* (Nashville, Tenn.: Cokesbury Press, 1940), Chapter 8.
9. A. Leonard Griffith, *What Is a Christian?* (New York: Abingdon Press, 1962), p. 12.

CHAPTER 9

The Objective

ANOTHER foundation of the sermon is the objective. The objective does not have to do with form and content; rather it has to do with results. It is the aim of the sermon. It is the goal of the sermon. It answers the question, "What life changes should result from the sermon?" In other words, "What does the preacher want to accomplish?" If something should happen because of preaching, exactly what does the preacher want to happen in the lives of the people before him because of one sermon?

This simple fact seems difficult for many preachers to grasp. The objective is confused with the subject or proposition. Preachers often state their objectives in terms of content, but the objective is concerned with action, changes, verdict. For example, a sermon on "The High Road to Salvation" would have this objective: to lead listeners to walk this high road and to receive salvation in Christ. A sermon on tithing would seek to bring the congregation to a commitment to tithe income.

While particular objectives are as varied as sermons, some general objectives characterize most preaching. (1) Perhaps the first objective is to please God. A sermon should first be an offering to God. A minister studies God's Word, prepares a message, and then first gives it to God in an act of worship. This has implications for discipline and preparation. (2) A second general objective is the salvation of souls. Jesus came to seek and to save the lost. The preacher tries to bring a saving gospel and lost souls together. (3) He is also to edify the church and to help his people mature in Christ through his preaching.

The objective will aid the pastor in the choice and arrangement of material. The end result of the sermon will determine how arguments are marshaled, how facts are presented. Primarily, however, the objective determines results. The person who aims at nothing always hits it. The preacher who has a definite aim and purpose may accomplish them.

Two rules should be kept in mind as the preacher prepares his objective. (1) The objective should be well defined. The preacher should know exactly what he is trying to accomplish, what verdict he is trying to win.

The first condition of an effective sermon is a definite object. Mark the difference between subject and object. In preparing a sermon the minister should define his object in his own mind. . . . What do I want to accomplish this Sunday morning . . . with this discourse? This is the first question for the preacher to ask himself.[1]

(2) Then the objective should be limited. Many sermons fail because the preacher tries to accomplish too much by one sermon. It may take ten single objectives to gain one major objective. For example, when a congregation has a poor concept of stewardship of money, the first sermon should not be on tithing. Sermons should be preached on God's sovereignty and God's ownership. Other sermons should follow on man's responsibility in many areas. Perhaps then a verdict may be won in the area of stewardship of money.

These foundations are basic to sermon preparation. Each of the five elements should be prepared for every sermon. Take note of the format that follows:

SERMON BEGINNINGS

1. Text:
2. Subject:
3. Title:
4. Proposition:
5. Objective:

*   *

Classification by method_____
Classification by subject_____

*   *

OUTLINE
Subject:

NOTE

1. Lyman Abbott, *The Christian Ministry* (New York: Houghton, Mifflin and Company, 1905), p. 208.

For Further Reading:
Foundations of the Sermon

Brown, H. C., Jr.; Clinard, H. Gordon; and Northcutt, Jesse J. *Steps to the Sermon*. Nashville, Tenn.: Broadman Press, 1963.

Davis, Henry Grady. *Design for Preaching*. Philadelphia: Muhlenberg Press, 1958.

Hall, Thor. *Future Shape of Preaching*. Philadelphia: Fortress Press, 1971.

Lenski, R.C.H. *The Sermon*. Grand Rapids, Mich.: Baker Book House, 1968.

Lloyd-Jones, D. Martyn. *Preaching and Preachers*. Grand Rapids, Mich.: Zondervan, 1971.

Macpherson, Ian. *The Burden of the Lord*. New York: Abingdon Press, 1955.

Reu, M. *Homiletics*. Grand Rapids, Mich.: Baker Book House, 1924.

Stevenson, Dwight E. *In the Biblical Preacher's Workshop*. Nashville, Tenn.: Abingdon Press, 1967.

Switzer, David. *Pastor Preacher Person*. Nashville, Tenn.: Abingdon Press, 1979.

Weatherspoon, Jesse Burton. *Sent Forth to Preach*. New York: Harper & Bros., 1954.

Part II

THE CLASSIFICATION OF SERMONS

THE wise builder studies plans or designs. The wise sermon builder also studies plans or designs. Having looked at the foundations of the sermon, it is important to examine designs or patterns before beginning consideration of actual sermon structure.

Sermon designs fall into many classifications and patterns. Dr. A. W. Blackwood has made this observation about sermon designs: "Needless to say, these labels fit poorly. Sometimes these overlap and cause confusion."[1] However, it is important for the sermon builder to study various plans in order that he may construct sermons from these plans and use them as a basis for still other plans. Examination of the sermons of great preachers is almost always disappointing to the student seeking perfect examples of any one design. Designs are always secondary to purpose and utility. They are tools, and in the shaping of tools and the techniques for handling tools, experimentation and invention are desirable. But these require intelligence and faithfulness to underlying principles. The streamline automobile preserves the essential elements of an oxcart. The student of preaching must not disdain but rather master the sermon patterns, following them closely in the days of his apprenticeship.

CHAPTER 10

Classification by Homiletical Structure

1. THE TEXTUAL SERMON

The primary classification of sermons is by structure. One of the most common methods is the textual sermon. In the textual sermon, the divisions come from the text. The text provides the subject and the major divisions of the sermon. A single subject is drawn from the text and then is discussed under the divisions the text furnishes.

An example of a favorite textual sermon is 2 Corinthians 8:9, "For you know the grace of our Lord Jesus Christ, that though He was rich, yet for your sakes He became poor, that you through his poverty might be rich." The divisions that usually evolve are:

I. He was rich.
II. He became poor.
III. He did this that you (man) might be rich.

In this instance, the text provides a logical order.

Another example of a textual sermon is Psalm 145:16, "Thou openest thine hand, and satisfiest the desire of every living thing" (KJV). The divisions are these:

I. God provides personally.
II. God provides easily.
III. God provides abundantly.

Here the divisions are drawn from the text without following the natural order of the text.

In many ways the textual sermon is the easiest format. The main divisions are in the text, yet there is considerable freedom in the choice of material and the development.

A few suggestions may help in the handling of the textual sermon. (1) Find a specific subject. Discover what the text is about. Some writers indicate that a subject may not be necessary for some kinds of textual preaching; however, it is impossible to attain unity without at least a general subject. (2) Then seek for exact divisions. Ideas in a passage may overlap. The sermon builder must find the separate ideas. (3) Then it is not always necessary to follow the natural order of the text. This may be easy and convenient, but it is not obligatory. A sermon which rearranged the order of the text was developed on Ephesians 5:20: "Giving thanks always for all things unto God" (KJV).

I. The Duty of Giving Thanks—"giving thanks"
II. The Object to Whom Thanks Are Given—"unto God"
III. The Extent of the Thanks—"for all things"
IV. The Time of Giving Thanks—"always"

This reordering of a text is common procedure and should be done when the end results are clarity and climax. (4) The preacher need not use every part of a text. He should have the wisdom to omit. The material omitted will be usable for another sermon.

2. THE TOPICAL SERMON

Topical (subject) sermons are those in which the divisions are derived from the subject. The topic may be derived from the text, but the divisions come from the subject. The subject is divided and treated according to its own nature.

This form of treatment has important advantages. It better

insures unity, which is indispensable to effective speaking. It trains the preacher's mind in logical analysis, an invaluable asset. It is more convincing and pleasing to an educated audience, since it is more logical and also more complete. Besides, there will often be practical occasion for so thoroughly discussing a subject. The needs of the congregation will make the preacher wish to present a full view of some doctrine or some topic of general or particular morality, and not merely the special aspects of it which one text or another may exhibit. The Scriptures do not present truth in a succession of logical propositions, any more than the objects of nature are found grouped according to scientific classification. This suits the design of the Bible as a book to be read and also leads to a rich variety in textual preaching. But it is frequently instructive and satisfactory to discuss some collective subject.

Now the different methods of dividing a subject are numerous and varied. Again Dr. Garvie is helpful here:

An abstract idea may be illustrated by concrete instances, scriptural, historical, biographical, literary. A personality may be sketched as regards heredity, environment, development, capacity, character, career, reputation. An event may be examined as regards time, place, antecedents, consequents, human conduct, or divine Providence. A nation's history falls into periods separated by crises. The moral quality of an action may be judged as regards motive, method, manner, intention, result; its religious significance may be determined in its conditions and issues as regards the relation of God and man. A vice, virtue, or grace may be analyzed psychologically as regards thought, feeling, will. A statement may be broken up into its parts; e.g., Evil company doth corrupt good manners (1 Cor. 15:33). (1) What is evil company? (2) Wherein do good manners consist? (3) How does the first corrupt the second? The enquiry might be extended thus. (4) Why does it corrupt? The expansiveness and pervasiveness of personal influence would be the answer. (5) How is this corruption to be prevented? A subject can be dealt with in its various relations, as love in relation to God, self, neighbor. The various reasons for a thesis may be stated in order, as for the statement that Christ is divine: (1) his sinlessness and perfect moral character, (2) his unique and absolute consciousness of divine sonship, (3) the constance and efficacy of his mediatorial function.[2]

Subject preaching is the orator's method par excellence. It lends itself to finished discourse. But it has its dangers. The preacher easily becomes interested in finding subjects that are interesting and readily yield a good oration rather than those that have a true Christian and scriptural basis or those that come close to the needs of his people. He is tempted to think more of his ideas and his sermons than of "rightly dividing the word of truth" and leading people into the Kingdom of God. He is in danger also of preaching in too narrow a field of truth and human need, since of necessity he will be drawn to those subjects that interest him personally or with which he is already familiar. Unless, therefore, he is constantly widening his horizon by diligent study, he will soon exhaust his resources. Accordingly, at the very beginning, the student should be warned against too exclusive use of this type of sermon.

3. THE TEXTUAL-TOPICAL SERMON

Still another method of classification by homiletical structure is the textual-topical sermon. Few writers on preaching list this method as one of the classic forms. Yet a careful examination of sermons by prominent preachers will reveal the frequent use of the textual-topical method.

If the textual sermon gets its divisions from the text, and the topical sermon gets its divisions from the topic, the textual-topical sermon gets its divisions from both the text and the topic. A sermon was developed from Isaiah 53:3, "He is despised and rejected of men" (KJV). The title was "Admired, Yet Rejected," and the subject was "Some Common Attitudes toward Christ." The divisions were as follows:

  I. He is despised and rejected.
 II. He is admired, yet rejected.
III. He should be admired and accepted.

The first division came from the text; the other two divisions came from the topic.

This method has a strong biblical base and yet allows for

freedom of development. It has many of the oratorical advantages of the topical sermon.

4. THE EXPOSITORY SERMON

The last classification by homiletical method is the expository sermon. If preaching is giving the Bible a voice, if preaching is the proclamation of God's message, then it would seem that the expository method would be the method most commonly employed. However, this is not true. The expository sermon has been the type most neglected. Over the years many lectures have made a strong case for expository preaching. In his book *The Heralds of God,* James S. Stewart addresses three pleas to ministers.

> The first is a plea for expository preaching. This is one of the greatest needs of the hour. There are rich rewards of human gratitude waiting for the man who can make the Bible come alive. Congregations are sick of dissertations on problems and essays on aspects of the religious situation; such sermons are indeed no true preaching at all. Men are not wanting to be told our poor views and arguments and ideals. They are emphatically wanting to be told what God has said, and is saying, in His Word.[3]

In recent years more ministers are doing expository preaching. Congregations are responding to a Bible-centered proclamation. Since the expository sermon is becoming an increasingly used method, it is important to understand its meaning. But there is not one definition of the expository sermon; there are many. A general definition is this: An expository sermon is one which is occupied mainly with the exposition of Scripture. Following the pattern of the definitions of the textual and topical sermons, the expository sermon may be defined as a sermon that draws its divisions and the exploration of those divisions from the text. In actual practice, the main points and the subdivisions of the sermon often come from the text. In other words, the entire thought content comes from the Scripture. This does not rule out explanation, illustration, and application from other sources, but the basic ideas come from the text.

It does not seem to be valid to define an expository sermon in terms of the length of text, usually three or more verses. While the expository sermon is frequently from a longer passage, an expository sermon may be based on a single verse or even on one word.

Dr. A. W. Blackwood cites one example of the expository sermon based on Isaiah 6:1–8 and entitled "A Young Man at Worship."

1. A young man's vision of God.
2. A young man's vision of sin.
3. A young man's vision of cleansing.
4. A young man's vision of service.[4]

This sermon uses eight verses as a text.

However, an expository sermon may be prepared on one verse. An example is Romans 8:6, "For to be carnally minded is death; but to be spiritually minded is life and peace." This could be organized in two ways. The two parts of the verse could be treated as two ideas.

1. To be carnally minded is death.
2. To be spiritually minded is life and peace.

Or the text could be rearranged in this manner:

I. Two minds are:
  1. The carnal mind
  2. The spiritual mind
II. Two results are:
  1. Death
  2. Life and peace

Sermons could be prepared on a single great word such as *agapé* and *charis.*

Actually, the different kinds of expository sermons are many. In addition to the word, the single text, and the paragraph, it may also be based on a chapter, a book, an episode, a drama, a narrative, or an incident. The expository method is limited only by the kinds of literature in Scripture.

What, then, is the prime requisite for effective expository preaching? The answer must be unity. Unity in a discourse is necessary to instruction, to conviction, and to persuasion. Without it, the taste of educated listeners cannot be satisfied, and even the uneducated, though they may not know why, will be far less deeply impressed. But unity in an expository discourse is never the goal of many preachers. They conceive of it as a mere series of disjointed remarks upon the successive verses.

In making a single, detached expository discourse, one can easily see to it that the passage selected has unity. In continuous exposition of the same book, it may sometimes be necessary to take a passage in which this is not the case; but even then, thoughts may be gathered and framed into one plan. There should be unity whatever the cost.

And not only is unity essential, but also order is important. Thanks to the influence of the Scholastics of the Middle Ages, the modern mind enjoys analysis and the regular construction of the materials which analysis has furnished, and therefore has a great preference for topical sermons. The homilies left us by the early church Fathers are frequently quite deficient in orderly structure and sometimes even lack unity. And some persons appear to imagine that there can be no "homilies" except upon the model of the Fathers, and with a total disregard of modern taste and modes of thought. But a discourse upon an extended passage of Scripture, well chosen and well handled, may have a definite topic and a distinct and orderly plan and yet not fail to be an expository discourse. An expository sermon may have, and must have, both unity and an orderly structure. The frequent practical neglect of these requisites is one principal cause of failure to use this method.

In order to achieve variety in sermonic method, the preacher should prepare sermons employing every kind of homiletical structure. This variety will be acceptable and pleasing to the listening congregation.

NOTES

1. A. W. Blackwood, *The Preparation of Sermons* (New York: Abingdon-Cokesbury Press, 1948), p. 101.
2. A. E. Garvie, *The Christian Preacher* (Edinburgh: T. & T. Clark, 1920), p. 433.
3. James S. Stewart, *The Heralds of God* (New York: Charles Scribner's Sons, 1946), p. 109.
4. Blackwood, p. 68.

CHAPTER 11

Classification by Subject

1. THE THEOLOGICAL SERMON

A second way to classify sermons is by subject matter or content. Because of the nature of the Christian faith, the theological or doctrinal sermon may be the primary classification by content. The theological sermon is one which expounds some basic Christian beliefs with the purpose of gaining its understanding and acceptance.

The phrase "doctrinal sermon" is constantly used by some pastors to denote sermons on points of denominational peculiarity or controversy. Such a limitation, implying that these are the only doctrines, or that doctrine cannot be discussed other than polemically, is a grave error and should be carefully avoided.

Doctrine, i.e., teaching, is the preacher's chief business. Truth is the life blood of piety, without which we cannot maintain its vitality or support its activity. And to teach people truth, or to revive what they already know into freshness and power, is the preacher's great means of doing good. The facts and truths which belong to the scriptural accounts of sin, providence, and redemption, form the staple of all scriptural preaching. But these truths should not have an incidental or miscellaneous place in our preaching. The entire body of scriptural teaching upon any particular subject, when collected and systematically arranged, has come to be called the doctrine of Scripture on that subject, as the doctrine of sin, of atonement, of regeneration, etc.; and in this sense the pastor should preach frequently on the doctrines of the Bible.

It is important that the preacher should himself have sound views of doctrine; is it not also important that he should lead his congregation to have just views? In this time of confusion and agitation, in these days of somewhat intense religious activity, real doctrinal preaching does not have the place it deserves. To a certain extent, it is proper that we should conform to the tastes of the age, for they frequently indicate its real needs and always affect its reception of truth; but when those tastes are manifestly faulty, the preacher should earnestly endeavor to correct them. The preacher who can make doctrinal truth interesting as well as intelligible to his congregation and gradually teach them the doctrines of the Bible is rendering them an inestimable service.

The Christian preacher should not neglect the great doctrines. True, they are familiar; but sermons upon them need not be commonplace. The sunlight is fresh every morning, and so the great doctrines of the gospel are forever new. Our task is, loving these truths ourselves, to make others love them. Many a preacher could tell how, in the early months or years of his untutored ministry, he was sometimes driven from sheer lack of a novel topic to fall back upon familiar doctrines and make what he felt to be a poor sermon, and how, long afterwards, he heard of good results from those sermons rather than from others which he, at the time, considered much more striking and impressive. Of course, one should not make a hobby of a particular doctrine, as some men do with the doctrine of election, or baptism, or perfection, or the witness of the Spirit, or the second coming of our Lord. In regard to preaching unpopular doctrines, such as election (before some audiences), future punishment, depravity, and even missions (before others), one comprehensive rule may be given: Be faithful and fearless, but skillful and affectionate.

In recent years, it has become much more popular to preach a full range of doctrines. Perhaps a renewed emphasis on biblical studies and biblical theology has contributed to this change in attitude.

Some practical suggestions may help in performing this great task. (1) For one thing, theological preaching should be comprehensive. It should cover both the major and minor doctrines of the Christian faith. A pastor who plans his preaching may have a series of theological sermons as a part of his plan each year for five years. (2) Theological preaching should be positive. As has been noted, it need not be polemical. It should be a straight forward presentation of the truth. Positive truth has a way of eliminating error. (3) Then theological preaching should be clear. It cannot be the book of theology chapter or the theological lecture reproduced. The doctrine must be assimilated and then presented in simple terms which the average person in the congregation can understand.

2. THE ETHICAL SERMON

Another classification by subject matter is the ethical sermon. The ethical sermon deals primarily with Christian living—personal and social. It sets forth Christian ideals for life's relationships and offers guidance for attaining those ideals.

Sometimes pious people speak with severe reprobation of ethical sermons. It has often been the case that morality would be preached with little or no reference to the atonement and the work of the Spirit, a mere morality taking the place of the real gospel. This has established an association in many minds between moral discourses and opposition to the doctrines of grace. But our Lord's personal teachings consist mainly of morality; and Paul and Peter, while unfolding and dwelling on the salvation which is by grace through faith, have not merely urged in general a holy life but have given many precepts with reference to moral duties. But there is in many quarters a reluctance to preach much upon particular questions of moral obligation. A preacher of the gospel certainly should not preach morality apart from the gospel. While he may present other than strictly evangelical motives, he must be inspired by the motive of grateful love to Christ and consecration to his service. He must first, as an ambassador for Christ, call his parishioners to be reconciled to God; he must insist upon the indispensable need of regeneration through the Holy Spirit. Then, speaking to those who are looked upon as regenerate, he must, with all his might, urge them to true and high morality, not only on all other grounds, but as a solemn duty to God their Savior. For Christianity has a distinctive ethics as well as a theology, and the preacher cannot escape the dual responsibility of making clear the moral principles that are basic in Christian living and of guiding his people in the application of those principles to personal and social problems. The only question is how far he should go into details. As above intimated, our Lord and his apostles did go into details very freely. And preaching often suffers from the fact that, while inculcating Christian morality in general, practical application of ethical principles is not brought home to the hearts and daily lives of the people.

As is true of the theological sermon, the ethical sermon on particular problems is much more acceptable now than in the recent past. Personal and social problems are acute. Many pastors are trying to bring the light of biblical truth to the dark needs of this generation.

As a preacher presents ethical sermons, some suggestions for this kind of preaching may prove helpful. (1) The ethical sermon should generally be positive. It may be necessary to deal with the problem or error before presenting the Christian ideal. But many listeners are aware of the problems. They want answers; they want to know the teaching of the Christian faith. (2) Ethical preaching should be constructive rather than destructive. Present a Christian plan. Try to answer the question "How?" It is much easier to talk about the problem of divorce than to tell people how to build strong marriages. (3) The preacher of ethical messages should try to win the love and confidence of his people before challenging them to dramatic life changes or radical social action. It takes time and care and love to become the shepherd of a flock. Congregations will listen to a true shepherd. (4) The preacher of ethical sermons must be willing to begin where people are and move from the real to the ideal. Many serious problems are solved one step at a time. (5) Then the preacher of ethical sermons should reveal in his sermon delivery that he also is struggling to attain the Christian ideal. He, too, has not yet attained the Christian ideal, but like Paul, he is striving to attain.

3. THE CHURCH PROGRAM SERMON

Another classification by content is the church program sermon or the ecclesiastical sermon. The church program sermon seeks to promote some phase of the program of the church so that the church can fulfill its function. This type of sermon should be used infrequently. It does not have the importance of the theological or ethical sermon. Nonetheless, present-day church life has many activities, and often these need support.

Some rules should be followed for church program preaching. (1) The preacher should be certain of the motive behind such preaching. Is he trying to promote self, or the local church, or the Christian faith? (2) The pastor should remember that church program preaching is not an end in itself. It is a means to a much bigger end. (3) Then the church program sermon should have a strong biblical base. Otherwise, it may sound very secular and much like "hardsell" advertising.

The theological sermon, the ethical sermon, and the church program sermon may merge into each other. Often hybrids are produced. A sermon may begin in theology and end in living. A sermon may begin with a Christian ideal and support it with theological truth. Both theological and ethical sermons may provide the base for church program sermons. The sermon type and variation really do not matter as long as the preacher has a clear concept of his goal in mind.

CHAPTER 12

Classification by Pattern

SERMONS have been classified by structure and subject matter. Sermons may also be classified by pattern or format. Sermon plans have been many and varied. Surely new formats are yet to be discovered or invented.

When Dr. Halford Luccock suggested certain patterns of outline, he indicated that they were offered "without undue solemnity, or any pride of parentage."[1] These patterns are suggested in the same spirit.

1. *The diamond outline.* One sermon pattern is the diamond outline. This has been called the jewel sermon and the one-idea sermon. The development of the diamond outline consists of turning an idea around so that the different sides of it may be seen. Or a single idea may be illustrated in different ways. One pastor preached a sermon entitled "You Can't Bribe God." He examined each facet of the idea as each facet of a diamond might be examined.

This pattern is usually interesting. It is especially effective for the brief sermon and for the devotional sermon.

2. *The ladder outline.* Another sermon pattern is the ladder outline. To move up a ladder, the climber should take one step at a time, and each step depends on the step below. In the ladder sermon, each idea builds on the previous point, augmenting it and moving to a climax.

A commonly used evangelistic outline builds in this manner.

I.   All men have sinned.
II. Christ suffered and paid the price for man's sin.
III. Through Christ, man may be forgiven his sin.

The ladder sermon is ideally adapted to persuasion and appeal. If the first idea is accepted, it is likely that each succeeding idea will be more readily received.

3. *The label outline.* Yet another sermon pattern is the label outline. This is also called the classification sermon. Various persons and things are labeled or classified. The parable of the soils or hearers may be so developed. Each type of soil or hearer is labeled.

One pastor preached a sermon entitled, "What Kind of Spring Are You?" In this sermon, springs and Christians were classified as big, small, seasonal, and former (with explanation of terms).

This type of sermon is usually interesting. It is also easy to understand and easy to follow.

4. *The contrast outline.* Yet another sermon pattern is the contrast outline. This is always a two-point sermon in which contrasting ideas are stated. Common contrasts are wrong-right, negative-positive, bad-good.

This sermon type is excellent for reproof and correction. It is often used for the Christian life sermon and for the church program sermon.

5. *The question and answer outline.* One of the oldest sermon patterns is the question and answer outline. This plan involves raising questions and then giving answers to the questions. This pattern has been called the "adverbial plan." In practice, the preacher may raise one question and give several answers, or he may raise several questions and answer each question.

For example, in response to the question, "Who is Jesus?" there could be many answers. Also, questions such as what, where, when, and who may be raised about many subjects.

While some writers doubt the value of the question and answer method, it is still a viable plan. However, the preacher should keep in mind that it is only a plan. The question is really a method of transition; the answer to the question is the division or subdivision. Moreover, when the pastor raises a question, he should give an immediate answer. Occasionally, a pause gives someone in the congregation opportunity to answer the question. If the answer given differs from the preacher's answer, the result may be disastrous. On the other hand, in a dialogue sermon, the preacher may want one or more people to answer the question.

6. *The chase outline.* The chase outline is yet another plan that may be used. This method is also called the guessing-game sermon. This method consists of raising the question, "Is it this? Is it this? Is it this?" and giving negative answers until the proper answer (according to the speaker) is reached.

Dr. Clarence Edward Macartney employs this method in a book of sermons entitled *The Greatest Words in the Bible and Human Speech.* In one sermon, "The Most Beautiful Word," he begins with the question, "What is the most beautiful word, in the Bible or out of it, spoken in heaven, or upon earth?"[2] After considering many answers, Dr. Macartney concludes that the most beautiful word is forgiveness. Each sermon in the book follows the chase format.

The preacher leads the people to a conclusion and then develops it as the sermon. In this instance, the chase method provides an introduction to a sermon. However, it may give the plan for an entire sermon.

7. *The diagnosis-remedy outline.* This method consists of making a diagnosis of a problem or need and then giving the remedy to this problem or need. This pattern has also been called the problem-answer outline or the problem-solution outline. Naturally the sermon consists of two major parts, giving a diagnosis and then suggesting a remedy.

This sermon plan is quite useful in dealing with problems in Christian living or in church programs. This is the place for the "how" sermon. The people can be shown how to solve the problem.

Because of the directness of this method, it may be offensive to some people, but it need not be. The preacher should give an honest diagnosis, and then he must offer a helpful remedy. Some preachers are much more effective in diagnosis than in prognosis. It is especially important that an answer or a solution be presented.

8. *The "Hegelian" outline.* This sermon plan has been suggested by the methodology of the philosopher Hegel. It follows the order of thesis, antithesis, and synthesis. An example of this technique is seen in a sermon on "The Nature of the Gospel." This sermon has these ideas:

1. The gospel is personal.
2. The gospel is social.
3. The gospel is both personal and social.

In using this method the preacher tries to present a thesis which will be accepted by the congregation, and then he adds an antithesis about which some members of the congregation may have doubt. He then will add the synthesis, hoping that the synthesis will be accepted by the congregation. This method is especially valuable because it usually begins where people are and then seeks to add to their understanding.

9. *The analogy outline.* The analogy plan is a method of presenting truth by analogy or by comparison. For example, many sermons have been preached on "Jesus, the Good Shepherd." An analogy is created by first revealing the characteristics of a good shepherd and then showing that Jesus has all of these characteristics in a spiritual sense. One pastor preached a sermon on "The Church as a Lighthouse." He had unusual knowledge of lighthouses, and he was able to make a careful analogy between the lighthouse and the church.

This sermon plan has a high interest content. Since it is often based on a picture or story, it is easy both for the preacher to present and for the congregation to retain.

10. *The proof outline.* Yet another sermon type is the proof outline. This method offers proof of the preacher's subject or affirmation. It often follows the format "This is true because. . . ." This method will often have more than the usual three ideas. A pastor may give several reasons to support his assertions. One pastor preached an evangelistic sermon entitled "Tomorrow May Be Dangerous." The outline consisted in a listing of five reasons why tomorrow was dangerous for the unbeliever.

The value of this method is that it offers a reasoned basis for the preacher's proposition. It also gives the preacher opportunity to prove his assertions.

11. *The rebuttal outline.* The rebuttal outline is just the opposite of the proof outline. It seeks to tear down or to disprove. A pastor may learn that some of his people have been subjected to false doctrine. Therefore, he tells them why that doctrine is not true.

This method of preaching has often been used as a way of dealing with personal or social problems. The pastor will tell his congregation why a habit or practice is wrong or harmful. For example, pastors have used this technique in presenting the dangers of alcohol or other drugs.

The rebuttal outline has the advantage of offering a reasoned basis for a decision. The pastor does much more than make an appeal. He gives practical reasons to show the harmfulness of a habit or practice.

12. *The refrain outline.* The refrain outline is an outline that has a theme or a refrain running through it. This technique has been called the symphonic sermon. It has also been classified as a thematic sermon. The refrain is usually presented in the introduction of the sermon, and then it is repeated after each idea of the sermon. For example, a pastor preached a sermon entitled "Just as He Said." This was based on Luke 19:28–35, the incident of Jesus's sending the disciples out to get the colt. The disciples were given unusual directions, but they found things to be "just as he

said." After each division in the sermon, the refrain came again and again, "It was just as he said."

While this is not a common method of outlining, it can be highly interesting. Because the theme is presented again and again, this sermon outline is easy for the congregation to remember.

13. *The "series of statements" outline.* Another commonly used sermon plan is the series of statements outline. The body of the sermon consists of a "succession of statements or observations related to the truth under consideration."[3]

An example of this type of outline is a sermon by the title, "Worship Can Make a Difference!" The preacher presented different ways in which worship can make a difference. While the series of statements made do not exhaust a subject, they give it a fair and adequate treatment.

Generally, this method of preaching will offer an orderly and reasonable treatment of the subject under discussion.

14. *The "dog fight" outline.* This sermon technique is akin to the rebuttal outline. The pastor will make a sharp attack of some subject. Dr. Frank A. Caldwell, who suggested this plan, indicated that people will turn from almost anything to give their attention to a dog fight.[4]

To say the least, this suggests a vigorous treatment of a subject. The preacher "grabs" the subject and "shakes" it for the people to see. The preacher is on the attack. Preachers in another generation often employed this method when they preached against sin. While this method could not be used regularly, its occasional use should create high interest.

15. *The interpretation-application outline.* The interpretation-application outline is another two-part sermon. It consists in giving an interpretation of Scripture, and then applying the truth of that Scripture to life.

This is one of the ways of doing expository preaching. The introduction leads to the passage; the passage is carefully interpreted; then its applications are made to the congregation. One pastor has used this technique with a series of sermons on the miracles of Jesus and on the parables of Jesus. In the series on the parables, each parable is interpreted and then applied. In the series on the miracles, the story is amplified, and then lessons are drawn from the incident which relate to the needs of the congregation.

The interpretation-application method is one of the easier methods of preaching. It has the distinct advantage of presenting real biblical content.

16. *The "subversive" outline.* The subversive outline is the plan whereby the preacher appears to be accepting a proposition that he does not believe. While appearing to be on the wrong side of a proposition, he gradually undercuts that proposition by presenting weak arguments for it. For example, a preacher could appear to be for social drinking. But along with his reasons for, he would make certain "damaging admissions," which would gradually make the case ridiculous.

Dr. W. E. Sangster suggested the subversive plan as one of his psychological methods. However, he offered this counsel for the use of the subversive method.

This is a method to be used sparingly and only after men have had a great deal of experience in preaching. Even then it requires an unusual congregation if it is to achieve its full effectiveness.[5]

This listing of patterns for sermons is not intended to be a complete listing. There have been many, many types of sermon outlines. There are many yet to be discovered. The preacher must always work for variety in sermon plans. A congregation should never be able to predict the sermonic method the preacher will use Sunday by Sunday. Variety heightens anticipation and interest.

NOTES

1. Halford Luccock, *In the Minister's Workshop* (New York: Abingdon-Cokesbury Press, 1944), p. 134.
2. Clarence Edward Macartney, *The Greatest Words in the Bible and Human Speech* (Nashville, Tenn.: Cokesbury Press, 1938), p. 21.

3. Illion T. Jones, *Principles and Practice of Preaching* (New York: Abingdon Press, 1956), p. 105.
4. Frank A. Caldwell, *Preaching Angles* (Nashville, Tenn.: Abingdon Press, 1954), p. 113.
5. W. E. Sangster, *The Craft of the Sermon* (Philadelphia: Westminster Press, 1951), p. 115.

For Further Reading:
The Classification of Sermons

Abbey, Merrill R. *Living Doctrine in a Vital Pulpit.* New York: Abingdon Press, 1964.

Ford, D. W. Cleverley. *A Theological Preacher's Notebook.* London: Hodder & Stoughton, 1962.

——————. *An Expository Preacher's Notebook.* New York: Harper and Bros., 1960.

Koller, Charles W. *Expository Preaching Without Notes.* Grand Rapids, Mich.: Baker Book House, 1962.

Mark, Henry C. *Patterns for Preaching.* Grand Rapids, Mich.: Zondervan, 1959.

Mitchell, Henry H. *The Recovery of Preaching.* New York: Harper & Row, 1977.

Stewart, James S. *A Faith to Proclaim.* New York: Charles Scribner's Sons, 1953.

Wedel, Theodore O. *The Pulpit Rediscovers Theology.* Greenwich, Conn.: Seabury Press, 1956.

White, Douglas M. *The Excellence of Exposition.* Neptune, N.J.: Loizeaux Brothers, 1977.

Whitesell, F. D. and L. M. Perry. *Variety in Your Preaching.* Westwood, N.J.: Fleming H. Revell, 1954.

Part III

FORMAL ELEMENTS
OF THE SERMON

CHAPTER 13

Importance of Arrangement

THE effective arrangement of the materials in a discourse is no less important than their intrinsic interest and force. This is a distinct part of the speaker's work and should be contemplated and handled as something apart from invention on the one hand and from style on the other, although it is closely connected with both. In fact, the task calls for a specific talent. Some preachers exhibit from the outset a power of constructing discourses which is quite out of proportion to their general abilities; others find it extremely difficult to acquire or to exercise skill in arrangement.

In this respect the speaker is an architect. Out of gathered materials he is to build a structure, and a structure suited to its specific design. The same or nearly the same materials may be made into a dwelling, a jail, a factory, a church. But the difference is the plan of the building. It is important that it be built with special reference to the design. In like manner, substantially the same materials may be wrought into a story, a dialogue, an essay, or a speech; the same thoughts may make a very different impression according to the plan of each. What the blueprint is to a building, the plan is to the sermon.

1. VALUES OF A PLAN

1. Arrangement is of great importance to the speaker himself. It affects one's creative ability. One has not really studied a subject when he has simply thought it over in a desultory fashion. The attempt to arrange his thoughts upon it suggests other thoughts and can alone give him just views of the subject as a whole. Good arrangement assists in working out the details, whether this be done mentally or in writing. Each particular thought, when looked at in its proper place, develops according to the situation, grows to its surroundings. If one speaks without manuscript, an orderly arrangement of the discourse greatly helps him in remembering it. One reason why some preachers find extemporaneous speaking so difficult is that they do not arrange their sermons well. And not only to invention and memory but to emotion also is arrangement important. Whether in preparation or in delivery of sermons, a person's feelings will flow naturally and freely only when he has the stimulus, support, and satisfaction which come from conscious order.

The speaker who neglects arrangement will rapidly lose, instead of improve, his power of constructing or organizing a discourse; and he will have to rely for the effect of his sermons entirely on the impression made by striking particular thoughts or on the possibility that high emotional excitement may produce something of order. When a pastor has been forced to preach with inadequate preparation, he may be unusually helped by passionate emotion. It is very proper that a preacher should sometimes give himself up, for a small portion of discourse, to the suggestions of deep feeling. But to rely on this habitually is very unwise.

2. Still more important is good arrangement as regards the effect upon the audience. It is necessary, first, in order to make the discourse intelligible.

Hearers generally, when the preacher has a poor plan, feel the difficulty, though they may not be able to trace it to its real source; and one of the reasons why a man of truly philosophical mind is able "to make things plain" even to illiterate hearers is that he presents clear thoughts in a proper order.[1]

Many persons appear to think that intelligibility is altogether an affair of style, when in fact it depends quite as much on clear thinking and on good arrangement as on clear expression. It is sad to think how large a portion of the people, even in favored communities, really do not understand most of the preaching they hear. Not a few would say, like Tennyson's "Northern Farmer," if they spoke with equal frankness, that they had often heard "parson a bummin' awäy."

Besides, something worse may happen than that the discourse should not be understood; it may be misunderstood, and with deplorable results. The preacher must strive to render it not merely possible that the people should understand but impossible that they should misunderstand.

Again, organization greatly contributes to make the discourse pleasing. "Order is heaven's first law." Even those phenomena in nature which seem most irregular and those scenes which appear to be marked by the wildest variety are pervaded by a subtle order, without which they would not please. Chaos might be terrible but could never be beautiful. Discourses which are pleasing but appear to have no plan will be found really to possess an order of their own, however unobtrusive or peculiar. A poorly arranged sermon may contain particular passages that are pleasing, but even these would appear to still greater advantage as parts of an orderly whole, and the general effect of that whole must be incomparably better.

A well-arranged discourse will much more surely keep the attention of the audience. And this not merely because it is more intelligible and more pleasing but also because, being conformed to the natural laws of human thinking, it will more readily carry the hearer's thoughts along with it.

Further, good arrangement makes a discourse more persuasive. Both in presenting motives and in appealing to feeling, order is of great importance. He who wishes to break a hard rock with his sledge does not hammer here and there over the surface but multiplies his blows upon a certain point or along a certain line. They who lift up huge buildings apply their motive power systematically, at carefully chosen points. It is so when motives are brought to bear upon the will. And the hearer's feelings will be much more powerfully and permanently excited when appeals are made in some natural order.

We may, by a word or an isolated act, give a movement to the soul, inclining it immediately to a certain object, to perform an act of will; but this movement is only a shock. By the same means we may repeat, multiply these shocks. . . . Eloquence consists in maintaining movement by the development of a thought or proof, in perpetuating it, according to the expression of Cicero, "What is eloquence but a continuous movement of the soul?"[2]

And finally, it causes the discourse to be more easily remembered.

Hearers are edified, other things being equal, just as the sermon sticks. No food feeds the flock as that which is distinctly remembered, which the mind can carry away from the sanctuary for the heart to feed on afterwards. This sometimes makes the difference, between failure and success in a pastorate.[3]

2. QUALITIES OF GOOD ARRANGEMENT

The importance of arrangement may be further seen by observing the principal qualities of good arrangement. They appear to be unity, order, proportion, and progress.

1. *Unity.* It might seem quite unnecessary to urge the importance of unity in a discourse, but it is often neglected in practice, particularly in text-sermons and expository sermons, which are frequently made up of two or three little sermons in succession. Whether the unity be that of a doctrinal proposition, of an historical person, or of a practical design, in some way there must be unity.

A work of art may express a variety of ideas, but it cannot remain a work of art unless this variety is held together by the unity of a single idea. The sermon, too, may and should present a variety of thoughts; yet it dare not be a barrage of heterogeneous and arbitrarily assembled elements but must form an organic unity.[4]

Unity is a sense of oneness. The sermon presents one subject, one major idea.

2. *Order*. While unity concerns the sermon as a whole, order concerns the various parts in relation to the whole and to each other. All that is said might be upon the same subject, while the several thoughts by no means follow one another according to their natural relations, or according to the design of the discourse.

We know not how to name a composition without order. It is disposition, it is order which constitutes discourse. The difference between a common orator and an eloquent man is often nothing but a difference in respect to disposition. Disposition may be eloquent in itself, and on close examination we shall often see that invention taken by itself, and viewed as far as it can be apart from disposition, is a comparatively feeble intellectual force. Good thoughts, says Pascal, are abundant. The art of organizing them is not so common. . . . I will not go so far as to say that a discourse without order can produce no effect, for I cannot say that an undisciplined force is an absolute nullity. We have known discourses very defective in this respect to produce very great effects. But we may affirm in general that, other things being equal, the power of discourse is proportional to the order which reigns in it, and that a discourse without order (order, be it remembered, is of more than one kind) is comparatively feeble. A discourse has all the power of which it is susceptible, only when the parts proceeding from the same design are intimately united, exactly adjusted, when they mutually aid and sustain one another like the stones of an arch. . . . This is so true, so felt, that complete disorder is almost impossible, even to the most negligent mind. In proportion to the importance of the object we wish to attain, or the difficulty of attaining it, is our sense of the necessity of order.[5]

Good order requires first of all that the various ideas comprising the unit of consideration be carefully distinguished from one another; secondly, that they follow one another in sequence, making for continuity; and, thirdly, that the order of thought shall move toward a climax.

The climactic arrangement is especially in place when the appeal is to the will, so that each successive point will bear with stronger and ever stronger impact upon the will until the last crowns the whole. . . . This should be borne in mind especially by beginners, who commonly bring up their heaviest troops first, only to be left later in the lurch; unless they husband their resources they will give out before reaching the conclusion, and their powers will be spent when they should be at their height.[6]

What Horace said, speaking of poetry, is also true of the sermon: that the power and the beauty of order consist in saying just now what ought to be said and postponing for the present all the rest.

3. *Proportion.* This involves two things. The several parts of the discourse, whether they are distinctly indicated or not, must be so treated as to make up a symmetrical whole. They are not to be all discussed at the same length, but at a length proportioned to their relations to each other and to the entire discourse. And besides this proportion of natural symmetry, there is that of specific design. One may treat substantially the same topic in essentially the same manner and yet greatly vary the length of particular parts and the stress laid upon them, according to the object.

Disregard for proportion is one of the faults apparent in the sermons of younger ministers, especially those who do not write their sermons. In the ardor of the discussion they give so much time to the less important points that they do not have the necessary time for those of greater weight. Writing the sermon and constant care in the delivery, if the style is extempore, are the most useful ways by which to avoid the danger.[7]

Coquerel says that the lack of method is the most common fault of preaching and the most inexcusable because it is usually the result of insufficient labor.

A man cannot give himself all the qualities of the orator; but by taking the necessary pains he can connect his ideas, and proceed with order in the composition of a discourse.[8]

4. *Progress.* Progress refers to movement, usually to forward movement. The sermon is to move toward a climax. Some sermons have been called "ferris wheel" sermons. They move "round and round," but they do not move forward to a climax. This climax will be determined by the objective of the sermon. What does the preacher want to accomplish by the sermon? The material will be chosen and arranged accordingly.

Without specific talent for building discourse, one will not find it an easy task and may never be able to write out plans that will be remarkably felicitous; but a fair degree of success in arrangement is certainly within the reach of all, provided they are willing to work.

3. STUDY OF ARRANGEMENT

The importance of studying arrangement is accentuated by the fact that for greatest effectiveness every preacher must be the author of his own forms. The patterns, the blueprints which have been examined, are not final. They were arrived at through the experience of many preachers and by long study of the best ways to present truth to people. They are always subject to further experience and more complete knowledge. No one form is adequate in all circumstances. And no set of forms can anticipate changing mental habits and satisfactions. Forms, therefore, are but suggestive helps and should be regarded as flexible. They will naturally be influenced by the individual preacher's manner of thinking, the peculiar requirements of an audience, and the various purposes of particular sermons. In the forms as well as in the materials of preaching, there is room for originality and freedom. Rules are instruments, not masters. The essential qualities of discourse—unity, order, proportion, and progress—are the limiting factors; the form is subservient to them as they in turn are subservient to the moral and spiritual ends of preaching.

However, for the preacher to possess the freedom to create forms that satisfy his own sense of proper expression, he must accept the disciplines of an art student. He must be familiar with the formal elements essential to every sermon and become a master of the principles of construction that are illustrated in typical forms. To know the causal why of historic forms will not only give the preacher an appreciation of their worth, but also will give him authority to venture in expressing a new, effective how. But to venture without knowledge, merely in rebellion against old forms, whether we call it vanity or anarchy, is a perilous assertion of freedom. Therefore, the next four chapters will be devoted to a study of the formal elements—discussion, introduction, conclusion, and transition.

NOTES

1. Henry J. Ripley, *Sacred Rhetoric* (Boston: Gould & Lincoln, 1859), p. 185.
2. Alexander Vinet, *Homiletics,* 3rd ed. (New York: Ivison, Blakeman, Taylor, 1871), p. 289.
3. Herrick Johnson, *The Ideal Ministry* (New York: Fleming H. Revell, 1908), p. 342.
4. M. Reu, *Homiletics* (Minneapolis: Augsburg Publishing House, 1924), p. 390.
5. Vinet, pp. 264, 265.
6. Reu, p. 393.
7. O. S. Davis, *Principles of Preaching* (Chicago: University of Chicago Press, 1924), p. 225.
8. Athanase Coquerel, *Observations on Preaching* (Paris: J. Cherbuliez, 1860), p. 163.

CHAPTER 14

The Discussion

THE discussion, or body of the discourse, must be constructed on some plan, or it is not a discourse at all. Even if there are no divisions and no formal arrangement of any kind, the ideas must follow each other according to the natural laws of thought. People who rely on their powers of absolute extemporizing or who imagine themselves to possess a quasi-inspiration usually stagger and stray in every direction, following no definite line and accomplishing little, except where passion comes in and strikes out an order of its own.

The plan of a discourse in the broadest sense includes the introduction and the conclusion, but since these are to be considered separately, the plan is here spoken of as belonging rather to the discussion, or body of discourse, with its divisions and subdivisions.

After excluding the introduction and conclusion, the remainder is called by various names, such as the division, the development, the argument, the treatment, and the body; but *discussion* seems to be, upon the whole, the best term. Nevertheless, the present concern is to consider the fact that the discussion must have a plan.

1. THE PLAN

Sometimes a plan will come with the subject or on very little reflection. In other cases only a variety of separate thoughts will materialize. It is well then to jot them down as they occur, to make the thoughts objective so that the preacher may examine them, and sooner or later a plan of treatment will present itself. This effort to make out an arrangement will often suggest new thoughts, which is helpful.

One ought to seek not merely for some plan but for the best.

There are plans, energetic and rich, which, applying the lever as deeply as possible, raise the entire mass of the subject; there are others which escape the deepest divisions of the matter and which raise, so to speak, only one layer of the subject. Here it is, especially here, in the conception of plans, that we distinguish those orators who are capable of the good from those who are capable of the better—of that better, to say the truth, which is the decisive evidence of talent or of labor. . . . Every one should strive, as far as possible, for this better, and not be content with the first plan which may present itself to his thought, unless, after having fathomed it, he finds it sufficient for his purpose, suited to exhaust his subject, to draw forth its power—unless, in a word, he can see nothing beyond it.[1]

The plan ought to be simple, not only free from obscurity but free from all straining after effect. Yet it should, as far as possible, be fresh and striking. So many sermons follow a beaten track, so as to make it difficult even for devout hearers to listen attentively. It is only a plan which gets the audience's attention that has any chance of being remembered. Still, sensational or odd plans should be avoided. Great formality of plan should also be avoided.

Robert Hall, in a striking passage, criticizes very justly the stiff and minute method of analysis and statement prevalent in his day.[2] Many of the older English and American preachers doubtless erred in this direction. There has been much improvement during the present century, but many preachers are still stiff, uniform, and monotonous in their plans.

In making the plan, a well-formed proposition is an almost indispensable aid. Although it does not mark out the pathways and intersections of thought, it does fix the boundaries, thus promoting unity and proportion. Often, also, it will be directly suggestive of the order of presentation itself. It would be worthwhile at this point in study to review the discussions of the proposition and the qualities of good arrangement.

2. THE QUESTION OF DIVISIONS

It is a question of much practical importance whether the plan of a discourse should include divisions. The Greek and Roman orators, greatly concerned to make the speech a finished work of art and often anxious to hide the labor bestowed upon the preparation, seldom made clearly marked divisions. Yet, in all cases they followed a definite plan and advanced in an orderly manner. In much the same manner the Christian Fathers preached. But the great Schoolmen of the Middle Ages, applying the most minute logical analysis to all subjects of philosophy and religion, established a fashion which was soon followed in preaching. The young preachers, being trained by the books they read and by the oral teaching at the universities, made the mistake of carrying lecture room methods into the pulpit. Analysis became the rage. Scarcely anything was thought of but clear division and logical concatenation, and to a great extent all oratorical movement and artistic harmony was sacrificed. Too much of the preaching of all the modern centuries has been marred by this fault. Analytical exposition of topics and elaborate argumentation have been the great concern to the comparative neglect of simplicity and naturalness, of animated movement and practical power. Preachers have too often regarded instruction and conviction as the aim of their work, when they are but means of leading men to the corresponding feeling, determination, and action. And the custom being thus established, it has been followed simply because it was the custom by many practical and deeply earnest preachers who limited and overcame the evils of the method as best they could.

Two centuries ago, when the excessive multiplication of formal divisions and equally formal subdivisions was almost universal in France as well as in England, Fénelon inveighed vehemently against the whole fashion, urging a return to the methods of the ancient orators, and on this question almost all subsequent writers have taken sides. Yet, a certain formality of division and of general order has continued to be common in France and Germany, and for the most part in England and America. Dr. Arnold of Rugby set the example and urged others to avoid divisions and make the sermon a very informal address. Since his time, many preachers in the Church of England have followed that course. But it is worthy of special notice that two of the ablest and most generally admired preachers the Church of England has produced, Robertson and Liddon, both regularly made divisions and commonly indicated them in passing. Robertson frequently stated his divisions beforehand and also marked numerous subdivisions. Dr. John Watson, better known as Ian Maclaren, said:

Three detached sermonettes do not make one sermon; but, on the other hand, a handful of observations tied together by a text are not an organic whole. It all depends on whether the heads advance, ascend, cumulate, or are independent, disconnected, parallel.[3]

Concerning the tendency of his time in America, Phillips Brooks made the following observation and judgment:

One prevalent impression about sermons, which prevails now in reaction from an old and disagreeable method, is, I think, mistaken. In the desire to make a sermon seem free and spontaneous there is a prevalent dislike to giving it its necessary formal structure and organism. The statement of the subject, the division into heads, the recapitulation at the end,—all the scaffolding and anatomy of a sermon is out of favor, and there are many very good jests about it. I can say that I have come to fear it less and less. The escape from it must not be negative but positive. The true way to get rid of the boniness of your sermon is not by leaving out the skeleton but by clothing it with flesh.

True liberty in writing comes by law, and the more thoroughly the outlines of your work are laid out, the more freely your sermon will flow, like an unwasted stream between its well-built banks.[4]

From these principles and facts, what is one to conclude?

1. While not necessary, distinctly marked divisions will usually be of service, not only in making the train of thought plain to the hearers but also in serving the preacher himself by encouraging logical correctness and thorough preparation, and by helping him to remember in extemporaneous delivery. In every particular sermon or class of sermons, the case must be decided upon its own merits; but it will commonly be best to make divisions. John Oman suggests these beneficial divisions:

> They help the preacher to clarify and develop his thought, to proceed easily from one part to another, and to secure a right proportion of the whole; and they give the hearer resting places and points of outlook by the way, and help to recall what he hears.[5]

Whether they shall be subtle or obvious and how carefully the introduction of a new division should be indicated must also be decided according to the merits of the case. Where the subject specially requires explanation and argument, it will commonly be advantageous to have clearly stated divisions and frequently subdivisions also; but these must not be so multiplied or so stated as to prevent the discourse from standing out as a living whole, or to interrupt its progressive movement towards the practical end in view.

2. As to the number of divisions, one must consider simplicity and, at the same time, vividness and variety. It is of course more simple to have few, and in many cases two divisions will be most natural and pleasing. But as a habitual method, using only two divisions lacks the requisite variety. It is also highly desirable that the divisions, as stated, should be interesting, having the vividness which belongs to concrete or specific thoughts, and this can often be attained only by having several divisions, since the reduction to a smaller number would render them abstract or general. Yet, when the heads become as many as five or six, they must follow each other in a very natural order, or the

average hearer will not easily remember them. Accordingly, judicious and skillful preachers seldom have more than four heads of discourse.

Why is it that sermons have three divisions more often than any other number? This is a fact long observed and made the subject of small wit—"three heads, like a sermon." No doubt many preachers have tried to make out three divisions, even where nothing called for it, simply from habit or from blindly following a custom. But the custom itself must have had some natural origin. Now a principal reason for it is seen from the considerations stated above; three divisions will give variety without distracting attention or burdening the memory. And in many directions one meets with similar or analogous facts. Thus one of the most common schemes of discourse will naturally be What, why, what then?—i.e., explain, prove, apply. A syllogism, when fully stated, furnishes three propositions. There cannot be a climax without at least three steps. Three gives the idea of completeness—beginning, middle, end. When racers start in a race, the signal is always "One, two, three," neither more nor less. The Scriptures often use a threefold repetition as the most emphatic and impressive: Holy, holy, holy; ask, seek, knock; etc. Often logical and rhetorical reasons combine to fix three as the number. Thus, the resurrection of the body is (1) possible, (2) probable, (3) certain. To carry religion into daily life is (1) possible, (2) desirable, (3) obligatory. Piety is for every young man (1) a thing to be respected, (2) a thing to be desired, (3) a thing to be sought. These considerations go to show that it is not accidental and not strange that elaborate discourses so often have three divisions. The fact that this is the most common number may incline the preacher to avoid it unless required by the natural arrangement of the subject; but when it is so required, as must very frequently be the case, let the sermon builder use it without hesitation. In general, then, one should make the most natural division, considering the subject and the practical design of the discourse.

3. CHARACTER OF THE DIVISIONS

The character of the divisions must be determined by their relation to the subject proposed and to each other. (1) As to the former, it is obvious that no one division should be coextensive with the subject; and yet inexperienced sermonizers sometimes unconsciously have it so. More important is the inquiry whether the divisions should exhaust the subject. This depends upon what is meant by the subject. The general subject treated will very seldom be exhaustively divided in a sermon; but the view of it proposed in the sermon should be exhausted by the divisions. That is to say, they ought to exhaust the proposition or, one might say, the subject proposed. Yet, even in this narrower sense the oratorical division and subdivision of a subject will not commonly exhaust it as a logical analysis would do. The latter must rigorously set forth "all and singular" the contents of the proposition. The former requires that its divisions shall with a certain general completeness cover the whole ground of the proposition, so as to make the discourse a structure, but does not always demand scientific accuracy in that respect; and, as to subdivisions, it is very easy to extend analysis beyond what contributes to practical effect in speaking. The complete logical analysis of a subject, dividing and subdividing, will sometimes be useful as a part of the preparation for preaching on it; but the oratorical division is distinct from this and often very different, especially as to subdivisions.

(2) The relationships of the divisions to each other must be distinct and symmetrical. It is not uncommon for unpracticed speakers to have one division that really includes another, and it is very common to see one that includes some part of what also comes under another. The preacher is sometimes greatly tempted, while treating one branch of a subject, to go on with some closely related matter which yet properly belongs to another branch. The incongruity is not always obvious and requires attention. Sometimes, in fact, it is difficult to decide where an idea properly belongs; but it must be confined to one head or fairly divided between the two, so that, in whatever

way, the heads shall be kept distinct. Furthermore, ideas are frequently stated as distinct divisions which are not sufficiently distinct to be divided at all; and ideas which are distinct will be so stated as to glide into each other, without any clear line of demarcation.

Words the most different do not always convey essentially different ideas, as in this division: "It is characteristic of Christian faith, that it excites, guides, supports." To prove successively that a thing is contrary to good sense and contrary to our own interests is to condemn ourselves to be in presence of nothing after finishing the first part.[6]

Besides being distinct, the divisions should be symmetrical. It is insufficient to say that they must not be incongruous, though preachers of some ability do at times throw together matters which have as little congruity as the human head, a horse's neck, a body composed of parts brought from all directions and covered with many kinds of feathers, and the whole ending in a fish's tail—according to the well known warning of Horace. But the important precept is that the divisions must all sustain the same kind of relationship to the subject proposed. Nothing is more common among the faults of inexperienced preachers than to see three divisions, one of which is not coordinate with the other two but only with some other proposition of which those two are really subdivisions; some of the divisions are branches of the tree, and others are but branches of branches. This fault should be carefully guarded against. In some respects, the idea of symmetry is often pushed too far. Of course the subdivisions of any one division should all have the same relationship to it. Some try too hard to give each division the same number of subdivisions in order to make the plan symmetrical. Even when this is natural, it is very apt to appear artificial, particularly if the number of divisions and subdivisions is considerable. When it is really artificial, the effect is not good. Pascal compares such matters inserted merely for the sake of symmetry to false windows in a building, a poor attempt to hide internal lack of symmetry, offensive as soon as we know what they are. Another mistaken notion of symmetry requires that each division and sometimes even each subdivision be discussed at about the same length. When natural, this is pleasing. But it will not often be natural. A mere external symmetry is far less important than proportion to the internal relationship of the topics and to the specific design of the course.

4. PROBLEMS OF ORDER AND MANAGEMENT

1. The order of the divisions will be controlled not merely by logical but also by practical considerations. Even where instruction and conviction are especially the goal, there is always a practical effect proposed in preaching, and usually instruction and conviction are quite subordinate to the object of impressing the feelings and determining the will. As to instruction, it is obviously proper that those divisions should precede, which will help to understand the succeeding ones; and it is commonly convenient that negative considerations should precede the positive. So far as conviction is concerned, a sermon should arrange arguments according to the general principles which regulate the order of arguments and which apply here no less than in the essay or treatise. In respect to practical effect, we must endeavor to clearly discern the particular end proposed and then consider what selection and arrangement of points will be most likely, by inspiring the imagination and eliciting passion, to induce the hearers to resolve and to act as the truth requires. For this purpose the abstract must precede the concrete, the general precede the specific or particular, and instruction and conviction must precede appeal. The appeal, however, may either come in mass after the whole body of instruction and argument, or it may immediately follow each leading thought as presented. This last method has sometimes considerable advantages. The successive waves of emotion may rise higher and higher to the end. And besides, while thought produces emotion, it is also true that emotion reacts upon and enlivens thought, so that the impressive application of one division may secure for the next a closer attention. Yet, the interest must steadily grow as we advance, or the effect will be bad. Where we cannot feel sure that it will grow, point by point, the application had better be postponed till towards the close.

The preacher who repeats a sermon ought to consider whether he cannot advantageously rearrange it or, at any rate, improve the plan.

2. The statement of the divisions and subdivisions, like that of the proposition, ought to be exact, concise, and as far as possible, suggestive and attractive. Without straining after effect, one may often state a division in terms so brief and striking that the hearer's attention will be at once awakened. It is well that the several divisions should be stated in similar forms of expression where this can be done without artificiality. Such similarity of statement brings out the symmetry of the division, making them clearer and more pleasing. Alliteration is often quite felicitous in making the divisions memorable. But one must always guard against artificiality and inaccuracy.

It is dangerous, and *p* is a specially dangerous letter, though *q* runs it hard. The result is apt to be what an address which had two heads with *p's* and two with *q's* was called, "a very peculiar speech." But while it is a fond thing to search for alliteration, there is not reason for rejecting it if it arrive for a better reason than ingenuity.[7]

3. Shall the divisions be announced beforehand? This was once almost universal and is still the regular practice of many preachers. At one time in some parts of Germany, the plan of the sermon was printed and either published in the newspaper of the previous week or handed in slips to the congregation as they entered the church. To make a minute announcement of divisions and subdivisions and repeatedly recall them in passing is very appropriate when lecturing to a class on some difficult subject where the object is not persuasion but only instruction and conviction. But in preaching these purposes are commonly subordinate to persuasion. Now three cases may be noted in which it is desirable to announce the divisions at the outset. First, when the train of thought is difficult, the announcement may aid in following it. Sometimes this would but increase the difficulty, the hearer finding it easier to comprehend each division by itself as it is presented. But, in other cases, the divisions will throw light on each other when placed side by side. Secondly, an announcement is helpful when it is particularly desir-

able that not merely the practical impression be permanent but that the successive steps in the exposition or argument be remembered. Thirdly, it is good to announce the divisions when we judge that the announcement would awaken interest and attention rather then abate them; and here every case must be decided upon its own merits. Unless one of these three conditions exists, no previous announcements should be made. It must be remembered that there are many different methods of announcing, beginning with the formal statement of numbered divisions (and sometimes of subdivisions also) and extending through numerous gradations to the perfectly informal and perhaps very slight mention of the divisions as the points it is proposed to consider. Between these limits one may devise a great variety of methods by the exercise of imagination, judgment and good taste. As a general rule, recapitulation is better than preannouncement, because it is more intelligible, more impressive, and more easily remembered. In many cases, this is true. In many others, the preannouncement is best. Sometimes, it is even well to employ both. To announce at the outset the subdivisions, also, would be scarcely ever desirable, and that only in very peculiar cases where the train of thought was in itself very important.

NOTES

1. Alexander Vinet, *Homiletics,* 3rd ed. (New York: Ivison, Blakeman, Taylor, 1871), pp. 276–77.
2. Robert Hall, "Sermon on the Discouragements and Supports of a Christian Minister," *Works,* Vol. 1 (New York: J. & J. Harper, 1832), p. 140.
3. John Watson, *Cure of Souls* (New York: Dodd, Mead & Co., 1896), pp. 41–42.
4. Phillips Brooks, *Lectures on Preaching* (New York: E. P. Dutton & Co., 1907), pp. 177–78.
5. John Oman, *Concerning the Ministry* (New York: Harper & Bros., 1937), p. 151.
6. Vinet, p. 282.
7. Oman, p. 152.

CHAPTER 15

The Introduction

SERMONS should generally have an introduction. Listeners have a natural aversion to abruptness and appreciate a somewhat gradual approach. A building is rarely pleasing in appearance without a porch or some sort of inviting entrance. An elaborate piece of music will always have a prelude of at least a few introductory notes. And so any composition or address which has no introduction is apt to seem incomplete. But there is more than an aesthetic reason for an introduction. A book needs a preface to introduce to the reader the subject, the author's reason for writing, his point of view, his approach, or his plan. So the subject of a sermon usually needs to be introduced as a significant idea into the conscious mind of the hearers. Dr. Oman observes that

even if your subject need no introduction, your audience does. If for nothing else, they need a little time to settle down. But also they start the better for being first drawn both to you and your subject, and they will travel more hopefully if they can survey the scene for a little before taking the road.[1]

Moreover, the preacher himself needs, for the sake of self-possession, certitude, and deliberate movement, to walk or step into his message rather than to run or plunge headlong into it.

1. OBJECTIVES OF THE INTRODUCTION

The introduction has two chief objectives: to interest the hearers in the subject and to prepare them for understanding it.

1. As to the former, a preacher may usually, it is true, count on a certain willingness to hear. Not many come to worship who are hostile to the truth, but many come who are sadly careless about it. And a much more alert attention may be created by an interesting introduction.

We all know how much depends in the ordinary affairs of life upon first impressions. The success of his sermon often depends upon the first impressions which a preacher makes upon his hearers in his exordium. If these impressions be favorable, his audience will listen to the remaining part of his discourse with pleasure and attention and, consequently, with profit.[2]

The aim should be to excite not merely an intellectual interest but, so far as possible at the outset, a spiritual and practical interest—to bring the hearers into sympathy with the preacher's feeling and bring their minds into harmony with the subject to be presented. One may sometimes expressly request attention, as did Moses (Deut. 4:1), Isaiah (Isa. 28:14), Stephen (Acts 7:2), and Jesus (Matt. 15:10); but such a request, if often repeated, would lose its force, and it is usually best to aim at saying something which will at once interest the hearer's mind. "What is the best way," asked a young preacher of an older one, "to get the attention of the congregation?" "Give 'em something to attend to," was the gruff reply.

2. The other object, to prepare the audience for understanding the subject, is obviously very important and to some extent can often be effected. But efforts in this respect must be carefully guarded against the danger of anticipating something which properly belongs to the body of the discourse. What such preparation involves will be suggested later in the consideration of sources of introduction.

German preachers traditionally gave an introduction before announcing the text. This custom would appear to have originated in the fact that most of them were required to take their text from the pericope, or lesson appointed for the day, so that it could be assumed as to some extent known already before it was announced. Frequently the same custom is observed in the American pulpit, sometimes, one is inclined to think, as a timid compromise with some moderns who avoid texts altogether. The habitual practice of beginning with an introduction is apt to make it too general, or pointless, or farfetched; but some introductions of this sort are exceedingly helpful, and the practice is well worthy of occasional use.

There are cases in which it is best to dispense with introduction and plunge at once into the discussion; for example, when the sermon is long, or when nothing seems to make a really good introduction. In familiar addresses, as at prayer meetings, Sunday school meetings, and the like, this course is quite often preferable. In all preaching let there be a good introduction or none at all. "Well begun is half done." And ill begun is apt to be wholly ruined.

2. SOURCES OF INTRODUCTION

The sources from which the preacher may draw introductions are many and varied. There may, however, be some advantage in classifying them as follows:

1. *The text.* Wherever the meaning of the text requires explanation, this explanation may form the introduction. So, too, an introduction is advisable when an explanation of the context would throw light on the meaning of the text. These seem to be very natural sources; and Robert Hall, with his severe taste, commonly began with some explanation of the text or the context, preferring this to more ambitious introductions. And if not for explanation proper, there may be occasion for illustration of the text by means of historical and geographical knowledge that will make its meaning, though not more clear, more vivid and interesting. In other cases, some account of the writer of the

text or of the condition of any particular persons whom he addressed (as in the case of Paul) may serve to interest hearers in the text or to prepare them for understanding it.

2. *The subject to be discussed,* if obvious from the mere statement of the text, or if announced at the outset, may then furnish an introduction in various ways. The preacher may remark on its relation to some other subject, e.g., "to the genus, of which the subject is a species," or to some opposed or similar subject, or one related to it as cause, or consequence, or case in point. Where the sermon is designed to be explanatory or practical, an introduction on the relevance of the subject to some present need or problem will often be appropriate; where the sermon is to establish the truth of a proposition or to exhibit its importance, the introduction will frequently explain the nature of the subject involved. The preacher

may state the intellectual advantages to be derived from discussing such a theme. The subject may be the doctrine of moral evil or that of divine sovereignty. It may be stated at the beginning that these are the greatest problems of the human mind meeting the philosopher as well as the theologian, that they have called forth the strength of the best intellects of the race, that no problems are more difficult and therefore none more deserving of the attention of thinking minds. He may state the connections of the subject with other more practical spiritual truths. He may remove the prejudice that the doctrine has no immediate practical bearing or utility, even as depravity, for instance, or the doctrine of sin lies in one sense at the base of the whole Christian system, of the atonement, regeneration, holiness, and the Christian life. He may make some *historical allusion* naturally connected with the theme, which always forms an attractive introduction.[3]

And so in many other ways.

3. *The occasion.* If the sermon has reference to some particular season of the year or is preached at some special religious meeting, in connection with the administration of an ordinance or the like, the preacher may begin by remarking upon the occasion. Allusions to the character of the times in which we live or to recent events or existing circumstances may show why the particular text or subject has been chosen or may awaken

a livelier interest in it. Or the pastor may speak of doubts known to exist on the subject, or hostility to the truth in this respect, or of some common mistake, or some prevailing or growing error, or evil practice with reference to this subject. In other cases, allusion is made to the religious condition of the church or congregation or cheering news from some other church or part of the country. Sometimes one may refer to a subject or subjects formerly discussed as reason for the present subject; and the hymn which has just been sung or a passage of Scripture (not containing the text) which has been read will occasionally afford an interesting introduction. In rare cases the preacher may begin by speaking of himself, whether it be of his feelings as a preacher, of his interest as a pastor, of some particular time in his connection with this church, or of something in his personal experience as a Christian. However, the preacher should beware of apologies. These often create the suspicion of insincerity where it is undeserved because they are sometimes in fact sincere and because the preacher who feels at the outset oppressed by ill health or unfavorable circumstances may, quite unexpectedly to himself, rise to the subject and succeed remarkably well. A preacher should never say that he feels unusually embarrassed on the present occasion. Apologies are like public rebukes for disorder in the congregation in that one will very seldom regret having omitted them, however strongly tempted at the moment to speak. When there is any real occasion, whether in beginning or ending the sermon, for what might be called apology, let it never proceed or seem to proceed from anxiety as to the preacher's reputation; let it be brief, quiet, and as it were, incidental.

One must often decide whether any of these remarks upon the occasion shall be made in the introduction or in the conclusion. The pastor must consider whether a particular remark of this kind will cause interest in the discussion or deepen the impression. Moving personal allusions, in which the preacher might be interrupted by his emotions, are in general better reserved for the conclusion.

4. *The problem.* The problem or need being addressed may

be the source of introduction. There are many "problem-answer" sermons or "problem-solution" sermons. The problem or need is stated in the introduction, and the body of the sermon presents a solution or an answer. For example, a congregation may have a poor concept of the stewardship of money. This problem is stated in the introduction. The body of the sermon offers a program or a plan to correct their concept of the stewardship of material things.

5. *The objective.* The objective of the sermon may occasionally provide the sermon introduction. This method should be used only rarely. But now and then the preacher may begin with absolute candor and state his objective. The introduction is a statement of the aim of the sermon. In an evangelistic sermon, the preacher may say in effect, "Some of you who are listening need Jesus Christ. I am going to present Jesus Christ that you may receive him as your Savior." Whenever the objective is used for the introduction, the preacher must convey a sense of intense earnestness.

6. *The life situation.* Another source of introduction is the "life situation." The life situation sermon begins with real life problems and experiences. Dr. Halford Luccock suggested "preaching to life situations" as one kind of preaching.[4] In actual practice the sermon begins with a life situation, and this becomes an introduction or starting point. Dr. A. W. Blackwood cites an example of how a life situation sermon may begin.

> You overhear a businessman telling a friend, "John, the way you and I are living is not worth what it costs." Since you do not know either man, and since you have heard the conversation on a bus, you feel free to start with these words. Then you discuss the subject "Is Life Worth What It Costs?"[5]

The life situation may provide a rich and varied source of introduction.

7. *The story.* The story or illustration is still another source of sermon introduction. These should not be unrelated stories or audience warm-up stories. Rather they should be stories that lead to a discussion of the subject. Stories are interesting and

catch attention. If the climax of the story is a statement of the subject, then the introduction is natural. For example, a man came to his minister and told him of all the troubles he had during the past year. He ended by declaring, "I tell you, preacher, it's enough to make a man lose his religion." "Seems to me," replied the preacher, "it's enough to make a man use his religion." This story could well introduce a sermon on "using your religion."

8. *Striking statement.* The striking statement is yet another good source of sermon introduction. A quotation, a sign, a placard, a quip, or a song title may provide a natural lead-in for a sermon. When the gospel song "Put Your Hand in the Hand of the Man" was popular, a pastor studied all gospel records of the hand of Jesus, and then used the song and its title to introduce a sermon on the hand of Christ.

9. *Imagination.* If all else fails, the preacher should use his imagination. In other words, he should create his own introduction. Out of the stored materials in his mind he can develop an introduction that fits the sermon. A brief radio devotional on 2 Corinthians 8:9 began with an introduction created by imagination.

I want to tell you an unusual story—the story of two men. One man was wealthy. He owned a profitable business; he lived in a beautiful home; he had a large bank account. Everything he did seemed to prosper. The other man was poor. He had a struggling business; his home was barely comfortable; he was deeply in debt. Each year he went farther behind.

One day the wealthy man came to the poor man and said, "You take my business, my home, my bank account, and I shall take your business, your home, and your debts." The trade was made. The rich man was poor, and the poor man was rich.

I doubt if you have ever heard a story like that because men are inherently selfish. We are interested in ourselves and our families. But the Apostle Paul in his second letter to the Corinthians tells of one who did even more than that. Paul was urging the Corinthian Christians to be generous to their poor brethren in Jerusalem. In the midst of his fervent appeal, he suddenly gave the highest example of love and self-sacrifice, "For ye know the grace of our Lord Jesus Christ, that, though he was rich, yet for your sakes he became poor, that ye through his poverty might be rich" (2 Cor. 8:9, KJV). That is more than an example. It contains a summary of the good news of the gospel. Jesus Christ gave up his riches that we who are poor might be rich.[6]

3. QUALITIES OF A GOOD INTRODUCTION

1. The introduction must present some thought closely related to the theme of discourse, so as to lead to the theme with naturalness and ease, and yet a thought quite distinct from the discussion. Inexperienced preachers very frequently err by anticipating in the introduction something which belongs to the body of the discourse; and the danger of doing this should receive their special attention.

The design of the introduction is altogether preparatory. The preacher will often find himself tempted, especially in introductions drawn from the text or context, to remark in passing upon interesting matters which are somehow suggested but are foreign to his purpose on that occasion. This temptation should be resisted, except in very peculiar cases. When the preacher has determined to carry the audience along a certain line of thought, hoping to arrive at a definite and important conclusion, he should not stray from the chosen direction.

2. The introduction should generally consist of a single thought; one does not want a porch to a porch. But there are many exceptions to this rule, and it is frequently appropriate to present some introductory thought and afterwards give an exposition, which in such cases becomes a part of the body of the discourse or else constitutes a sort of halt while the way is cleared for the discussion.

3. It is desirable to avoid the practice of beginning with some very broad and commonplace generality, as with reference to human nature or life, to the universe or the Divine Being. Of course, there is sometimes real occasion for this, but many preachers practice it as an habitual method, and it is apt to sound like a platitude, an opening promise of boredom.

4. On the other hand, the introduction must not seem to promise too much in its thoughts, style, or delivery. It should excite interest and awaken expectation, provided the expectation can be fairly met by the body of the discourse. It should not be highly argumentative or highly emotional. As to the latter, it must be remembered that even if the preacher is greatly excited at the outset, the audience usually is not, and he had better restrain himself so as not to get beyond the range of its sympathies. When Cicero broke out with his opening words against Catiline, the Senate was already much excited; and so with Massillon at the funeral of Louis the Great.[7] Such exceptional cases must be decided as they arise.

It is the privilege of talent and the fruit of study and experience, to know when to venture and when to abstain. It cannot be allowed to teaching, strictly so called, to set aside talent or anticipate the dictates of experience.[8]

Moreover, while earnestly seeking to make the introduction interesting and engaging, one must shun the sensational and the pretentious. Ostentation is exceedingly objectionable in a preacher, and particularly at the outset. And he should begin not merely with personal modesty but also with official modesty, reserving for some later period of the sermon anything which may be proper to state with the authority belonging to his office.

5. A good introduction would, in general, be exclusively adapted to the particular discourse. In some cases, a certain general thought might with equal propriety introduce several different subjects. Thus some account of Paul might form the introduction to sermons on various passages of his writings; yet the account must in almost every case be at least slightly varied if it is to be exactly adapted to the design. Descriptions of a Scripture locality and, to some extent, introductions personal to the speaker should be varied. Lawyers make many speeches on very similar subjects or occasions; and this fact partly explains Cicero's statement that he kept some introductions on hand for any speech they might suit—as was also done by Demosthenes.[9]

The preacher should beware of set phrases and stereotyped forms of introduction; the people very soon begin to recognize them, and the effect is then the opposite of awaking interest and exciting curiosity. Nowhere is it more important to have the stimulus and charm of variety, and this is best attained by habitually seeking to give the introduction a specific and exact adaptation.

6. The introduction must not be long. An eminent preacher, much inclined to this fault, was one day accosted by a plain old man as follows: "Well, you kept us so long in the porch this morning that we hardly got into the house at all." And it was said of John Howe by someone: "Dear good man, he is so long in laying the cloth that I lose my appetite, and begin to think there will be no dinner after all." Of course the introduction may sometimes be much longer than would be generally proper; and the attempt of some writers to tell how many sentences it should contain is exceedingly unwise. But "where one sermon is faulty from being too abruptly introduced, one hundred are faulty from a long and tiresome preface."[10]

7. The introduction, though simple, should be carefully prepared. Quintilian remarks that a faulty proem may look like a scarred face and that he will certainly be thought a very bad helmsman who lets the ship strike in going out of the harbor.[11] The extemporaneous speaker should know exactly what he is to say in the introduction. But it is very doubtful whether he ought, as is frequently recommended and practiced, to have the introduction written when the remainder of the discourse is unwritten. It is too apt to seem formal and the transition to the unwritten to be abrupt and precipitous, something like stepping from a wharf into deep water, as compared with quietly wading out from the shore. However, it is good advice that at least two sentences should always be written: the first sentence, that the preacher may be sure of his beginning; and the last, that he may be sure of his ending. It will sometimes happen that at an early stage of the preparation, an introduction will come to mind; more commonly, it has to be selected after the principal materials have been gathered. That is, its materials may be

the last to be gathered. But as to the composition of the sermon in detail (whether it be written or unwritten composition), the introduction should be composed after the body of the discourse is fully perceived. The preacher must know the body to be introduced before he can do it properly. However, when the final writing is done, the introduction will be written first.

The discussion of this subject may close with a useful remark from Vinet:

Among experienced preachers we find few examples of exordiums altogether defective; we find few good ones among preachers at their beginning. We hence naturally infer, that there is in this part of the discourse something of special delicacy, but nothing which demands peculiar faculties.[12]

NOTES

1. John Oman, *Concerning the Ministry* (New York: Harper & Bros., 1937), p. 155.
2. Thomas J. Potter, *Sacred Eloquence* (New York: Pustet, n.d.), p. 97.
3. James M. Hoppin, *Homiletics* (New York: Funk & Wagnall, 1893), pp. 342–43.
4. Halford Luccock, *In the Minister's Workshop* (New York: Abingdon-Cokesbury Press, 1944), Chapter 5.
5. A. W. Blackwood, *The Preparation of Sermons* (New York: Abingdon-Cokesbury Press, 1948), p. 145.
6. Unpublished radio devotional.
7. "My brethren, God only is great" were his first words.
8. Alexander Vinet, *Homiletics*, 3rd ed. (New York: Ivison, Blakeman, Taylor, 1871), p. 105.
9. Compare Vinet, p. 301.
10. William G. T. Shedd, *Homiletics and Pastoral Theology* (New York: Charles Scribner's Sons, 1867), p. 182.
11. Quintilian, *The Institutio Oratoria of Marcus Fabius Quintilianus* (Nashville, Tenn.: George Peabody College for Teachers, 1951), IV, 1, p. 61.
12. Vinet, p. 297.

CHAPTER 16

The Conclusion

PREACHERS rarely neglect to prepare some introduction to a sermon, but they often neglect to prepare the conclusion. Yet the latter may be as important as the former. John Bright, who was one of the foremost political orators in his time, stated that however little preparation he may have made for the rest of a speech, he always carefully prepared the conclusion. Lord Brougham said that the conclusion to his celebrated speech before the House of Lords in defense of Queen Caroline was composed twenty times over, at least. The peroration of Burke's first speech at the trial of Warren Hastings was worked over sixteen times. The great orators of Greece and Rome paid much attention to their perorations, seeming to feel that this was the final struggle which must decide the conflict. But often the opposite is true of the preacher, especially on the part of the preacher who extemporizes. The beginning and earlier progress of the sermon show good preparation, but towards the close the preacher loses the way. He wanders, struggles, and flounders. The conclusion should move like a river, growing in volume and power. It should not be like a stream that loses itself in a marsh. It has several important functions to fulfill. In reference to the sermon, the purpose of the conclusion is to bring the discussion to a fitting end. Like love among the virtues, it is to complete and join all together. In reference to the hearers, its function is to relate the truth helpfully and lastingly to life as they face it. In reference to the preacher, the conclusion is a leave taking, in which he commits vital and eternal issues to the decision of those who have heard him. He leaves the responsibility of action to them. And he can be at peace only if he has said his best word.

1. GUIDING PRINCIPLES

How may these high purposes be fulfilled? They may be fulfilled by giving careful attention to some guiding principles.

1. The first of these principles is careful preparation. Years ago a group of travelers in China went one day in rickshaws to see a famous pagoda that was located several miles from the railway station. Unused to being hauled about by men instead of motors, they watched the coolies as they traveled along, with an uncertain feeling that soon crystallized into pity. With the miles the pace lagged and shoulders drooped. Finally, returning, they came again in sight of the railway station. Suddenly, to the surprise of every rider, the coolies straightened their shoulders, lifted their heads and trotted briskly to the journey's end. Why? They wanted, by ending well, to get a friendly tip and more business. To end well was their best strategy. Many preachers are careless about the way they end their sermons because they do not have a coolie's understanding of the importance of ending well. Rhetorically, psychologically, and spiritually the conclusion is a most vital part of the sermon. It is not an addition to the sermon but an organic part of it, necessary to its completeness of form and effect. It gathers up the various ideas and impressions of the message for one final impact upon the minds and hearts of the hearers. "The conclusion makes possible the oratorical drive."[1] In most cases it is the place of the sermon's climax—or anticlimax.

Let it be the rule, then, that the conclusion should be carefully prepared. There may be occasion to modify it in delivery, according to the state of feeling which has then been reached by the preacher and the hearers. But one can usually determine, when preparing, precisely the thoughts with which the sermon ought to conclude though he may leave the mode of stating them to be controlled by the feelings of the moment. In every case he ought to have something well-prepared ready that will make an appropriate and effective conclusion.

2. The conclusion should be a natural and appropriate termination of the discussion. It should seem to the congregation to be the inevitable thing to be said, a logical end of all the arguments, a considered proposal in the light of all the facts. The most effective conclusion rests wholly upon the cumulative force of the discussion without the introduction of new or extraneous material. Any deviation from this rule is apt to divert the audience at the moment when concentration is desired, and so to lose the full impact of the line of thought pursued in the discussion. The true connectives between discussion and conclusion bear the meaning of such words as *therefore, so, consequently, surely then*—words that may not be spoken but are nevertheless felt by those who hear.

3. The conclusion should be unmistakably personal in its aim. Preaching is personal encounter. It is through one person to others. Sometimes in the midst of the sermon the preacher, becoming conscious of his oratory, gets off the track and soars around impersonally to the delight of himself and his audience, making little progress toward his destination. But, whatever he may do elsewhere, in the conclusion the preacher must be very conscious of his hearers and must speak very directly to them. He is a messenger and advocate of God, beseeching, exhorting, persuading, counseling, guiding, challenging. His conscious aim is not oratorical but personal and spiritual. "I remind you," "I beseech you," "I plead with you," "I challenge you" are the words of his heart. The second personal pronoun will be in his mind and often spoken. Dr. Herbert H. Farmer in his discussion of the sermon as personal encounter says:

If there is no point where you can say "you," then it is strongly suspected that your discourse is not a sermon but an essay or a lecture. It is at the points of focus, where you seek to draw your message together and drive it home in challenge or appeal or succor, that the pronoun "you" is indispensable.[2]

4. The conclusion should be alive and energetic. "It is not enough just to stop, . . . words of wisdom are to be as nails fastened in a sure place and your last word should be the right word to fasten them."[3] Weakness in manner, thought, or words draws the nails instead of driving them deeper. Deep passion, thoughts that burn, strong words are the instruments required, whether the conclusion be a direct drive on the will or an appeal to the heart. Strength, of course, does not mean bombast or uncontrolled emotion but life and energy, by which deep passion may express itself in compassion as well as in compelling challenge, and thoughts may burn with tenderness as well as fury, and words may have the power of gravitation as well as the shock of an earthquake. It is a fault of some energetic speakers that they exhaust themselves before they reach the conclusion and come up panting and hoarse and with no banner but a moist handkerchief. Some end weakly through lack of forethought or lack of courage, and still others because in the sermon they have laid no strong foundations. If the preacher has any regard for the vital effect of his sermon, he ought to conclude strongly. No better examples of what this means can be found than in the conclusion of Joshua's address to his people (Josh. 24:14–16) and the closing paragraph of the Sermon on the Mount (Matt. 7:24–26).

5. The conclusion should be definite and clear in thought and expression. Precision is a proper standard for the preacher at every point in the sermon. It cannot be abandoned in the conclusion. If there is any place for clear statement and definite counsel along carefully chosen lines, it is there. It is easy for the extemporaneous preacher who does not write his sermons, after he has fixed upon his main ideas or divisions, to leave the conclusion to the inspiration of the moment. That indicates indefiniteness concerning the objective of his message and is an unnecessary hazard. Without accurate cutting beforehand (i.e., precision) the conclusion may become a confusion of generali-

ties. Unexpected circumstances may blunt for the moment the keen edge of thought and make one's vocabulary a jumble. In the emotion of the moment words that wound may appear where words of healing ought to be, and soft words where there ought to be challenge. If one has self-mastery and keen sensitivity, and can think accurately on his feet, and has a large and intelligible vocabulary, one has less to fear. But no preacher should gamble with "the moment." To go into the pulpit knowing precisely to what ends he seeks to guide his people and having conceived those ends in terms that they will understand gives to the preacher, all the way through, an invigorating confidence and liberty. It is there, not in haphazardness, that one finds spiritual fervor.

2. METHODS OF CONCLUSION

One element in the conclusion of a sermon will often be recapitulation. If the discourse has consisted chiefly of careful explanation or argument, and if it is important that its several divisions be remembered, and doubtful whether they will be, then the divisions and occasionally even certain subdivisions may be distinctly restated. But this must be so managed, to use a phrase of Cicero, "that the recollection may be revived, not the speech repeated." Too much recapitulation is as unnecessary as it is tedious. Though perhaps anxious at the moment to return to some favorite point, recapitulation must be confined to its proper use. In most sermons, however, there is no desire to reproduce the several thoughts and fix them separately in the hearer's mind, but rather to gather them all together and concentrate their force on one final effort of conviction or persuasion. In such cases it is better not to make any formal recapitulation, but in a freer way to restate the train of thought or the principal points of it, sometimes using very different forms of statement. This appears to be what Vinet would call *résumé,* as distinct from recapitulation.[4] For properly oratorical purposes, it is preferable. The recapitulation or the *résumé,* especially the latter, may sometimes form the entire conclusion; but in most cases it only draws the whole message together in one focal point that will support the preacher's final word. It is often better, particularly where the discourse includes many points, to give some recapitulation before reaching the conclusion, usually when passing to the last division.

The conclusion will, for the most part, consist of application, i.e., pointing out the bearing of the truth preached on the lives of the hearers in some particular manner or at some particular point. Application usually includes also practical counsel in reference to some opportunity, duty, or challenge that emerges from the truth of the sermon.

Application is often made elsewhere than in the conclusion, sometimes, indeed, forming a large portion of the sermon, enlarged at some point or distributed throughout. Yet, it is evident that the application concentrates itself, so to speak, in the conclusion. This concluding application requires, even more than the other parts of the discourse, that the preacher should have strong faith, warm religious experience, intense earnestness.

Often the claim of the sermon will be articulated in a direct appeal. Prophetic and apostolic preaching were characterized by it. And it is not a good sign that many preachers have lost the unembarrassed urgency of importuning men for God. Appeal is necessary, particularly in evangelical preaching. In many American churches the appeal is made in the form of an invitation to men to confess Christ publicly or to repent of unfaithfulness and pledge themselves to faithful living. Too often this method, one fears, becomes a custom without a sense of timeliness and without any inspiring emotion.

It is quite wrong to suppose, as some preachers appear to do, that every sermon must end with a pathetic or overwhelming appeal. It is not infrequently best to end quietly, yet still impressively. And whatever the subject might require, a person should not speak with emotion unless he really feels it. An effort to work oneself up into feeling because it is desirable at this point will usually fail; and if it succeeds, it is not likely to make a good impression on the hearers. If an impassioned conclusion was prepared and the speaker now finds that his own feelings and those of the audience have slowly subsided till there is no good prospect of exciting them, he should omit the prepared conclusion or modify its tone so as to attempt nothing but what can be achieved. Few things are so painful or so injurious as the reaction produced by passionate words which are not felt by the hearers or even by the speaker. "Do not preach the corpse of an appeal."[5] And let it never be forgotten that the preacher must not aim to excite emotion merely for its own sake, as if that were the end in view, but to make it a means of determining the will and stimulating to corresponding action. Even love to God will not subsist as a mere feeling.

Again, the conclusion may center in pastoral exhortation, encouragement, or warning. A concluding exhortation should, as a rule, be specific, keeping itself in relation to the subject which has been treated. There is great danger that a fluent and fervid speaker will wander into mere general appeals, equally appropriate to almost any other subject or occasion. This may be sometimes allowable, but a more specific exhortation would almost always be more effective. When the sermon has been one of solemn warning, it is sometimes well in concluding to speak words of comfort and encouragement in view of the divine promises; or when the discourse has dealt mostly with earnest invitation, it might be best for the conclusion to speak frankly of the difficulties of discipleship to Christ, so as to discourage a hasty profession. The preacher must judge in every case, whether this combination will deepen the general impression, or whether the two will neutralize each other in the hearer's mind and leave him unaffected by either. It may be added that warnings, and all that is alarming in gospel truth, should be uttered not as if the pastor delighted in denunciation, but with special tenderness, showing that he speaks in the faithfulness of love.

The final words of the conclusion may sometimes consist of a comprehensive and impressive restatement of the subject which has been discussed.

It is very effective when, in our final appeal, we can strongly and vividly reproduce the leading idea of the whole discourse. It has a very great effect upon our hearers, after so many solid proofs and so many skillful strokes of oratory have been devoted to it, to see the great leading truth, the parent idea, appear once more at this crowning moment in all the force of its beautiful simplicity, in all the strength of its unity.[6]

Or the text itself may be the last words. When the discourse has been developed out of the text and has exhibited all its wealth of meaning, then the emphatic repetition of the text in closing will impressively sum up all that has been said. Or one may end with another passage of Scripture, or with part of a hymn, or a poem. There seems to be an increasing tendency in America to close sermons either with a story or a poem. Neither should become a habit. And the requirements for their effective use are great. One must have good taste for choosing, skill in the telling, and a pure heart to keep his motive high and centering outside his own vanity. A story or poem ought to be appropriate to the main thought without the necessity of a build-up. And it ought to be brief and clear. Again, to close with an invocation of the divine blessing is sometimes natural and impressive but should never become a regular form. Very often, however, the general contents or design of the conclusion will require that it close with some particular thought. The last sentence, of whatever it may consist, ought to be appropriate and impressive, but its style ought not to be elaborate and ambitious. In most cases it should be the preacher's own. It is a very solemn moment. Do not be thinking of your reputation but of your responsibility and of your hearers' salvation.

3. RELEVANT QUESTIONS

Attention must be given briefly to several questions: (1) How long should the conclusion be? (2) Should it be announced? (3) Should it always register a positive note? (4) When should the conclusion be prepared? The length of the conclusion, like that of the introduction, is dependent on circumstances, and no rule can be laid down.

1. Because of the limited time allotted to the sermon in the modern service of worship, the tendency is toward brev-

ity in conclusion, so much so that one writer issues a warning. He says:

Most conclusions are too brief. To impress people properly with any idea, it is not enough to state it clearly or beautifully; one must repeat it often enough and long enough to let it sink into their minds. Twenty-nine minutes of sermon and one minute of conclusion is not a good proportion—not if it has been a real sermon from which a real conclusion can be drawn.[7]

But there is great danger of making it too long, especially in hortatory appeals and in sermons which have not been thoroughly prepared. The feeling of the speaker inclines him to continue, but the feelings of the hearers cannot be long kept up to a high point. If the sermon has been long, the conclusion should certainly be brief, except in very peculiar cases. Sometimes the close of the last division really brings the whole train of thought to an end and gives it a practical turn; any extended conclusion is then unnecessary and commonly undesirable. Sometimes an abrupt conclusion is very effective, when well managed, with good taste and unaffected solemnity. Sometimes the preacher will be overcome by emotion, and then tearful silence will be more powerful than speech.

Excessive length is a common fault of the conclusion of extemporaneous preachers and writers; in fact, of all who do not govern themselves both in the preparation and delivery of sermons by well-defined plans. New thoughts occur to them, and they are hitched on to what has gone before. What is worse, sometimes the preacher becomes conscious that he has failed to accomplish the object of his discourse, or to awaken the degree of interest he ought to have excited, and he struggles on in the vain endeavor to compensate the fault, until at last he is forced to terminate further from his object than when his conclusion began.[8]

2. It is generally better to use some other connective than "Now, in conclusion" to mark the transition from the discussion. Phillips Brooks began the conclusion of a sermon by saying, "Thus, then, I have passed through the ground which I pro-

posed. See where our thoughts have led us." Other examples are: "We are not proposing, then, this Christmas morning, an easy thing—to let him in, to make room for him—but we are proposing a glorious thing."[9] "But what of this sense of guilt, this inward sense of shame that comes down on the soul like a great shadow? Can that ever be lifted? Ought we to want to have it lifted?"[10] "Now, all this gives me what I am always so glad to find, a new fresh way of conceiving our function as believers in our own particular age."[11] The stereotyped "In conclusion" is often spoken for no reason at all, which is an excellent reason for not saying it. Any announcement of a conclusion inevitably calls attention to time and to the stage of the sermon at which the preacher has arrived. Whether anything is gained by that the preacher must judge. As with illustrations, it is usually best to proceed with the conclusion without calling attention to the fact. Pause and vocal inflexion, a single transitional word or sentence will be enough. Certainly the conclusion ought not to be announced if, already, the last point of discussion has been announced with a "finally." Most of all, it is unwise to give indication that one is about to conclude and then start again or keep dragging on.

3. In most instances the conclusion should be positive rather than negative. What Patton says is generally true:

Negative statements belong in the early part of the sermon. These may often be very important. We teach by contrast. It is frequently necessary to clear the ground before one can put up his own structure; but one should not still be clearing ground in his concluding sentences or bring in at that place things which he wants to warn his hearers away from.[12]

But there are times when one must end with a warning, to carry his people with him in a great condemnation of their own sin. Recall the conclusion of the Sermon on the Mount and Bushnell's sermon of "Unconscious Influence" whose final sentence is "I only warn you here of the guilt which our Lord Jesus Christ will impute to them that hinder his gospel." In every such case however, the preacher must make sure his love and solicitude are obvious.

4. As to the time of preparation, the general character of the conclusion ought to be determined before the detailed composition (whether written or unwritten) of the discourse is begun. Then the development of the concluding details may be suitably limited and directed by the proposed use of the whole. If the other materials have been provided and arranged and no conclusion has yet suggested itself—a thing which will not often happen—the preacher may look again over the thoughts he has presented, asking himself distinctly the question, "What will be the most suitable conclusion to all this?" Or perhaps a renewed examination of the text or of its connection or of parallel passages will furnish something suitable. The problem is not to find some conclusion, but that one which will be most appropriate and effective. It is plain that the conclusion cannot be composed in detail till it is reached in composing the discourse. In fact, some better conclusion than was originally contemplated may have presented itself in the course of composition. And the same thing may happen in the course of delivery. The great requisite is that the body of the discourse and the conclusion be adapted to the other; and this may be accomplished by fixing the general contents and design of the conclusion when laying out the plan of the discourse, and then allowing the style and tone of the conclusion to be modified, or its very character changed, in any way that may have been suggested in the progress of composition or of delivery. This relation of the conclusion to the whole sermon is well expressed by Dr. Oman.

As the introduction should be like the porch, first in execution and last in conception, the conclusion should be like the spire, last in execution but first in conception. As you have to prepare for the spire by laying foundation strong enough to bear it and erect thereon pillars, buttressed by the whole building, able to support it, so every word you say should not only be leading up to the conclusion, but have throughout power to sustain it. Though preaching is more than mere pleading, there is a sense in which, like a barrister addressing a jury, you should be out, from the beginning to end, for a verdict. And the conclusion should only be, like his most impressive, most telling appeal, to clench all that has been already said.[13]

NOTES

1. O. S. Davis, *Principles of Preaching* (Chicago: University of Chicago Press, 1924), p. 217.
2. Herbert H. Farmer, *The Servant of the Word* (New York: Charles Scribner's Sons, 1942), p. 64.
3. John Oman, *Concerning the Ministry* (New York: Harper & Bros., 1937), p. 158.
4. Alexander Vinet, *Homiletics*, 3rd ed. (New York: Ivison, Blakeman, Taylor, 1871), p. 323.
5. Austin Phelps, *The Theory of Preaching* (New York: Charles Scribner's Sons, 1893), p. 576.
6. Thomas Potter, *Sacred Eloquence* (New York: Pustet, n.d.), p. 228.
7. C. S. Patton, *Preparation and Delivery of Sermons* (Chicago: Willett, Clark & Co., 1938), p. 54.
8. D. P. Kidder, *Homiletics* (New York: Carlton & Porter, 1866), pp. 229–30.
9. H. E. Fosdick, *The Power to See It Through* (New York: Harper & Bros., 1935), p. 247.
10. James Reid, *Facing Life with Christ* (Nashville, Tenn.: Cokesbury Press, 1940), p. 57.
11. John A. Hutton, *The Victory over Victory* (London: Hodder & Stoughton, 1922), p. 121. In his conclusions Dr. Hutton often speaks in terms of what the truth of the sermon means to him.
12. Patton, p. 64.
13. Oman, p. 156.

CHAPTER 17

Transition

HAVING discussed the body of the sermon, the introduction, and the conclusion, it is important to consider movement from part to part within the sermon. This movement is called transition. Transition may be formally defined as both the act and means of moving from one part of the sermon to another, from one division to another, and from one idea to another. Transitions are to sermons what joints are to the bones of the body. "They are the bridges of the discourse, and by them"[1] the preacher moves from point to point.

Needless to say, transitions are important to the sermon. O. S. Davis declared, "Transition is vital to the sermon."[2] Ability in transition is also the mark of a skilled homiletician. "No part of the preacher's work requires greater skill and delicacy than this."[3] However, though many writers mention the value of transition, only a few writers give it even limited treatment.

What then are the values of transition? One value is that transition saves the preacher from obscurity. Transition shows relationship; it clarifies meaning. When a preacher moves about in a sermon without showing connections, the people are lost and cannot follow the ideas. Dr. James Black asserted,

I think the one thing hearers never follow easily is a "leap" or "jump" in one's thinking. In fact, this leap is very often the reason why some speakers are charged with obscurity.[4]

Transition also helps the preacher keep the congregation's attention. Attention is highly mobile. It shifts with the preacher or away from him. If a preacher has been discussing one idea and then suddenly he is talking about another subject, the listeners may be confused. While they try to establish relationship, they miss what is then being said. The preacher who makes careful transition keeps the attention of the congregation.

Transition will aid the preacher in recalling the sermon. It is difficult to remember unrelated ideas. Vinet pointed out that well planned transitions will help the preacher recall ideas.[5] The actual preparation of the transitions will tend to fasten ideas in the mind. In the delivery of the sermon, when the preacher comes to the planned transition, the idea is also remembered. This association of the means of transition and of the ideas to be connected greatly aid the memory.

Moreover, transition will contribute to progressive movement. One of the qualities of a good plan is movement. Transition will reveal that the preacher is moving about in the sermon. Whether announced or unannounced, transitions will indicate progress.

Finally, transition will test the unity of a sermon. If it is difficult to move about in a sermon, the ideas may have no real relationship. No good transition can be made between topics that do not have a real and natural relation. Therefore, when transition is difficult, it is well to check for a defective arrangement. A discourse is not a mere conglomeration of unrelated matters. From whatever source its materials may have been derived, they must be made to unite and grow together. Like sap in the plant or blood in the body, the vital current of thought must flow through the whole discourse, giving it animation, flexibility, and strength.

The transitions from one part of a discourse to the next are most felicitous when least noticeable. The ideal of excellence would be that the parts would fit perfectly together, "like well-cut stones, needing no cement," to use Cicero's image, or that each should grow out of the preceding by a process of natural development. This ideal can seldom be realized. The preacher will need to add the connective or build the bridges. Here are some of the means that may be employed.

One method of transition is the relation method. It is inherent in the ideas to be united. Each division seems to move out of the division immediately before it. For example, in a sermon previously mentioned entitled, "Admired, Yet Rejected," the transitions grow out of the ideas. The outline is

I.   He is despised and rejected.
II. He is admired, yet rejected.
III. He should be admired and accepted.

In this instance the ideas fit together like stones that require little or no mortar.

Another means of transition is the connecting word. The most common connecting word is the numeral, e.g., first, second. Numerals have been used in a variety of ways. Other connecting words include now, then, also, therefore, again, besides, furthermore, moreover, finally, and lastly. Sermons should be studied in an effort to build a long list of connecting words.

Still another means of transition is the connecting phrase. Examples of such phrases are "in addition to," "in the next place," "not only that but also," and "on the other hand." Again sermons should be studied to develop a complete list of connecting phrases.

Still another means of transition is the third idea or the bridge. It will frequently happen that the practical design of a sermon or the exigencies of preparation will require the preacher to bring together thoughts between which there is not a perfect fit or a spontaneous vital connection. It may then be necessary to interpose some third idea, related to both and forming an easy transition. Such an idea must not have any separate prominence. The transition can be effected by a single brief sentence. To manage this with simplicity, grace, and variety is a task of some delicacy, but attention and practice will enable anyone to perform it with some success.

Still another method of transition is the use of summary. After completing some of the ideas of a sermon, the preacher may repeat them and add yet another idea. Occasionally preachers will use a summary of the divisions as a means of transition from the body of the sermon to the conclusion. Summary is one of the better means of making transition.

Yet another means of making transition is the use of the question. In discussing the "question-and-answer" outline, it was noted that the question is a means of transition. The preacher uses the question in order to answer it and thereby give his idea or division. In a sermon on 2 Corinthians 8:9 which has already been used as an example of a textual sermon, the preacher used questions to make transitions to the second and third points. How did Jesus become poor? The answer was a discussion of the ways that he became poor. How does he make man rich? The answer was a discussion of the ways in which he makes man rich.

Still another method of transition is by the use of rhetorical devices. Transition was defined as the act or means of moving. In the use of rhetorical devices, it becomes only the act of moving. The preacher may make transition by a change in posture or position. He may indicate transition by pausing. He may make transition by the use of inflection or volume or pitch. To use rhetorical devices as methods of transition will require considerable skill, but experienced preachers make use of the method frequently. This gives additional variety to transition.

As to this whole matter of the plan of discourse, it may be noted that in the present time there is no established and dominant custom; rather there is much flexibility and freedom. The preacher, particularly in his youth, should study and practice different methods, following mainly those which he finds best suited to his abilities. However, frequently he should practice others so that no one method will become a necessity to him. On the other hand, he need not always follow the fashions of the time. Taking into account the nature and purpose of pulpit discourse, he should give free scope to his own individuality and create his own plans. He should be neither eager to appear independent and original nor afraid to try experiments.

NOTES

1. T. Harwood Pattison, *The Making of the Sermon* (Philadelphia: American Baptist Publishing Society, 1898), pp. 117–18.
2. O. S. Davis, *Principles of Preaching* (Chicago: University of Chicago Press, 1924), p. 247.
3. Samuel McComb, *Preaching in Theory and Practice* (New York: Oxford University Press, 1926), p. 72.
4. James Black, *The Mystery of Preaching* (New York: Fleming H. Revell, 1924), p. 102.
5. Alexander Vinet, *Homiletics,* 3rd ed. (New York: Ivison, Blakeman, Taylor, 1871), p. 288.

For Further Reading:
Formal Elements of the Sermon

Baumann, J. Daniel. *An Introduction to Contemporary Preaching.* Grand Rapids, Mich.: Baker Book House, 1972.

Brastow, Lewis O. *The Work of the Preacher.* Boston: Pilgrim Press, 1914.

Caemmerer, Richard R. *Preaching for the Church.* St. Louis, Mo.: Concordia Publishing House, 1959.

Grasso, Domenico. *Proclaiming God's Message.* Notre Dame, Ind.: University of Notre Dame Press, 1965.

Jones, Ilion T. *Principles and Practice of Preaching.* New York: Abingdon Press, 1956.

Reindorp, George. *Putting It Over.* London: Hodder & Stoughton, 1961.

Sangster, W. E. *The Craft of Sermon Construction.* Philadelphia: Westminster Press, 1951.

Sweazey, George E. *Preaching the Good News.* Englewood Cliffs, N.J.: Prentice-Hall, 1976.

Part IV

FUNCTIONAL ELEMENTS
OF THE SERMON

CHAPTER 18

Explanation

WHAT are the functions of preaching? The answer is to be found in the spiritual needs of mankind, which are many. People need to be converted; they need to be instructed in the truth about God and man, about their relation to God and to their fellowmen; they need to grow in character and spirit; they need to be enriched in their devotional life, sentiments, and ideals; they need to be inspired and guided in Christian action, in home, church, and community life; they need to have the horizons of Christian interest and responsibility constantly lifted. It is among such needs as these that sermons must find point and purpose. The functions of preaching, therefore, may be classified as evangelistic, theological, ethical, devotional, inspirational, and actional.

In order to fulfill any one or more of these functions, a sermon must use the instruments that are supplied jointly by psychology, logic, and rhetoric—which are explanation or exposition, argument, application, and, as largely auxiliary to the others, illustration. These functional elements are not entirely distinct from one another; they often overlap. Therefore, certain processes which are always classed under explanation, such as narrative and description, are often used at the same time and mainly for proof or persuasion. They are not proper categories for the classification of sermons, although a sermon may be predominantly characterized by one or another. They are instrumental or functional elements to be used in the proportion that best suits the purpose of the particular sermon. For example, an evangelistic sermon will naturally appeal to emotion more extensively than a didactic sermon; a devotional sermon will be more explanatory and persuasive than argumentative; a theological sermon of the apologetic type will be largely argumentative, while the simple instructional sermon will be mainly explanatory; inspirational sermons will be strengthened by illustrative examples. In order to be able to adapt content to function, the preacher should become thoroughly familiar with the elements discussed in this chapter and the three subsequent ones.

1. EXPLANATION IN GENERAL

There is in preaching a frequent need for explanation. Numerous passages of Scripture are not understood or are even misunderstood by our hearers, and many have become so accustomed to passing over these that they are no longer aware that they present any difficulty. Some of the most important doctrines of the Bible are in general very imperfectly understood; those who believe them need clearer views of what they profess to believe, and those who object to them are often in fact objecting to something very different from the real doctrine. The plan of salvation is seldom comprehended till one is really willing to conform to it, so that there is constantly arising new occasion for answering the great question, "What must I do to be saved?" And a thousand questions as to what is true and what is right in the practical conduct of life perplex devout minds and call for explanation. Preaching ought to be not merely convincing and persuasive, but eminently instructive. The preacher often belabors men with arguments and appeals, when they are much more in need of practical and simple explanations of what to do and how to do it. And while some persons present may have repeatedly heard us explain certain important matters, the pastor must not forget that there are others—children growing up, strangers moving in, converts entering the church—to whom such explanations will be new and necessary.

But just here the inexperienced minister may profit by several homely cautions. Do not attempt to explain what is not assuredly true. One sometimes finds great difficulty in working out an explanation of a supposed fact or principle because it is really not true. Do not undertake to explain what you do not understand. In preaching, as well as elsewhere, this happens so often as to be ridiculous if it were not mournful. How can the housewife cook what has never been caught? How can the preacher explain what he does not understand? Never try to explain what cannot be explained. Some things taught in the Bible are in their essence incomprehensible; such as the nature of the Trinity or the coexistence of absolute divine predestination with human freedom and accountability. In such a case it is very important to explain just what the Scriptures really do teach to remove misunderstandings; and it may sometimes be worthwhile to present any remote analogies in other categories of life perhaps to diminish the hearer's unwillingness to receive the doctrine; but attempts to explain the essential difficulty must necessarily fail, and the failure will only strengthen doubt and opposition. Do not waste time in explaining what does not need explanation. A conspicuous instance is the nature of faith. Men frequently complain that they do not understand what it really is to believe, and preachers are constantly laboring to explain. But the complaint is in many cases a mere excuse for rejection or delay, and the real difficulty is, in most cases, a lack of disposition to believe. Elaborate explanations do not lessen this indisposition, but do strengthen the supposed excuse, and may even embarrass the anxious inquirer with the notion that there is something very mysterious about faith, when it is in fact so simple that it does not need to be explained. Our main duty is to tell the people what to believe and why they should believe it.

2. EXPLANATION OF TEXTS

To explain the Scriptures would seem to be among the primary functions of the preacher. And there will often be occasion to explain not merely the text of the sermon but various other passages of Scripture which may be introduced into the discussion. The power of making such explanations attractive as well as clear will, of course, depend largely upon the preacher's ability. But the most gifted in this important task should seek constant improvement, and they who have great difficulty must exert diligent and optimistic efforts to overcome it. What nobler work is there than that of "opening" the Scriptures, as Paul did at Thessalonica (Acts 17:3)?

1. The exegesis of texts, as the process by which the preacher himself comes to understand them, has already received attention. Pulpit exegesis, or exposition, is in certain respects a different thing. It is necessary, except in exceptional cases, to present results and not processes. Various matters should be omitted because they would not interest the people or are not applicable to the object of the present discourse. Preachers sometimes allow themselves, in the introduction to the sermon or as a digression, to give long explanations of something in a passage or its connection which have no bearing on their subject and thus impair unity and distract attention. There must, of course, be no parade of knowledge with the original languages, and there should be no morbid fear of being charged with such pride. Commentaries can be mentioned if the people know something of them and would be more readily satisfied, or if it is desirable to bring good popular authors to their notice. To repeat lists of strange and impressive names in favor of this or that interpretation is always useless and is in general a very pitiful display of cheap erudition, which with the help of certain books can be put together in a few minutes. One may very easily indicate, without any array of authorities, that this is the view of the best writers or of some good commentators. It is important that one take the results of the most careful investigation, select from them the appropriate points, and present these clearly, briefly, and in such a way as to be interesting. Sometimes the text or another passage introduced may be amply and admirably explained by a few words; but such words do not come by themselves; they result from careful thought and choice of expressions. Sometimes passages may be intro-

duced without a word of explanation to give them new meaning and preciousness. It is a fault in many able ministers that they comparatively neglect to bring in and explain the relevant sayings of Scripture which would both give and borrow light. And however congregations may shrink from elaborate exegesis or bungling and tedious attempts to explain, they will always welcome the simple introduction and quick, vivid elucidation of passages from God's Word.

2. Narration has in preaching a peculiar character. Modern works on rhetoric consider it almost exclusively as practiced in writing—historical, biographical, fictional, dramatic, and the like. Ancient writers discuss oratorical narration and are therefore more valuable for our purpose, although they are chiefly concerned with the narrative in judicial oratory. The preacher, of course, narrates as a speaker and deals mainly with scriptural history. A speaker must always subordinate narration to the object of his discourse, the conviction or persuasion which he wishes to effect. He must not elaborate or enlarge upon some narrative merely because it is in itself interesting or follow the story step by step according to its own laws.

In an epideictic speech, narration is not continuous, but intermittent. Some account there must be of the actions that give rise to the speech, for the speech consists of two elements. One of these, namely the actions, is not supplied by the speaker's art, for of the actions he is in no way the author. The other is supplied by his art.[1]

That is, the facts are independent of the speaker, but he breaks them up and presents them according to his object.

The reason why it is sometimes undesirable to make the narration continuous, and exhaustive, is that the exposition thus becomes hard to recollect. Accordingly, it is well to make a selection from the facts. ... A speech thus devised will be simple as compared with the former, which is involved and profuse.[2]

And so when the sermon is on the minor and less familiar personages of Scripture, it is proper enough to narrate all the facts concerning them. But when it is about one of the great characters, one must choose between two courses. The salient or characteristic points of his history may be selected and narrated to exhibit the chief lessons of that history, introducing the details that are relevant and rigorously omitting all others. Thus, the history of Joseph, of Job, or of John the Baptist may be conveniently treated. In such a case, every speaker will mention or enlarge upon different parts of the history, according to his particular object, like Stephen's speech and that of Paul at Antioch in Pisidia sketch very differently the history of Israel. Paul, in the two speeches narrating the story of his conversion, expands in each of them certain matters which in the other are but slightly touched, adapting the narration to the character and needs of his audience. But it is generally better to narrate some one event of the man's history or some one trait of his character. In preaching upon the meekness of Moses, there would be occasion to state briefly those circumstances of his training and career which were particularly unfavorable to the development of meekness and then to narrate the leading instances in which his meekness was exhibited, as well as those in which it temporarily failed. The discourse would properly close with a somewhat extended application of the whole matter to ourselves. In this way, the history of Moses would be much more impressively told, than if one attempted an outline of his whole story.

Narration is often given in the introduction to the sermon. In such a case, one should not have the narration too long, should not wander into parts of the story which have no bearing upon the design of the discourse, and should not pause, except in very rare cases, for remarks upon outside topics which the narrative may suggest. Be sure, also, that the particulars of the narrative are interesting, plausible, and of evident value to the ends of the sermon. There is special danger here of violating the laws of unity and proportion.

Besides the instances in which some history in the Bible is the theme, there will be constant occasion to take illustrations from biblical history and great demand for skill in the brief and interesting narration of those events. Happy is the preacher who can, in this way, keep those beautiful and sacred stories fresh in the minds of his hearers, because they are not only interesting to children and full of instruction for youth, but when understood correctly, they assume new interest and meaning at every stage of life.

It is a rather common fault in the pulpit to narrate in a declamatory way. The preacher becomes excited and states a plain fact or tells a simple story with a vehemence that is extremely incongruous. Quintilian keenly satirizes those who think it beneath their dignity to state facts in everyday language, who do not seem eloquent to themselves unless they have thrown everything into agitation by boisterous vociferation, and, instead of simply narrating, imagine that they have here a field for showing off and "inflect the voice, set back the neck, and fling the arm against the side, and riot in every variety of ideas, words, and style."[3]

3. Description is usually necessary for separate scenes of a narrative. There is also frequent occasion to describe scriptural scenes apart from their connection in the narrative, as in the introduction to a sermon, in the use of historical illustrations from Scripture, etc. And while narration and description of only the events and scenes of biblical history are spoken of here, it is obvious that the same skill must be applied to that great variety of illustrative matter from every other source, which must be vividly narrated in order to make any impression. The old adage, "He is the best speaker who can turn an ear into an eye,"[4] is still true.

Power of description is, of course, partly a natural gift; but many intelligent people lament that they cannot describe, when they have never fairly tried—never given themselves any general training in narration, never really studied any one scene or object which they attempted to describe. Such people are aware that they cannot work out an argument without much previous thought but seem not aware that corresponding effort is necessary to achieve a good description.

He who would describe anything must have seen it, not necessarily with literal vision but with imagination. He must begin, then, by getting correct information about the scene or object; and this information must extend, if possible, to details. With regard to biblical scenes, one often needs a familiarity with biblical geography and with the manners and customs of the Jews. While gathering such information and after doing so, he must concentrate on the scene so that the imagination can picture it; he must look at it as he would at a landscape or a painting, first surveying the whole, then inspecting the most interesting details. This should be continued, with varied points of view till the whole scene is clear and vivid in the imagination; only then is he prepared to describe it.

Remember now that a speaker does not describe as the writer of a poem, a novel, or a book of travels might. His description should be brief and subordinate to the objects of his discourse. The outlines of the picture should be briefly, but distinctly, described. Then, certain prominent or characteristic points of the scene must be presented with some of the most suggestive details which will arouse the hearer's imagination to fill in the picture. In this lies the great art of description, especially for speakers—to stimulate the hearer's imagination into seeing for himself. Sometimes there are a few details so characteristic that they need only the slightest indication of outline to make a picture; as in a caricature, one or two peculiar features, somewhat exaggerated, and a few simple lines will be more interesting than a finished picture. And even where there are no remarkably striking details, one may contrive slight touches here and there which will give life to the whole. If these are not available in our knowledge of the facts, they may be avowedly imagined, care being taken to have them suggest only what will harmonize with the facts. Thus, in that remarkable home-scene at Bethany, after describing Mary seated at Jesus' feet and hearing his word, one might imagine Martha as coming to the door of the room, her face heated with excitement and vexation, and, after vainly trying to get Mary's attention and call her, finally stepping straight to the Master himself with her complaining request; and this slight glance at her before she enters will help in imagining the scene.

Avoid elaborate description. The preacher is expected always to cherish a practical design, and to be so earnest that he does not have time for painting finished pictures. An educated audience will always consider them inappropriate. As regards the temptation to give elaborate descriptions to show one's talent in that respect, this must of course be resisted like all other temptations to be ostentatious. But the preacher cannot use to advantage the historical portions of Scripture or other narrative and pictorial illustration without cultivating powers of narration and description. He who will discipline himself, under the guidance of correct principles, first to see clearly and then to describe suggestively, may soon surprise himself by the ease and pleasure with which he can describe, in not many words, some story or scene from the Bible.

3. EXPLANATION OF SUBJECTS

Here again there will be included not merely the general subject of a discourse but any other ideas which enter into the discussion. Both the former and the latter must often require explanation. Many matters of truth and duty are obscure and, without explanation, practically unintelligible to the popular mind; many questions are sadly perplexing. To answer such inquiries, to clear up difficulties, and make as plain as possible the ways of truth and duty are an important part of the preacher's work as well as the explanation of Scripture.

1. One means of explaining subjects is by definition.

Definition is defined by the etymology of the word. It marks the limits of an idea. To define definition positively, we say that it teaches of what elements an idea, as a whole, is composed. It consists in bringing together many general ideas, of which one is limited by the others. When the idea, so to speak, is fortified, entrenched, so that on all sides it repels ideas which would mix themselves with it, the object is defined. We must not confound definition and judgment. Definition does but verify identity; judgment expresses a relation. . . . Definition aims to make us know; judgment, to appreciate. Very often, however, definition appreciates, and involves judgment; and judgment is equivalent to a partial definition. We must not, however, confound with definition those judgments which give force to a characteristic of an object, and are only designed to excite toward it such or such a sentiment. Examples:

"Rivers are roads that move and carry us whither we would go."

"Hypocrisy is a homage which vice pays to virtue."

"Time is the treasure of the poor."

"A tomb is a monument placed on the boundary between two worlds."

"Love is the fulfilling of the law."

When the notion of the attribute does not exhaust that of the subject, and one cannot be put indifferently for the other, we have not a definition, we have a judgment. . . . A definition is indeed a judgment, but a judgment which contains or begets all the judgments which may at any time be pronounced upon an object. And reciprocally, by combining all the judgments which at any time may be pronounced on an object, we have a definition.[5]

Vinet proceeds to give examples of definition, including one which is very often called a definition but surely without propriety: "Faith is the substance of things hoped for, the evidence of things not seen" (Heb. 11:1, KJV). Other judgments may be given to the word faith besides this. Faith is the substance of things hoped for, etc., just as love is the fulfillment of the law. It may be said that faith is the means of union with Christ, but that is not defining faith.

In preaching, an idea may most easily be defined by connecting it with another idea, either in the way of distinction or of comparison. And instead of or in addition to definition, it is often well to use exemplification.

Definition is not only a means of perspicuity, an element of instruction, the basis of argumentation; it is often the beginning of proof. Demonstration, at least, is firm and sure in proportion to the exactness and clearness of the definition.[6]

Everyone has observed how important it is in beginning a controversial discussion, public or private, to define the question; otherwise, confusion of ideas is inevitable. Now, it is equally, though not so obviously, important in conducting a discussion alone that one should clearly define to himself the subject in hand. In fact, it is more important in this case because controversy will sooner or later force two parties to realize that they have not clearly understood the question or understood it in the same way, while the solitary thinker or the unanswered speaker may remain permanently involved in the confusion or error produced by his lack of well-defined conceptions at the outset. And the same thing applies to the definition of leading terms. But while the preacher must always define for himself, it is not always necessary for him to define for the audience. The proposition of the subject, if felicitous, may often be sufficiently perspicuous and precise; or one may see that the discussion itself will effectively give clear and definite views of the subject. In all definitions stated, formality should be avoided, and the preacher should "avoid too subtle distinctions and classifications, which assume a great habit of abstraction and an exact knowledge of language on the part of the hearer."[7]

2. A second means of explaining ideas is by division. The methods of dividing a subject and of stating divisions have already been discussed.

3. Exemplification is often necessary and almost always useful in the work of explanation. The common mind does not easily understand general definitions expressed in abstract terms; and even to the most cultivated thinkers, an idea will become more vivid and interesting when some apposite example is added to a precise definition. It would be difficult to present to a popular audience a clear distinction between pride and vanity by definition; but by supposing certain circumstances and showing how the proud person would act and how the vain person in such a case, or by taking up some particular action of a well-known character and inquiring whether the motive here was pride or vanity, one can quickly make the difference plain. So, instead of undertaking to explain faith, one may describe a believer or, in addition to stating in general terms what will make a Christian happy, may give an ideal portrait of a Christian who was happy. And still more useful are examples from real life. Every

preacher uses his observation of life in this way, and some do so with very great effectiveness. But, besides what the preacher has personally observed, examples can be derived from wide fields of history and especially of biblical history. In selecting those to be used, the preacher must inquire not only what is most apposite, but what will be most intelligible and interesting to the particular audience and what he himself can most effectively handle. Historical examples which would thrill one congregation will make little impression on another, not being familiar to them or not linked to them by any ties of sympathy. In this, as in most respects, examples from biblical history are the best. They are more generally familiar than most others, and if any time be consumed in bringing the example vividly before the hearers, it is time well spent because it promotes general acquaintance with the Scriptures.

4. Among the commonest and most useful means of explanation is comparison. Comparison may be classed with contrast and also analogy, which depends on a resemblance, not in objects themselves, but in their respective relationships to certain other objects. Analogy, however, is more frequently used for the purpose of proof and will be considered in the next chapter. Contrast needs no special remark.

The great mass of our Lord's parables are comparisons. "The kingdom of heaven is like. . . ." "Unto what shall we liken this generation?" Some of them are in the form of narrative; but others are mere statements of comparison, and he uses many striking comparisons which are never called parables. The comparison of his coming to that of a thief (Matt. 24:43, 44) is an instructive example of the fact that comparison is all the more striking where there is one point of resemblance between objects or events which in other respects are very different. Several of the parables are cases of exemplification rather than of comparison, as, for instance, the Rich Man preparing to rest, the Pharisee and the Publican, the Good Samaritan. Many of them are introduced for other purposes in addition to that of explanation. But they are chiefly comparisons and are mainly used to explain. Therefore, they impressively show us the importance of explanation and the value of comparison as a means of effecting it.

NOTES

1. Lane Cooper, *The Rhetoric of Aristotle* (New York: D. Appleton-Century Co., 1932), p. 228.
2. Cooper, pp. 228–29.
3. Quintilian, *The Institutio Oratoria of Marcus Fabius Quintilianus* (Nashville, Tenn.: George Peabody College for Teachers, 1951), IV, 2, pp. 37–39.
4. John Nichols Booth, *The Quest for Preaching Power* (New York: Macmillan Co., 1943), p. 136.
5. Alexander Vinet, *Homiletics,* 3rd ed. (New York: Ivison, Blakeman, Taylor, 1871), pp. 161–63.
6. Ibid., p. 164.
7. Ibid., pp. 164, 165.

CHAPTER 19

Argument

EXPLANATION does not in itself meet the full requirement of preaching. Events must be related to present life situations and needs. Ideas made clear, if they are to have their full force, often must be established as true by relating them to other already accepted ideas in such a way as to win acceptance for them also. In so relating ideas, the preacher is expressing a judgment—that they are related, and how they are related—and, to quote Dr. Garvie,

it often happens that the connection between the two ideas in a judgment cannot be taken for granted, or be simply imposed by the preacher on his hearers. He must justify the connection; he must so present the connection as to win the assent of his hearers. He must, therefore, give reasons, or links of connection between the two ideas which are not obviously immediately related to one another.[1]

He must sometimes follow a line of reasoning, i.e., make an argument, to support his judgment and so establish the truth and justify the application he would make of it. Argument, therefore, in the logical and at the same time popular sense of the term, forms a very large and very important element in the materials of preaching. There are preachers, it is true, who seem to consider that they have no occasion for reasoning, that everything is to be accomplished by authoritative assertion and impassioned appeal. And this notion is not new, for Aristotle complained that previous writers on rhetoric had concerned themselves only with the means of persuasion by appeals to feeling and prejudice. But preachers really have great use for argument, and there are many reasons why its importance in preaching should be duly considered.

1. IMPORTANCE OF ARGUMENT IN PREACHING

There are many who deny and doubt who must be convinced of both the truth of Christianity and the truth of what is represented to be its teachings. There are many who in both respects believe but whose religious affections and activity might be encouraged by convincing and impressive proofs that these things are so.

Even in the cases in which reasoning seems superfluous, it may be greatly useful, since its object is not so much to prove what is not yet believed as to fill the mind with the evidence, and, if we may so speak, to multiply the brightness of truth.[2]

And besides, there is in Christian countries a multitude of people who say they believe because they do not disbelieve or question, whose minds remain in a negative state towards the gospel which is often the most fatal form of unbelief. Argument, concerning the truth and value and claims of the gospel, concerning the peril and guilt of their position, is often useful in arousing feelings of contrition and desire. This is, therefore, one of the means by which the preacher must strive to bring them, through the special blessing of the Spirit, into some real, operative belief.

Some forms of error which exalt the intellectual at the expense of the spiritual gain much acceptance, particularly with a certain class of minds, by their use of argument. The teachers of these errors come to men accustomed to a sleepy acquiescence in truths which they have never heard vigorously discussed, use their powers of argument well, and they win. Even those who maintain sound doctrine sometimes support it by very unsound reasoning and thereby leave the way open for some shrewd opponent to overthrow their arguments, and thus appear to overthrow their doctrine.

Every preacher, then, ought to develop and discipline his powers of argument. If averse to reasoning, he should discipline himself to practice it; if by nature strongly inclined that way, he must remember the serious danger of deceiving himself and others by false arguments. One who has not carefully studied some good treatise of logic should do so. It will make his mind sharper to detect fallacy, in others or in himself, and will help him to develop the habit of reasoning soundly. The fact that, as so often sneeringly remarked, "preachers are never replied to," should make it a point of honor with preachers not to mislead their hearers by bad logic and should make them very anxious to avoid those self-deceptions, which they have no keen opponent to reveal. One must constantly remind himself to argue for truth rather than for victory and, as a rule, never to maintain a proposition which he does not really believe. The delicate perception of truth and the enthusiastic love for it will inevitably be impaired by a contrary course.

Yet in preaching everything does not have to be proved, and every proof does not need to be a formal argument. Some things cannot be proved, some do not need to be, and others have been sufficiently proved before and should now be taken for granted. Elaborate argument which is not called for will only cause doubt or boredom and disgust. The preacher may usually assume the truth of Scripture. And as to whatever the Scriptures plainly teach, while he must sometimes argue, it is often true, as Spurgeon has said, that the preacher should "dogmatize," being careful, of course, to remember that the dogmatic use of a passage as a proof-text must be approved in the light of the whole scriptural teaching.

The accent of true authority is welcome to almost every one. We are prepossessed in favor of men who, in this world of uncertainty and perplexity, express themselves on a grave subject with confidence and command. . . . The person of preachers is nothing, their message is the whole; and not for their person, but for their message, do they claim respect; but they would be as culpable not to demand this respect for the divine thought of which they are the depositaries, as they would be foolish and ridiculous to demand it for their own thoughts.[3]

But the right to speak with such authority will be acknowledged, among Protestants, only where the preacher shows himself able to prove whenever it is appropriate all that he maintains.

2. PRINCIPAL VARIETIES OF ARGUMENT

It is not proposed to give a formal analysis and classification of arguments but to explain the nature and use of the leading varieties. These are, in the order of their natural development and usage, testimony, induction, analogy, and deduction.

1. Argument from Testimony. In establishing truth in the minds of one's hearers, the most direct and simple way is to tell one's own experience of the truth and one's own observation of the truth. The preacher himself becomes a witness of what he himself has seen and heard and handled and tested out to a final faith. It has often been said that no one should go further. Preach only what you have experienced! Yet every preacher does go further, and must. He expresses also his judgment. The man of experience inevitably becomes the man of opinion; having testified, "I was blind and now I see," and having given the details of the experience, he soon goes on to say, "He is a prophet." The testimony of fact is supplemented by the testimony of opinion or judgment.

The grain of truth in the old idea that we are to preach only what we have experienced is that we are not to preach anything that has not in some way become real to us. Guesses and hypotheses carry little weight. Speculations can never take the place of convictions. Yet, even speculation has a place in all human thought, religious or otherwise, and not all convictions are reached by experience.[4]

So in preaching, preachers may use the facts of experience and judgment and draw, also, upon the experience and judgment of others. This is the simplest proof, the beginning of argument. It is necessary in the use of testimony to distinguish clearly between fact and judgment or opinion. Common usage sometimes confuses these terms, even as men are very apt not to distinguish facts from their own judgments concerning them. In the alleged "spiritual manifestations," of which so much has been said, there is unquestionable testimony that tables rise and move without the application of any apparent and adequate physical force, that certain peculiar rapping sounds are heard, and that other strange things occur. Now upon the testimony, these matters of fact should be, without hesitation, accepted. But what causes these movements and sounds, whether some unknown physical force or some unknown spiritual agency, is purely matter of opinion. Those who have most frequently witnessed the phenomena are not necessarily the best prepared to decide upon their cause; while the supposed interpretation of the rapping noises and the correspondence of such interpretations with facts otherwise known are matters which open a wide door for all manner of self-delusions and deceptions. Pastors must educate the people to distinguish more carefully than is common between testimony on matters of fact and mere judgments, opinions, and hypotheses as explanation.

It is not appropriate to discuss here the general subject of testimony as relating to the administration of justice. And, yet, a minister does well to consider carefully the rules of evidence in the courts of justice, endeavoring, in every case, to find the principle involved so that he can apply it with the necessary adaptations to the matters with which he is concerned. Those parts of the subject with which the preacher frequently has to deal will be briefly discussed.

a. In testimony on matters of fact, the points to be considered are, on the one hand, the character and number of the witnesses and, on the other, the character of the things attested.

As to the character of the witnesses, we of course consider mainly their veracity, but also their intelligence, their opportunities of knowing the facts and their tendency to think in a certain way. A large number of witnesses will obviously make the evidence stronger, provided each speaks from his own knowledge and not from what others have told him. When there are several such independent witnesses, their testimony will differ on some points of detail. Where the details are numerous, no individual will be expected to remember and state them all; and each will select according to what he happened to observe, or what was specially noteworthy to him, or what he has had frequent occasion since to remember, or what is in agreement with the general design and drift of his statement or is suggested, point after point, by the natural association of ideas. If all were to agree in the details of an extended statement, we should feel sure that they had in some way learned from each other or had all drawn from a common source. These principles are familiar to the English and American mind.

The unintentional testimony of adversaries is frequently of great value. Thus the opposition of Christianity in the early centuries, both heathen and Jewish, in endeavoring to account for the miracles of our Lord as being magic, have shown that they felt it impossible to deny the reality of the occurrences.

On the other hand, there is to be considered the character of the things attested. Things in themselves improbable will, of course, require more testimony in order to gain our credence. Such is the case with miracles. That some spiritual force should so counteract the operation of great physical forces as for a time to prevent their otherwise uniform results is a thing which we are naturally slow to believe. This improbability, however, is greatly diminished where an important reason for such interference is noted, such as where miracles are done to authenticate a revelation. The Christian miracles have not only this but another advantage. The character and teachings of Christ are inseparably associated with miracles. He who denies the miracles denies the supernatural origin of Christ's character and teachings and must then account for these as merely human and natural, which the ablest and most ingenious infidels, after a great variety of attempts, have utterly failed to do. So the question of antecedent probability is here reduced to this: Which is more improbable, that miracles should have been performed upon such occasion as the introduction of Christianity, or that the character and teachings of Christ should be merely human and of natural origin? Thus the general improbability of miracles is in this case much lessened by the adequate reason for them and then is more than counterbalanced by a yet greater improbability if they are denied.

Moreover, the testimony of others to our Lord's miracles is not only strong and unquestionable in itself but has the unique and invincible reinforcement of our Lord's own testimony. Jesus professed to work miracles; he cannot by possibility have been deceived on the subject; and so either he did work miracles, or he was a bad man. His character shatters all the objections to miracles. And this is not arguing in a circle—not proving the miracles by Christ and Christ by the miracles. The concurrence of the two makes it easy to account for both; the denial of the miracles necessitates conclusions more improbable than the miraculous.

The evidence of Christian experience ought never to be overlooked. The believer finds a change in himself which testifies to the reality and power of Christianity, and he in turn bears witness to others that the change which they observe in him occurred in connection with believing.

b. Testimony on matters of opinion, as distinguished from matters of fact, might be conveniently designated by the term "authority." But this term is sometimes applied to testimony on matters of fact, especially where it is particularly strong and convincing testimony, and is also frequently used to denote some combination of testimony on fact and reliable judgment or opinion. But the basic distinction must not be overlooked. And it must be remembered that a reliable witness to facts is not thereby necessarily reliable in judgment. The so-called "authority" of the Fathers must be differently regarded in different cases. Concerning the question, What books were of apostolic origin? they afford testimony—though in the case of all but the earliest Fathers, it is not original but transmitted testimony—and also the authority of their judgment on the validity of the entire evidence known to them. In respect to such questions, they are known to have been very critical, and one may well attach great value both to their testimony and their authority. But concerning the interpretation of the sacred books, the question concerning what Scripture teaches, one has only their authority, their judgment. Some of them were loose interpreters, and they were all greatly influenced by philosophical opinions, prejudices of various kinds, and especially, with rare exceptions, by an extreme fondness for allegory. Except, then, the cases in which familiarity with Greek, with ancient customs, and the like gives special weight to the opinions of a Father, their authority concerning the meaning of Scripture is not great and, in fact, not justly equal to that of some later writers.

The Scriptures themselves are an authority, indeed. All that they testify to be fact is thereby fully proven, all that they teach as true and right is thereby established and made obligatory.

This is proof without arguing in the narrow sense. Somewhat similarly do all men prove by the direct appeal to consciousness. "You know that so and so is true" will in some cases settle the question. So, too, is the appeal to common sense, though it should be noticed that people often put forward as a judgment of common sense what is only some opinion of their own, some conclusion reached by a process of reasoning but by a process so obscure that it escapes their consciousness and thus hides its fallacies from their view. But the Scriptures furnish a standard of final appeal having a far more frequent and extensive application. This does not at all enable one to dispense with argument. Sometimes the preacher has to prove that the Scriptures are such a standard, and to show what the various passages of Scripture teach on a subject often requires not merely exposition but argument. Many truths have to be established partly by argument on other grounds, reinforced and confirmed by indirect teachings of the Bible; and it is appreciated by believers, and demanded by unbelievers, that the minister should, wherever it is possible, exhibit the concurrence of reason and experience with the teachings of revelation. But in all our reasoning, care should be taken to treat the authority of Scripture as paramount and, wherever its messages are distinct and unquestionable, as decisive. There are some subjects on which the Bible is our sole authority, such as the Trinity, justification by faith, the conditions of the future life, and the positive ordinances of Christianity, namely, baptism and the Lord's supper. The Christian reasoner should seek fully to appreciate this unparalleled authority and should maintain its proper relation to all other means of proof.

The generally received opinions of mankind and the proverbs and maxims which express the collective judgment of many have a greater or less authority according to the nature of the case. Those, for example, which are easily attributed to human superstitions or selfishness or express only half-truths have little weight.

2. Argument from Induction. Induction has been variously defined. John Stuart Mill says: "Induction is that operation of the mind by which we infer that what we know to be true in a particular case or cases will be true in all cases which resemble the former in certain assignable respects." Professor N. K. Davis defines: "Induction is an immediate synthetic inference generalizing from and beyond experience."[5] Every term in this statement is important, and when they are well understood the definition will be found to be exact and complete.

Induction has also been very simply defined as the process of drawing a general rule from a sufficient number of particular cases. Finding something to be true of certain individual objects, it is inferred that the same thing is true of other objects or of the whole class to which those individuals belong. Induction is, in popular usage, the most common form of argument. When carefully done, it results in reliable knowledge and, when carelessly done, often involves error. People in general do not argue from general principles or previously established truths nearly so often as from examples. These examples they indolently observe, and without extensive comparison or careful study, they hastily infer that what a certain person did is right for them, that what is true of certain individuals, or of all they happen to have noticed, is true of all the class. When they are strongly impelled to wish it so—by appetite, interest, or prejudice—and some powerful desire combines with indolence, it is not surprising, however deplorable, that a hasty induction is the result. In agriculture or in home remedies, all manner of rules are upheld and followed by people on the ground of imperfect observation and hasty induction. Certain choice specimens of what are called uneducated ministers surpass some very poor specimens of the educated, and this is thought to prove that ministerial education is unnecessary; a half-educated young preacher makes a foolish display of something he learned at college or seminary, and this shows that education is injurious. But who could catalogue or even broadly classify the instances of hasty or otherwise unwarranted induction which make up so sadly large a portion of human reasoning? Teachers of truth should guard against this source of error.

The question of what is a sufficient number of cases to warrant our drawing a general rule depends upon the nature of the subject matter. In regard to physical facts, a single example will sometimes suffice.

A chemist who had ascertained, in a single specimen of gold, its capability of combining with mercury would not think it necessary to try the experiment with several other specimens but would draw the conclusion concerning those metals universally and with practical certainty.[6]

But nothing like this applies to social facts or to moral and religious truth. In order for a safe induction, one must not merely aggregate a number of instances, he must analyze and compare them, so as to eliminate what is merely incidental, and ascertain the "material circumstances" in each case. The more clearly one can discern a causal relation accounting for the common element the smaller the number of instances is necessary to establish a rule. But the cause must be a real cause, not a mere hypothesis, not a matter having no real connection with the result in question, not an incidental circumstance. As an example of the last, it is frequently inferred that something found true in several cases of conversion will be true in all cases, but the question is whether this is something founded in the essential principles of human nature or merely the result of peculiar temperament, education, and other circumstances.

With due emphasis on the dangers of faulty induction, it must be recognized with Garvie that rich values are found in this kind of reasoning.

There is a very wide scope for the preacher in taking the individual instances of morality enjoined in the prophets, the Gospels, and the Epistles so as to discover the general principles implied, and in then applying these principles to the instances of duty for his hearers.[7]

In his moral teaching our Lord laid down general moral principles which often were the results of some concrete fact or experience, and also he gave particular teachings that fitted particular situations, leaving it to us to perceive and apply the embedded principle to other situations. For example, take his generalization about rich men after his experience with the rich young ruler. He laid down no abstract principle about private property, but all his remarks about wealth and greed and giving are particulars from which listeners may draw their conclusions. His generalization about paying taxes to Rome was based upon a fact of actual debtorship. The facts of human paternal love were his argument for faith in the beneficent love of the Heavenly Father. In the house of Simon the Pharisee, his parable and subsequent remarks were full of facts from which that astonished man had to infer an embarrassing fact about himself. Christ's preaching was concrete, closely related to life situations; and its authority was strengthened by the fact that it claimed at every point the support of the facts of human experience. The preacher will do well to remember such facts. "Consider the lilies of the field," and "Behold the birds of the heaven." And he should study induction—constructing strong bridges of facts that will bring people to some significant realization.

It is extremely important for the preacher to know how to correct those many erroneous inductions, whether in the arguments of other public speakers, in newspapers and conversation, or in their own thinking, by which the minds of his hearers

are so apt to be misled. And it is highly important that one see
and utilize the significance of assembled facts.

3. Argument from Analogy. Analogy is still too often confused
with resemblance, in spite of the earnest efforts of Whately and
some other writers to confine the term to its original and proper
sense. The primary meaning of the word is "proportion," and
in this sense only is it used in mathematics. It denotes not a
resemblance between objects themselves, but a correspondence between their ratios or relations to other objects. The leg
of a table does not much resemble the leg of an animal, but they
are analogous because the former sustains, in several respects,
the same relation to a table that the leg sustains to an animal.
The foot of a mountain is analogous to that of man, though
scarcely at all similar.

An egg and a seed are not in themselves alike, but bear a like
relation, to the parent bird and to her future nestling on the one hand,
and to the old and young plant on the other.[8]

But analogous objects will frequently be similar, also, and this
fact has helped to obscure the distinction—that which is really
due to the analogy being sometimes carelessly ascribed to the
resemblance. Further, an analogy is often all the more striking
from the fact that it exists between objects which in some other
respects are utterly unlike. So it happens that failing to see
clearly the difference between analogy and resemblance, and
observing, besides, that the term analogy is often used where
there is in some respects a great dissimilarity, many persons
have fallen into the habit of calling objects analogous which are
similar in some respects, but have a recognized difference in
others. Of course, an argument from a mere partial resemblance between objects is worth little. But the case might be
very different where there is a resemblance (sometimes even an
identity) in the relation which two objects bear to a third, or to
two others, respectively. Understand analogy in this strict and
proper sense, and the argument from analogy may have great
force. It is extremely desirable that good usage restrict the term
to its proper meaning. The point to remember is that one

should never say there is an analogy between objects unless there is a correspondence (identity or similarity) in their relations to something else, however like or however unlike the objects themselves may be. People are controlled by words; and unless the thoughtful can discern, avoid, and correct such confusions in the popular use of important terms, reasoning to a popular audience will constantly become increasingly difficult.

Has the argument from analogy any positive force? It may certainly afford a probable proof of positive truth. When two objects are observed to be analogous in many important respects, it is more or less probable that they are also analogous in some other respect not observed. But it is very doubtful whether this can in any case be an absolute proof. Many results of induction, as has been seen above, are simply in a high degree probable; and they become certain only when some cause of that similarity can be discerned which will operate also in the instances not examined. Now the same thing must hold in the case of analogy. If two objects should correspond in all their relationships to certain other objects, and if the reasoner were able to discern some cause of the agreement that must produce a similar agreement in other relationships not examined, then he might infer with certainty that in any of these other relationships they do correspond. In many cases of induction, a cause or at least an explanation of the common element can be found. Perhaps the same can be done in cases of analogy. Still, an argument from analogy will often add its force to that of other proofs and will make a result more or less probable, even where no other proof exists.

4. Argument from Deduction. The mental process called deduction is that by which we argue or infer from a more general truth. Its object, as involved in the etymology of the word, is to lead the mind from some general truth to other truth, general or particular. It is obvious that much of all our reasoning is of this type. Syllogistic reasoning is deduction fully and formally expressed and because of its rigidity is not often effective in the pulpit; but often in deductive argument one or another of the steps is not fully stated but assumed, either as generally ac-

cepted, or so clear as not to need formal statement. Doctrinal preaching has been very largely of this sort, consisting chiefly in deductions or inferences from Scripture. Fully expressed, the preacher's syllogism would be similar to this:

All Scripture is true and obligatory;
This particular doctrine is Scripture;
Therefore this doctrine is true and obligatory.

The major premise, All Scripture is true and obligatory, is usually and properly taken for granted and not expressed; the main contention in doctrinal preaching commonly is to establish the minor premise that the particular doctrine under consideration is scriptural, either by express statement or by legitimate inference.

Now such deductions must be made with great care. The reply often heard in conversational discussion, "Ah, but that is only an inference of yours," shows the common feeling concerning the danger that our inferences will be far less certain than the truths from which we infer. There is obviously need for great care that the deduction shall be strictly logical and, also, that what the preacher assumes to be a general truth is accepted by his hearers. If they do not agree with him in that, his argument is valueless. But another thing is important. In economics, it is found that the results deduced by abstract reasoning from general principles must at every step be compared with facts, or they will at length be found to have strayed from actual truth. Religious reasoning is similar. One can very seldom take a general truth and make a series of deductions from it as is done in geometry and feel safe about the results. Conclusions must constantly be compared with the facts of existence and with the teachings of Scripture. The love of purely abstract reasoning leads many minds away from religious truth. The idea of establishing some truth of religion by "a perfect demonstration" is commonly delusive. Human life is not really controlled by demonstrated truth, in this world or the next. A person must be content with those practical certainties which the conditions of existence allow him to attain; and while constantly drawing inferences, as it is right to do, one must be content to compare them with fact and Scripture to make sure that they are correct.

Pure reasoning handles ideas and not facts. It is a sort of geometry of intellectual space. This geometry, however, is less certain than the other, the import of signs here being less variable. Hence the necessity of not coursing entirely through the void, and of descending often to the earth, to set our feet on facts. Otherwise, we run the risk of proving too much, and losing, at length, the sense of reality. At the end of the most sound reasonings, when the reason of the hearer seems to be overcome, something more intimate than logic rises up within him, and protests against your conclusions.[9]

So precarious is the value of deductive reasoning in the pulpit, depending as it does on initial agreement, logical procedure, and the mental habit and mood of the hearer, that its use is becoming less general. Dr. Garvie says:

The deductive reasoning of the syllogism is out of place in the pulpit; and even argument from general principles is, as a rule, less effective than from concrete instances; for men want facts rather than ideas, observation rather than speculation.[10]

He adds, however, that there are general principles which are almost universally admitted, "from which the preacher may draw his inferences with the confidence that these will find general assent."

In respect to the whole matter of evidence and belief, it is important to remember the relationship between belief and disbelief. As regards many truths of Christianity, he who disbelieves them is compelled to believe something which takes their place. He who cannot accept the difficulties, real or alleged, in the Christian evidences, must not forget the difficulties of infidelity. We must believe something, must believe something about the problems of religion, and if we go away from Christ, "to whom shall we go?"

3. CERTAIN FORMS OF ARGUMENT

In addition to the principal varieties of argument, several of the forms which arguments often assume need to be mentioned and explained.

1. An argument *a priori* is an argument from cause to effect, whether it be from a proper physical cause or from something in the general nature of things which necessitates a certain result or from something in the nature of a particular object or person which tends to produce a certain result. Therefore, deduction (argument from a general truth) is *a priori* when the general truth or major premise is necessitating or producing the conclusion; and induction (argument from particular facts) is *a priori* when the particulars are shown to account for a known cause, as when in a case of crime particular facts are adduced to establish some motive as a cause.[11]

2. *A posteriori* designates an argument from effect to cause, i.e., an argument that "infers a yet unknown cause from observed facts recognized as effects." (See Luke 7:47 and 1 Cor. 10:5.)

3. There is a form of argument known as *a fortiori*, i.e., from the proposition which has the stronger considerations against it to the proposition which has the weaker considerations against it. This shows that something is true in a less probable case, real or supposed, and then insists that much more certainly must it be true in a more probable case. This form of argument is a favorite one with orators and is very often found in the teachings of our Lord and the apostles, where the arguments are chiefly analogical or deductive in nature. "If you then, being evil, know how to give good gifts to your children, how much more shall your Heavenly Father. . . " (Matt. 7:11). "If God so clothe the grass of the field, which today is, and tomorrow is cast into the oven, shall he not much more clothe you, O ye of little faith?" (Matt. 6:30, KJV). "If they do these things in the green tree, what will happen in the dry?" (Luke 23:31). "He who did not spare His own Son, but delivered Him up for us all, how

shall He not also with Him freely give us all things?" (Rom. 8:32). "For if the word spoken by angels was steadfast, and every transgression and disobedience received a just recompense of reward; how shall we escape, if we neglect so great salvation; which at the first began to be spoken by the Lord [i.e., the Lord Jesus], and was confirmed unto us. . . " (Heb. 2:2–4, KJV). "For the time is come that judgment must begin at the house of God: and if it first begin at us, what shall the end be of them that obey not the gospel of God? And if the righteous scarcely be saved, where shall the ungodly and the sinner appear?" (1 Peter 4:17, 18, KJV).[12] These are but a few examples out of many. They should impress us with the suitableness of such arguments in addressing the popular mind.

4. A form of argument from progressive approach has been pointed out and well illustrated by Whately. This is frequently a good form in which to put the argument from induction. In arguing the being of a God from the general consent of mankind, the speaker observes that, in proportion, as men have become cultivated and civilized, their ideas of the unity and moral excellence of the Deity have progressed; that there is a progressive tendency towards the most exalted monotheism, which is therefore inferred to be true. Or concerning religious tolerance:

> In every age and country, as a general rule, tolerant principles have (however imperfectly) gained ground wherever scriptural knowledge has gained ground. And a presumption is thus afforded that a still further advance of the one would lead to a corresponding advance in the other.[13]

5. The dilemma presents two assumptions of such a character that one or the other must be true; and yet whichever is considered true, there will follow as a deduction the result proposed. Such was Gamaliel's argument (Acts 5:38, 39): "If this counsel or this work be of men, it will come to nought: but if it be of God, ye cannot overthrow it" (KJV). It must be either from men or from God, and in either case the conclusion would be, "Refrain from these men, and let them alone."[14] The dilemma is

most commonly but not exclusively used for the purpose of refutation.

6. Similarly, the *reductio ad absurdum* (reduction to the absurd) is most frequently but not always used for refutation in moral reasoning; Euclid uses it very frequently for indirect demonstration. When it is argued that the church should not send the gospel to the heathen because if they reject it, their guilt and doom will be so much aggravated, the answer is that with that principle the gospel should not be preached to the destitute at home or to anyone, and it is a pity there ever was a gospel. The principle which necessarily leads to such an absurdity must be, by analogy or deduction, in itself erroneous.

7. The argument *ex concesso,* from something conceded by the opponent or known to be accepted by the persons addressed may be used as a deductive argument not only for refutation, but also to establish positive truth, when we are satisfied that the accepted idea is really true.

8. The argument *ad hominem,* "to the man," is legitimately used only in refutation.

Arguments different in nature or form will often be combined in one complex argument.

Different speakers will prefer one or another species of argument, each person being apt to manage best that which he prefers. But this preference should never become exclusive, or it will make the mind one-sided. Besides, it is necessary to consider what species of argument will best suit the intellectual nature, education, and tastes of the audience. We should therefore habitually seek to draw arguments from a variety of sources and develop them into various forms.

4. ORDER OF ARGUMENTS

The order of arguments is scarcely less important than their individual force. The superiority of an army to a mob is hardly greater than the advantage of a well-arranged discourse over a mere mass of scattered thoughts. The question of what arrangement is to be preferred in any particular case must depend upon a variety of circumstances. Here, as everywhere in rhetoric, one can only lay down rules concerning what is generally best.

It is obvious that the several distinct arguments should be kept separate. But in the practice of inexperienced reasoners, it is not uncommon to see portions of two different arguments combined, and two parts of the same argument separated by the interposition of other matter.

All arguments are used to prove one of three things: that something is true; that it is morally right or fit; that it is profitable or good. The appeal is to truth, duty, or interest.[15]

The consideration which must principally determine the order of arguments is their natural relationship to each other.

Some proofs are explained by others, which must be previously exhibited in order to the full effect of the reasoning. Some proofs presuppose others. Some, once more, have great weight if preceded by certain others, and are of little moment unless preceded by them.[16]

Proofs which spring from the very nature of the proposition should commonly come first because the exhibition of these will involve a full explanation of the proposition, and "after such an explanation the relevance and force of every other proof will be more clearly seen."[17]

The order of arguments from inference (deduction, induction, analogy) should consider, first, their abstraction, the more abstract and general usually being introduced before those that are based on concrete and particular facts, thus moving from the purely intellectual toward an emotional and practical appeal. There are cases, however, as in sermons whose object is primarily intellectual, in which it is better to present first some more tangible and popular proof of a proposition, such as testimony or example, and then show that this need not surprise us when we look at certain *a priori* considerations. Secondly, the order of inferences should consider the degree of probability which they establish. The more remote or weaker probability should precede the stronger.

The latter is in accordance with the general principle of climax. It is usually best, where nothing forbids, to begin with the weakest arguments used and end with the strongest, thus forming a climax, the power of which is well understood.

But the preacher must sometimes depart from the order which would be fixed by the natural dependence of the arguments upon each other because of the known disposition of the hearers. If they are unfriendly to his views, it is well to begin with one or more strong arguments, well suited to their minds, in order to command respect and secure attention. The speaker may next, according to the precept of the ancient rhetoricians, state the less important matter and close with the strongest of all for the sake of the final impression; or, beginning with the strongest arguments, and adding less important but confirmatory considerations, he may at the close recapitulate in the reverse order and thus gain the effect of a climax.

What position shall be occupied by arguments from Scripture, relative to those drawn from reason and experience? When a thing has been proven by the Word of God, then for the preacher the question is settled; he cannot admit, he must not seem to admit, that there is any need of further argument. So far, then, it would appear that Scripture proofs should regularly follow others and so constitute the climax of proof. But there will be cases in which this is awkward; and besides, to some of the hearers, proofs from reason may be more convincing, or proofs from experience more impressive, than the plainest declarations of the Bible. To meet these conditions the pastor may begin with the scriptural teachings and then observe that here, as in fact everywhere, reason and experience are in harmony with the Bible and so proceed to the arguments from those sources. In this way the preacher conforms to the hearer's mode of thinking and feeling and ends with that which will make the strongest impression on him, without abandoning his own position of the supremacy of Scripture—a position which even infidels will feel that the preacher himself ought to maintain. To hold firmly his own ground and yet put himself as far as possible in sympathy with the persons he would win is a thing often demanded in preaching and is an achievement worthy of much thoughtful effort.

In what part of a discourse shall the refutation of objections be placed?

When an objection lies against the view advanced in a certain part of the sermon, it should obviously, for the efficiency of that part, be disposed of, though as briefly as possible, before passing to another point.[18]

If there are objections against the general sentiment of the sermon, and they can be refuted independently of the discussion, and briefly, it is advantageous to clear them out of the way before entering upon the line of argument. Where the refutation depends upon the argument or would occupy much time, it must be postponed to the end.

5. GENERAL SUGGESTIONS FOR THE ARGUMENT

In concluding the subject of Arguments, it is proper to put together a few practical hints, though some of them are indirectly involved in previous statements.

1. First note some suggestions on cultivating the logical faculty of the mind. The importance of developing the reasoning powers is clearly enough involved in all the preceding discussions, yet some suggestions as to how it may be done might be helpful. Study books on logic. Study other books logically. There are many books of distinctively argumentative character which the preacher must read with care. He should make it his business to follow the arguments carefully, criticising, comparing, approving, or refuting, as the case may require. Besides this challenging reading, even general literature should for the most part be read observantly, analytically, and thoughtfully. And practice argument frequently. Disciplined thinking on the preacher's own part is a necessity; he should think subjects through, working out processes of reasoning in his mind. Debate in conversation is very useful and may be well managed.

By all means the disputant should be calm and courteous. The good George Herbert truly says:

Be calm in arguing; for fierceness makes Error a fault, and truth discourtesy.

2. Let us also note a few suggestions concerning the conduct of argument.

a. Do not undertake to prove anything unless you are sure it is true and you are satisfied that you can prove it.

b. Let your argument start from something which the persons addressed will fully acknowledge. This is obviously important, but is often neglected.

c. Use arguments intelligible to your hearers and likely to make an impression on their minds. The preacher, of all persons, should study the common mind and seek to understand fully not only its forms of expression but, what is still more important, its ways of thinking. He should strive to put himself in the position of his hearers and consider how this or that argument will appear from their point of view.[19]

These are the reasons why uneducated men are more effective than the educated in speaking to the masses—as the poets say that the unlearned "have a finer charm . . . for the ear of the mob." Educated men lay down abstract principles and draw general conclusions; the uneducated argue from their everyday knowledge, and base their conclusions upon immediate facts.[20]

How true it is now of many able and learned preachers that they can speak only of generalities belonging to the common stock of human knowledge and do not know how to speak in a manner which is familiar and agreeable to the masses. That this last can be done without the sacrifice of truly profound thought or the violation of refined taste has been shown by some ministers of every age and country, and most conspicuously by that Great Teacher of whom it was said "the common people heard him gladly."

d. In general, depend principally on scriptural arguments and prefer those which are plain and unquestionable. When the minister engages in religious controversy before a popular audience, he will usually do well to say little concerning that great mass of knowledge about which the people cannot personally judge and rely mainly on commonsense views of the plain teachings of Scripture. And apart from controversy, use arguments chiefly from Scripture. This is common ground between the preacher and his hearers. In general, no other arguments can be so appropriate or be so effective with the people. The Bible has a limitless store of material for argument.

e. Do not try to say everything, but select a suitable number of the most available arguments. It is true that sometimes the judicious combination of many comparatively slight arguments may have a great effect. "Singly they are light," says Quintilian, "but taken together they do hurt, though not as by a thunderbolt, yet as by hail."[21] Still, it is a very common fault to multiply arguments to excess. With great effort the preacher has brought all these into existence, and surveying them with parental affection, he thinks each of them too good to be abandoned. But how many thousand men did Gideon dismiss that he might conquer with three hundred? Where there are so many arguments, either the discourse will be excessively long, or they must be too hurriedly presented. Where it is really necessary to present many arguments, skillfully group them, and state the more obvious briefly in order to pause and spend time on those which demand special attention.

f. Avoid formality. Have the reality of argument, but as little as possible of its merely technical forms and phrases.

g. As to the style of argument, the chief requisites are, of course, clarity, precision, and force. But a simple elegance is usually compatible with these. And where the subject is exalted and inspiring, and the speaker's whole soul is on fire, some great thunderbolt of argument may blaze with an overpowering splendor.[22]

NOTES

1. A. E. Garvie, *The Christian Preacher* (Edinburgh: T. & T. Clark, 1920), p. 398. For New Testament examples see Matt. 5:3–10; 13:52; Heb. 11:6; John 20:29.
2. Alexander Vinet, *Homiletics* (New York: Ivison, Blakeman, Taylor, 1871), p. 176.
3. Ibid., pp. 228, 229.
4. Carl S. Patton, *The Preparation and Delivery of Sermons* (Chicago: Willett, Clark & Co., 1938), p. 10.
5. Noah Knowles Davis, *Elements of Inductive Logic* (New York: Harper & Bros., 1895), pp. 6–7, where a number of other definitions are given.
6. Richard Whately, *Elements of Rhetoric* (New York: Harper & Bros, 1853), p. 111.
7. Garvie, p. 407.
8. Whately, p. 115.
9. Vinet, pp. 174, 175.
10. Garvie, p. 402.
11. John F. Genung, *Practical Rhetoric* (Boston: Ginn & Co., 1886), pp. 417–18.
12. See Vinet, pp. 193–96.
13. Whately, pp. 104–9.
14. We are not here inquiring whether Gamaliel's assumptions are correct.
15. Paul B. Bull, *Preaching and Sermon Construction* (New York: Macmillan Co., 1922), p. 185.
16. Henry N. Day, *Art of Discourse* (New York: Charles Scribner & Co., 1867), p. 153.
17. Ibid, p. 154.
18. Henry J. Ripley, *Sacred Rhetoric* (Boston: Gould & Lincoln, 1859), p. 81.
19. In these respects much may be learned from the critical observation of able "stump speakers" and courtroom lawyers.
20. Lane Cooper, *The Rhetoric of Aristotle* (New York: D. Appleton-Century Co., 1932), p. 156.
21. Quintilian, *The Institutio Oratoria of Marcus Fabius Quintilianus* (Nashville, Tenn.: George Peabody College for Teachers, 1951), V, 12, 5.
22. Compare Quintilian, V, 14, 33.

CHAPTER 20

Application

THE application in a sermon is not merely an appendage to the discussion or a subordinate part of it, but is the main thing to be done. Spurgeon says, "Where the application begins, there the sermon begins." The preacher is not to speak before the people but to them. He must earnestly strive to make them apply what he says to themselves. Daniel Webster once said and repeated it with emphasis, "When a man preaches to me, I want him to make it a personal matter, a personal matter, a personal matter!"

Preaching is essentially a personal encounter, in which the preacher's will is making a claim through the truth upon the will of the hearer. If there is no summons, there is no sermon. Certainly this is true of evangelistic preaching. But, as Dr. H. H. Farmer says,

even in the instruction, edification, and confirming of the saints the note of claim and summons should not be absent, though it will make itself felt in a different way. Almost everything depends on the mood and intention of the preacher and on his whole conception of his task. If his message has been prepared in the right way, with a clear and serious perception of the "I-thou" relationship which must lie at its heart if it is to be real preaching, the note of summons is certain to get through, even though nothing is said about it in explicit terms. It must be realized that in this sphere of our life instruction without this note does not instruct, edification does not edify, confirmation does not confirm.[1]

In application this note of summons is made articulate.

In the chapter on Conclusion, application was discussed briefly as comprising a large part of the conclusion. But the two are not identical. Application may and often should appear in other parts also. As a goal it properly involves every element of the sermon and dominates the whole process of preaching. As illustration is the servant of all, application is the master of all. The sermon is always moving within the purpose of making truth vitally effective. In many sermons, especially when the discussion is a close-knit unity, the conclusion is the natural place for application. In such cases, it should be said in passing, too much formality should be avoided. In England two centuries ago, from the passion for logical analysis in preaching, it was common to make a great number of inferences in concluding, sometimes twelve, sometimes twenty, and sometimes fifty. These were called uses: (1) of information, (2) of instruction, (3) of examination, (4) of reproof, (5) of encouragement, (6) of comfort, (7) of exhortation, etc.[2]

The sermons of Jonathan Edwards, with all their power, show the evil of always having a regular "application," formally announced or indicated. Often a brief and informal application is best. Often, too, it is better not to reserve the application for the latter part of the discourse, but to apply each thought as it is presented, provided they all conspire towards a common result.

Application is not a perfect word for this element of the sermon. Some prefer the term persuasion, but if application is too limited in one direction, persuasion is limited in another. It is perhaps better, therefore, to use the more familiar term and give it a technical connotation. As used here, then, the application includes three distinct things: (1) application proper, in which one shows the hearer how the truths of the sermon apply to him; (2) practical suggestions concerning the best mode and means of performing the duty urged; and (3) persuasion in the sense of moral and spiritual appeal for right response. Or, more succinctly, it is (1) focusing the claims of truth, (2) suggesting ways and means, and (3) persuading to vital response.

1. FOCUSING THE CLAIMS OF TRUTH

Application, in the strict sense, is that part, or those parts, of the discourse in which it is shown how the subject applies to the persons addressed, what practical instructions it offers them, what practical demands it makes upon them.

Such application may draw the meaning down only to certain areas of life, leaving more particular application to the individual. This was largely the practice of Dr. Alexander Maclaren, whose modesty and respect for people's right and ability to see and choose for themselves, as well as his belief that truth, understood and accepted, would speak for itself inwardly through conscience, restrained him from drawing too sharp a focus. That, however, is not for the ordinary people of this world. The finger must often be put on the very spot of the illness. If truth is not focused sharply enough to "spot light" some particular principle, or habit, or practice, or motive, or sentiment, or prejudice, or disposition, or need, it will not be very effective. And sometimes it must be made sharp enough to burn. Sometimes this is effected by means of what are called remarks, that is, certain noticeable matters belonging to or connected with the subject, to which attention is now especially directed. These should always be of a very practical character, bearing down upon the feelings and the will. And the remarks must not diverge in various directions, but should have a common aim and make a combined impression. In sermons upon historical subjects, it is acceptable to bring out several distinct lessons, but these had better be pretty closely related. It is obvious that while some subjects may be applied to the congregation as a whole, others will be applicable only to particular classes or will have to be applied to distinct classes separately, as converted and unconverted, old and young. But it is not necessary, as some preachers seem to imagine, always to make some kind of application to the unconverted, or some remark to them in conclusion. A sermon addressed throughout to pious people will often specially instruct and impress the unconverted. What men apply to themselves, without feeling that it was aimed at them, is apt to produce the greatest effect. It is never judicious to make an application to any particular individual, and very rarely to a small and well-defined class. What is popularly called "hitting at" some person or some few persons will almost always do more harm than good.

Application also frequently takes the form of inferences. This form of making application of the subject ought to be carefully limited in two directions. Nothing should be presented as an inference which does not logically and directly follow from the subject discussed. The other limit is that no inferences should be drawn in applying a subject which are not of practical importance. It is not a preacher's business to exhibit all the matters which may be inferred from his discussion, as if he were attempting an exercise in logic, but only to draw out those which will appeal to the feelings and the will of his hearers and move them to action. Of course, in other parts of the sermon than the application, these merely logical inferences may be allowable and instructive.

Again, application is often best presented in the form of lessons. This term implies that the practical teachings of the subject are more thoroughly developed and more fully applied than would be done in mere remarks, while it does not restrict the application to those teachings which appear as logical inferences from the propositions established. This way of applying the truths of the discourse would seem, therefore, to have some advantages over the other methods. These lessons must, of course, be thoroughly practical and must not be too formal or have a magisterial air. The preacher is not a dignitary, speaking *ex cathedra* to his inferiors. He had better speak, in general, of lessons which "we" may learn.

Of course, there are applications which would not be proper to designate by any one of these terms—remarks, inferences, or lessons. Nor is it necessary, or even advisable always, to use these somewhat formal phrases even where they are appropriate. The preacher must study naturalness, simplicity, and variety in the manner of presenting applications.

2. SUGGESTING WAYS AND MEANS

Another way of making application consists of suggestions as to the best means and methods of performing the duty or duties enjoined in the sermon. To give good practical suggestions is a task often calling for experience and the results of thoughtful observation, and sometimes demanding delicate tact, but is certainly, when well managed, a most important part of the preacher's work. When one has argued some general duty, as that of family or private prayer, of reading the Bible, or of relieving the needy and distressed, it is exceedingly useful to give suggestions about the actual doing of the particular duty, to make it seem a practical and a practicable thing, to awaken hope of doing better, and thus stimulate effort. Many a Christian duty seems to most people impracticable for them; and the most effective application in such cases is to show that it is practicable. This should not often be done by reproof, as if the preacher was wishing simply to take away excuses for neglect, but with a sympathizing recognition of real difficulties which are "common to man."

When the problem raised by truth involves conduct that reaches beyond person-to-person relations to social institutional relations, the preacher's task grows more problematical. We live not only in a world of persons but of powerful social organizations and institutions which exert constant and relentless pressure upon the moral and spiritual life of individuals. The preacher cannot be indifferent to these wider and more complex areas. He must pass unflinching judgment upon the wrongs of society; he must voice the Christian principles of righteousness and justice and good will; he must stir the consciences of men to meet the conditions and practices of the social order with unselfish devotion to truth and honor and common humanity. This duty has already been emphasized in the discussion of ethical preaching. But what should he propose in a practical way? Devise strategies and programs for labor or for capital? Write platforms for the political parties? Propose and advocate particular statutes for legislative bodies? Agitate for particular solutions of the race problems? Become expert in international procedures? Obviously such things are beyond his ability and outside his function. He is not an expert social planner. He is a prophet, a seer, and critic, and voice of conscience in the name of God. He should not be complacent in the belief that society is impersonal organization and natural process. Society is composed of men, women, and children. The forms of society are created and managed by persons. The human factor determines many things, including principles and goods. Human responsibility for the social order is therefore real, and the preacher must not permit complacency in himself or in those who hear him. He must ask burning questions of persons: "Where is thy brother?" "What meaneth this bleating of the sheep?" But he must ask in knowledge, not ignorance, speaking out of an understanding of conditions and problems understood by diligent study. With such understanding, he will be able to affix blame where blame lies and to propose with boldness the ways and means that brotherhood, honesty, high motive, and reverence for God will suggest. Such is the preacher's function. It is within his province and responsibility to bring every kind of evil, individually and corporately upheld, to the light and judgment of Christ's moral principles, and then to insist that men put these principles to the test in their lives, taking paths which an enlightened conscience can choose.

3. PERSUASION TO RESPONSE

But the chief part of what is commonly called application is *persuasion.* It is not enough to convince men of truth, nor enough to make them see how it applies to themselves, and how it might be practicable for them to act it out; but we must "persuade men." A distinguished minister once said that he could never exhort; he could explain and prove what was truth and duty, but then he must leave people to themselves. The apostle Paul, however, could not only argue, but could say, "We beg you on behalf of Christ, be reconciled to God" (2 Cor. 5:20).

It is well known, from observation and from experience, that a person may see his duty and still neglect it. Has a person not often been led by persuasion to do something, good or bad, which he was avoiding? It is proper, then, to persuade, to exhort, even to entreat.

1. Persuasion is not generally best accomplished by mere exhortation but by urging, in the first place, some motive or motives for acting or determining to act. This is not properly called a process of argument. The motive presented may require previous proof that it is something true, or right, or good, but this proving is distinct from the act of presenting it as a motive; and if when bringing a motive to bear, the pastor has to prove anything concerning it, the proof ought to be brief and direct, or it will delay and hinder the planned effect.

A preacher must of course appeal to none but worthy motives that are harmonious with Christian moral ideals. The principal motives he is at liberty to use may be classed under various headings.

The minister may lawfully appeal to the desire for happiness and its negative counterpart, the dread of unhappiness. Those philosophers who insist that we ought always to do right simply and only because it is right are no philosophers at all, for they are either grossly ignorant of human nature or else are indulging in mere fanciful speculation. No doubt some preachers err in that they treat happiness as the almost exclusive or chief motive. In the beatitudes and elsewhere, Jesus spoke of the blessedness of the poor in spirit, the meek, the pure in heart, the peacemakers, and indicated why they would be "blessed." Happiness was to be desired, but it was not something to be sought as an end. Experience testifies that when it is directly sought, it evades the seeker; it overtakes him when he is absorbed in duty and service. Certainly happiness should always be subordinated to duty and affection; but when subordinated, it is a legitimate desire and a legitimate basis of appeal. The Scriptures appeal not only to feelings of moral obligation, but to hopes and fears, for time and for eternity. "It is profitable for thee" is a consideration which Jesus repeatedly uses in encouraging self-denial. A desire for the pleasures of piety in this life or even for the happiness of heaven would never, of itself alone, lead people to become Christians or strengthen them to live as such; but, combined with other motives, it is good and useful. And there is here included not only the pleasure derived from the gratification of our common wants, but that of taste and of ambition.

There is in us a spark of desire, and often a deep longing for holiness or, as most would express it, goodness. The most abandoned person sometimes wishes to be good and even persuades himself that in certain respects he is good; and the great mass of mankind fully intend, after indulging a little longer in sinful pleasure, to become thoroughly good before they die. This is to say that conscience is a reality. Man, however wicked he may be, has a sense of difference between right and wrong, and something in his nature, his better part, votes for the right.

Here, then, is a great motive to which the preacher may appeal. The thorough depravity of human nature should not make him forget that goodness can always touch at least a faintly responsive chord in the human breast. He ought to hold up before his listeners the beauty of holiness, to educate the regenerate into doing right for its own sake and not merely for the sake of its rewards. The minister should stimulate and at the same time control that hatred of evil which is the natural and necessary counterpart to the love of holiness. And as regards the life after death, he should habitually point men not only to its happiness but still more earnestly to its purity and strive by God's blessing to make them desire its freedom from all sin and from all fear of sinning. It is the preacher's duty and privilege to cherish such noble and ennobling aspirations in his hearers by the very fact of appealing to them.

Another basic motive is the desire for recognition or prestige. Like so many things, this drive must be sublimated. In this day of mechanization, millions of people feel a sense of insignificance but want a sense of recognition; they want a sense of importance. How can one appeal to this desire? The answer is simple. A person reaches his highest worth in Christ. God loved and gave his Son for each of us. God knows everyone. He takes notice of all our needs. To God each of us is a person, each is significant. Christ proved this when he died for all.

Another basic motive is security. Does Christianity offer us security? It cannot promise us freedom from care or longevity of life, but it can give us security. Jesus declared, "He that cometh unto me I will in no wise cast out" (John 6:37, KJV). The highest security, eternal security, is found in Christ and only in Christ.

And the greatest of all motives is love. In the relations of the present life, love is the great antagonist of selfishness. They who "have none to love" by any natural ties should become interested in the needy and the afflicted, or they will grow more and more narrow and selfish. Accordingly, the preacher may constantly appeal to people's love of their fellowmen as a motive for doing right. Parents may be urged to seek personal piety and higher degrees of it for the sake of their growing children, and so with the husband or wife, the brother or sister or friend. Now the gospel appeals to this motive in a very peculiar manner. Man ought to love God supremely, and such supreme love would be his chief motive to do right and to do good. But sin has alienated him from God so that he does not love him. And Christ presents himself, the God-man, the Redeemer, to win his love to him and thus to God. "Whosoever shall lose his life for my sake" are words which reveal the new and mighty gospel motive, love to Christ. To this, above all other motives, the preacher should appeal. Far from excluding others, it intensifies while it subordinates them.[3]

Closely akin to love is admiration.

Even where there is not what can be properly called affection, because the knowledge may be inadequate and the intimacy not close enough, there may be admiration for greatness, wisdom, goodness, as embodied in the tale of achievement, experience, character. By study of Paul's letters it is quite conceivable that a man may today even reach a personal affection for the great apostle, for he seems so close to us, lays his heart so bare. But the Holy Scriptures, biography, and history present to us many personalities who gain admiration rather than win affection. If this admiration depends on what is from the Christian standpoint admirable, the preacher need not hesitate about seeking to awaken it by the way he presents these personalities in his sermon.[4]

2. But the task is not merely the calm exhibition of motives so that people might act according to them. Many truths of religion are eminently adapted to stir the feelings, and to speak of such truths without feeling and awakening emotion is unnatural and wrong. And so great is the opposition which the gospel encounters in human nature, so averse is the natural heart to the obedience of faith, so powerful are the temptations of life, that the pastor must arouse his listeners to intense earnestness and often to impassioned emotion if he would bring them to overcome all obstacles and to conquer the world, the flesh, and the devil. Who expects to make soldiers enter combat without excitement? Many persons shrink from the idea of exciting emotions. "It seems to be commonly taken for granted, that whenever the feelings are excited, they are over-excited."[5] But while ignorant people often value too highly, or rather too exclusively, the appeal to their feelings, cultivated people are apt to shrink from such appeals quite too much. It may be that this is partly the fault of preachers, and the shrinking is not so much objection to having the feelings moved as to the kind of feelings appealed to, the character of the motives applied, and the way of manifesting feeling which is sought. Nevertheless, our feelings about religion are habitually too cold—who can deny it? And any genuine excitement is greatly desirable. Inspired teachers have evidently acted on this principle. The prophets made the most impassioned appeals. Our Lord and the apostles tried not merely to convince their hearers but to incite them to earnest corresponding action, and their language is often surcharged with emotion.

Yet, the preacher should never wish to excite feeling for its own sake but as a means of persuasion to the corresponding course of action. In this respect many preachers err—some from not clearly perceiving that emotion is of little value unless it excites to action, and others, it is to be feared, from an excessive desire for popular applause. These last give their hearers the luxury of idle emotion, as a pathetic novel or a tragedy might do, and hearers and preacher go away well pleased with themselves and each other. No wonder some preachers find that their pathetic descriptions and passionate appeals now make little impression upon persons who were once powerfully affected by them. The emotion was treated as an end, not as a means, and was habitually allowed to subside without any effect upon the hearer's actions; and a steady diminution of the emotion itself was the inevitable result. Surely that is not good preaching—whatever the unthinking may suppose—which excited a mere transient and unproductive emotion.

It is a matter of universal observation that a speaker who wants to excite deep feeling must feel deeply himself. Demosthenes sometimes spoke with such passionate earnestness that his enemies said he was deranged. Cicero remarks that it is only passion that makes the orator a king; that, though he himself had tried every means of moving men, yet his successes were due, not to talent or skill, but to a mighty fire in his soul so that he could not control himself; and that the hearer would never be kindled unless the speech came to him burning. It is said of Ignatius Loyola, the founder of the Jesuits, that he preached

with such an unction and emotion, that even those amongst his audience who did not understand the language in which he spoke, were, nevertheless, moved to tears by the very tones of his voice—the earnestness and burning zeal which appeared in his every gesture and look.[6]

Alas! it is often the preacher's chief difficulty in preaching to feel himself as he ought to feel. And a genuine fervor cannot be produced to order by a direct effort of will. Nor is it possible to conceal from the audience the deficiency of real emotion by high and loud or tremulous tones of voice, wild gesticulation, etc. He must cultivate his religious sensibilities, must keep his soul habitually in contact with gospel truth, and maintain by the union of abundant prayer and self-denial that ardent love of God and that tender love of man which will give him, without an effort, true pathos or passion. The famous John Henry Newman, in his *University Preaching,* speaks as follows:

> Talent, logic, learning, words, manner, voice, action, all are required for the perfection of a preacher; but "one thing is necessary,"—an intense perception and appreciation of the end for which he preaches, and that is, to be the minister of some definite spiritual good to those who hear him. . . . I do not mean that a preacher must aim at earnestness but that he must aim at his object, which is to do some spiritual good to his hearers and which will at once make him earnest.[7]

When the preacher does feel very deeply, his mere exhortation will have some power to move, especially where he has personal influence as a devout person or for any reason has the sympathies of his audience. There is, then, the inexplicable contagion of sympathy. But he must avoid getting too far away from the hearers in his passionate feeling, for then sympathy will give place to its opposite.

Apart from the people's sympathy with his emotion, the pastor can excite emotion in others by indirect means, not by urging them to feel, though he should urge with the greatest vehemence. He must present considerations apt to awaken emotion and let them do their work.[8] For this purpose the preacher may of course learn from the study of the basic human emotions those that originate in the instincts and are therefore most influential. Among them are fear, disgust, wonder, anger, subjection, elation, and tender emotion. The preacher may study their nature and the best means of exciting them and using them for spiritual ends. And he needs not only to know human nature in general but in most cases also needs to understand the peculiar circumstances, sentiments, prejudices, tastes of those whom he addresses. This is plainly demanded in the case of a missionary but is hardly less necessary at home. One reason why uneducated preachers often have such power with the masses is that they understand and fully sympathize with the persons whom they address, while educated men sometimes do not.

In order to excite any of the passions by speech, the minister has to operate chiefly through the imagination.

A passion is most strongly excited by sensation. The sight of danger, immediate or near, instantly rouseth fear; the feeling of an injury, and the presence of the injurer, in a moment kindle anger. Next to the influence of sense is that of memory, the effect of which upon passion, if the fact be recent, and remembered distinctly and circumstantially, is almost equal. Next to the influence of memory is that of imagination.[9]

In proportion to the excitation of the hearer's imagination, he seems to see that which is presented, and the effect upon his feelings approximates to the effect of sight.

In presenting an object so that it may stir imagination and effect the feelings, well-chosen details need to be presented. Without this it is impossible to make a narration or description impressive. But preachers sometimes so multiply details as to weary the hearer, offend his taste, or betray a lack of right feeling on their own part. It may be gravely doubted whether a man can carry through a minute description of the crucifixion, who is at the time cherishing an intense faith and love towards Christ. A few vivid details, presented very briefly and with genuine emotion, will usually make a far deeper impression. It is also true with elaborate descriptions of the day of judgment and the agonies of perdition. One who truly realized the scene and tenderly loved his fellowmen could hardly endure to dwell so long on the most harrowing details, and the preacher who does this is apt to be for the time (though unconscious of it) mainly alive to the artistic interest in his picture.

Comparison is often very effective in awakening emotion. Thus the pastor makes people feel more deeply how shameful is ingratitude to God by first presenting some affecting case of ingratitude to a human benefactor. The emotion excited by something meaningful to people is transferred to the object compared. For example, "Just as a father has compassion on his children, so the Lord has compassion on those who fear Him" (Ps. 103:13). The effect of climax, gradually working the feelings up to the highest pitch, may also be very great, as everyone has observed.

The preacher must not try to be highly impassioned on all subjects, on all occasions, or in all parts of a discourse. Appeals to the feelings will usually be made only at the conclusion, sometimes, after the discussion of each successive topic, but then he must be sure that the interest first excited can be renewed and gradually increased. It is a common fault with inexperienced preachers to make vehement appeals in the early part, even in the very beginning, of a sermon; in such cases there will almost inevitably be a reaction and a loss of interest before the close. If several impassioned passages are to occur, those which come first should be comparatively brief and followed by something calm or familiar. It is also important to avoid exhausting one's physical force before reaching that portion of the sermon which calls for the most passionate earnestness. An exhausted speaker not only cannot speak forcibly but cannot feel deeply. And a concluding exhortation should never be prolonged beyond the point at which the preacher is still in full vigor and the hearers feel a sustained interest.

NOTES

1. Herbert Farmer, *The Servant of the Word* (New York: Charles Scribner's Sons, 1942), p. 67
2. Jean Claude, *An Essay on the Composition of a Sermon,* Vol. 2, trans. Robert Robinson (London: J. Buckland, 1779), p. 457.
3. On the subject of motives, see profound and suggestive remarks in Alexander Vinet, *Homiletics,* 3rd ed. (New York: Ivison, Blakeman, Taylor, 1871), pp. 203–22.
4. A. E. Garvie, *The Christian Preacher* (Edinburgh: T. & T. Clark, 1920), p. 412.
5. Richard Whately, *Elements of Rhetoric* (New York: Harper & Bros., 1853), p. 215.
6. Thomas Potter, *Sacred Eloquence* (New York: Pustet, n.d.), p. 211.
7. Quoted by Potter, p. 213.
8. Compare Whately, pp. 216–19.
9. George Campbell, *Philosophy of Rhetoric* (New York: Funk & Wagnalls, 1911), p. 103.

CHAPTER 21

Illustration

STRICTLY speaking, one would not call illustration a distinct element of the sermon coordinate with explanation and argument, or with application. Its function is solely auxiliary, coming to the support now of one and now of another of the principal elements. As a means of explaining, proving, or awakening emotion, it would fall under the heads of explanation, argument, and application; as a means of elaboration, it would belong to elegance of style. But because the same illustration often subserves different ends, and because the proper handling of illustrations is a matter of great importance, it seems best to give the subject a separate discussion.

To illustrate, according to etymology, is to throw light upon a subject—a very necessary function of preaching. The preacher cannot rely upon his gift of lucidity and power in exposition, reasoning and persuading; he must make truth interesting and attractive by expressing it in transparent words and using it in revealing metaphor and story and picture.

The necessity of illuminating the sermon properly is found in the mental attitude of the people. Whether we like it or not, most of us preach to the "moving picture mind." It is the mind accustomed to images, pictures, scenes, rapidly moving. It certainly is not accustomed to deep thinking or long, sustained argument. Current magazines, bill boards, novels, drama, rapid transit, all add to this popular method of visual thinking. We as ministers may not approve of the daily fare of the people; we may regret their inability to pursue abstract logic; we may wish them to prefer theoretical reasoning. But whatever our wishes, we must recognize that they regard thinking which is not imaginary and concrete as dull and uninteresting.[1]

Illustration is a psychological necessity.

1. VARIOUS USES OF ILLUSTRATION[2]

Illustration has many uses or functions. An illustration will often serve two or more functions at the same time.

1. Perhaps the principal use of illustrations is to explain. This they do either by presenting an example of the matter in hand, a case in point, or by presenting something similar or analogous to it which will make the matter plain.

2. But illustrations are also very frequently used to prove. This is done in some rare cases by presenting an example which warrants an induction; commonly, it is an argument from analogy. In Romans 6 and 7, Paul introduces three illustrations as showing the absurdity of supposing that justification by faith will encourage sin: believers are dead to sin and risen to another life; they have ceased to be the slaves of sin and become the slaves (so to speak) of holiness, of God; they have ceased to be married to the law and are married to a new husband, Christ, for whom they must now be productive. Each of these is not merely explanatory of the believer's position but involves an argument from analogy.

The fact that an illustration may furnish proof at the same time that it serves for explanation, ornamentation, etc., calls for special attention. Some analogy may be so ornamental, so amusing, or pathetic, as to make one overlook the fact that it has an argumentative force also; and some comparison may be so beautiful an ornament that it is considered proof when in reality it is a mere simile founded on resemblance and presents no true analogy, and thus no argument. The preacher should look closely at illustrations employed for other purposes and see whether they also contain an argument.

3. Illustrations are valuable as an ornament. To make truth attractive and pleasing is legitimate and desirable, but one must make sure that a beautiful illustration really adorns the truth that is preached and does not itself become the center of interest. In the Mammoth Cave of Kentucky the guide throws colorful flares upon ledges of rock, not to display the flares but to reveal the grandeur of that natural wonder. The kind and amount of illustration used for this purpose must be governed by the general principles which pertain to elegance of style.[3] Those who find themselves much inclined to the use of ornamental illustration should exercise a rigorous self-control and so cultivate their taste that it will discard all but the genuinely beautiful. Those whose style is barren of such ornament should try to develop it.

4. Illustrations are an excellent means for arousing attention. Often they will happily serve this purpose in the introduction to the sermon, securing at the outset the interest of the audience. But perhaps they are in this respect even more serviceable in the progress of the discourse, particularly if the attention has been somewhat strained by argument or description and begins to decline. They thus, as Beecher says, afford variety and rest to the mind; and this is very important.[4]

5. They also frequently make a subject impressive, by exciting some kindred or preparatory emotion. Thus, in the parable of the Prodigal Son, the natural pathos of the story itself touches the heart and prepares it to be all the more impressed by the thought of God's readiness to welcome the returning sinner. Most preachers use illustrations very freely for this purpose. The story or description may have some value for explanation, proof, or ornament, but its chief purpose is to arouse the feelings. This is appropriate and useful, provided the occasion be used to plant the seed of truth in the receptive mind. But sometimes stories are told at great length which claim to be illustrations of sacred truth and yet have no other effect, and to all appearance no other design, than to awaken a transient and aimless emotion.

6. Another function of illustration is to move to action or to persuade. If the emotions of a hearer are aroused, he may respond to the claim of the preacher. Often an illustration may be chosen which will portray a person doing what the listeners are being asked to do. A picture of such action will prompt the hearer to act in the same manner. This use of illustration is especially effective in the conclusion. The objective of the sermon is stated in the form of an appeal. Then an illustration is shared showing a person fulfilling that objective. This makes it easier for the hearer to act.

7. Illustrations may also provide for various hearers. Congregations are generally composed of heterogeneous groups. The people may represent varied ages, education, vocations, and interests. How does the preacher offer something to each hearer? He does so by choosing illustrations that will catch the interest of each group. Henry Ward Beecher was an excellent extemporizer. In the act of delivery, he would note the various classes of people in the congregation. Then from a vast mental store, he would choose illustrative material that would interest each group.

8. Finally, illustrations greatly assist the memory of the hearer in retaining the lesson of the sermon. Good illustrations are far more easily remembered than bright sayings and trains of argument. It is a not uncommon experience with preachers to find that their finest sentences and most profound observations easily slip the memory, while some apparently trivial anecdote or illustration remains. If these can be made so apt as necessarily to recall the argument or train of thought, so much the better.

The importance of illustration in preaching is beyond expression. In numerous cases it is our best means of explaining religious truth, and often to the popular mind our only means of proving it. Ornament, too, has its legitimate place in preaching, and whatever will help us to move unreceptive people is unspeakably valuable. Besides, for whatever purpose illustration may be specially used, it often causes the truth to be remembered. Sometimes, indeed, even where its force as an explanation of proof was not at first fully apprehended, the illustration, particularly if it is a narrative, is remembered until subsequent instruction or experience brings out the meaning. Such was frequently the case with the first hearers of our Lord's parables. In preaching to children and to the great mass of adults, illustration is simply indispensable if we want to interest, instruct, or impress them, while good illustration is always acceptable and useful to talented and educated hearers. The example of our Lord decides the whole question; and the illustrations which so abound in the records of his preaching ought to be carefully studied by every preacher to understand their source, their aim, their style, and their relation to the other elements of his teaching. Among the Christian preachers of different ages who have been most remarkable for affluence and felicity of illustration, there may be mentioned Chrysostom, Jeremy Taylor, Christmas Evans, Chalmers, Spurgeon, Beecher, Peter Marshall, Clarence Macartney and Norman Vincent Peale.

2. THE KINDS OF ILLUSTRATION

Illustrations are not only varied in function, they are also varied in kind. Illustrations are of many kinds and types. Some preachers limit the form of illustration to a story or detailed example. Alan H. Monroe defined illustration in this manner: "A detailed example of an idea to be supported is called an illustration."[5] While many illustrations are detailed examples, this definition too severely limits meaning. An illustration is anything that throws light on an idea being discussed. If the preacher is to fulfill the functions of illustration in sermon after sermon, he will need to choose various kinds of illustrations.

1. The simplest kind of illustration is one word. One word may paint a vivid picture. For example, "It was a *bruising* battle"; "It was a *bloody* revolution"; "The day *snailed* by"; "The bells and clocks were *discussing* midnight." A countryside was portrayed as *redhaired* autumn. One word may throw light or add luster to ideas. Indeed, one word may suggest a great picture to the imagination.

The one-word illustration has not been widely used by most

preachers. The study of words has always been helpful, but the study of words for illustrative use would make an excellent private study.

2. A second kind of illustration is the brief combination of words. This type includes brief descriptions and the figures of speech. Tennyson wrote about "Sunset and evening fell and after that, the dark." Here just a few words reveal an entire panorama. The simile or comparison may add new dimensions to an idea. One writer sees an action "as irrevocable as a haircut"; another views a problem "as involved as spaghetti." One preacher declares, "Sins go not alone, but follow one after another as do the links of a chain." Another preacher writes, "A man away from God is like a leaf away from a tree." Jesus made great use of metaphors in the Sermon on the Mount. "You are the salt of the earth." "You are the light of the world."

Again, this kind of illustration has had limited usage. Study and development in this area would bring the preacher great rewards.

3. A third kind of illustration is quotations. These quotations may be poetry or prose. However, quotations are often used to illustrate ideas. For example, this anonymous "Tribute to the Bible" has been cited to show the value of the Bible.

This book contains the mind of God, the state of man, the way of salvation, the doom of sinners, the happiness of believers. Its doctrines are holy, its precepts are binding, its histories are true, and its decisions are immutable. Read it to be wise, believe it to be safe, and practice it to be holy. It contains light to direct you, food to support you, and comfort to cheer you. It is the traveler's map, the pilgrim's staff, the pilot's compass, the soldier's sword, and the Christian's character. Christ is its grand subject, our good its design, and the glory of God its end. It should fill the memory, rule the heart, and guide the feet.

Read it slowly, frequently, prayerfully. It is a mine of wealth, a paradise of glory, and a river of pleasure. It is given you in life, will be open at judgment, and be remembered forever. It involves the highest responsibility, rewards the greatest labor, and condemns all who trifle with its holy contents.

4. A fourth kind of illustration is the detailed example. It is the kind most frequently used, and it has many variations and comes from many sources. It may be a story, an incident, an anecdote, a personal experience, a historical event, a parable, or an imagined example. The variations are almost limitless.

Since the story type illustration is the type preachers use most, examples will not be cited. However, as principles are discussed, examples of this type will be used.

3. SOURCES OF ILLUSTRATION

Illustration of religious truth may be drawn from the whole realm of existence and of experience. It might seem useless to make any classification of the sources, but there are two reasons for doing so. The preacher may be stimulated to seek such materials in directions which he has comparatively neglected, and the attempt at classification will give an occasion for some useful suggestions in passing.

1. Observation. It is preeminently important that the teacher of religion be a close observer, partly so that he will know how to adapt religious instruction to the real character of his hearers and the actual conditions of their life, but also so that he will be able to draw from that inexhaustible store of illustration which lies open everywhere to the individual who has eyes to see and ears to hear.

Nature teems with analogies to moral truth; and the preacher should not merely accept those which force themselves on his attention but should be constantly searching for them. Besides those analogies which are embodied in familiar metaphors and those which belong to the common stock of illustration, there are others, almost without number, which every thoughtful observer can perceive for himself; and here, as elsewhere, what is even relatively original has augmented power. Several of our Lord's most impressive illustrations are drawn from his own close observation of nature, as, for example, the lily, the mustard seed, the birds. And notice that although these are all so stated as to be very beautiful, he employs them for higher ends, for explanation or for argument. There is here an important lesson, for preachers who derive illustration from nature are too apt to follow the poets in making it chiefly ornamental.

A still richer field, if possible, is human life with all its social relations and varied vocations and pursuits, its business usages, mechanical processes, etc., and with all its changing experiences. Here a person's personal experience will blend with his observation of others. And one who really and thoughtfully observes life in all its immense variety and the world within human beings can surely never be at a loss for illustration. Chrysostom, though somewhat ascetical in his views, overflows with allusions to real life which he had observed while serving as deacon and presbyter in the great city of Antioch before going to Constantinople. Beecher, who lived for years in the middle of a continent and a nation condensed within a few square miles, shows that he diligently carried out the lesson which he said that he learned from Ruskin—to "keep his eyes and ears open." He watched the ships and the sailors, acquainted himself with the customs, good and bad, of commercial life, curiously inspected a great variety of mechanical processes, often visited his farm and closely observed agricultural operations and the various phases of rural life, was constantly seeing and hearing what occurred in his home and in other homes that he visited, supplemented his own observation by asking others about all the manifold good and evil of the great world around him, and everywhere and always was asking himself till it became the fixed habit of his mind, "What is this like? What will this illustrate?" The boundless variety and the sparkling freshness of his illustrations formed a notable element of his power as a preacher. Spurgeon, though perhaps not equal to Beecher in this respect, was also a close observer and drew far more than Beecher from reading.

One should not forget that many of the best illustrations are derived from the most common pursuits and the most familiar experiences of life. The great mass of our Lord's illustrations are drawn from ordinary human life. Jesus referred to sowing wheat and various circumstances which help or hinder its growth, to harvesting, winnowing, and putting in barns, to the management of fig trees and vineyards, and to bottling the wine. In domestic affairs, he speaks of building houses, various duties of servants and stewards, leavening bread, baking, and borrowing loaves late at night, of dogs under the table, patching clothes and their exposure to moths, lighting lamps, and sweeping the house. As to trade, he mentions the purchase of costly pearls, finding hidden treasure, money entrusted to servants as capital, lending on interest, creditors and debtors, imprisonment for debt, and tax-gatherers. Among social relations, he tells of feasts, weddings, and bridal processions, the judge and the widow who had been wronged, the rich man and the beggar, the good Samaritan. Of political affairs, he alludes to kings going to war; and the parable of the ten pounds (Luke 19) corresponds in every detail to the history of Archelaus as it occurred during our Lord's childhood. The story of the prodigal son contains beautiful pictures of real life. And who can think without emotion of Jesus standing in some market place and watching children at their games, from which he afterwards drew a striking illustration? All these form only a part of the illustrative material which, in the brief records of his teaching, he derived from the observation of human life, and in nearly every case from matters familiar to everyone. The lesson is obvious, and it should be emulated.

The observation of children is particularly profitable to a religious teacher. They reveal much of human nature, and their words and ways are usually interesting to adults. But do not repeat a child's memorable sayings in his own presence or flatter children, as preachers sometimes do. The recollections of one's own childhood grow increasingly interesting as life advances; but one must be careful not to exaggerate and glorify those memories when using them, not to fall into egotism, not to imagine that these perhaps trifling matters will be sure to interest others as much as ourselves.

Narrations of actual experience of the religious life are apt to be generally interesting and will often, as cases in point, furnish admirable illustration. The great revival preachers usually have many such narratives drawn from their observation at other places, and they often use them with great effect. This is one secret of the power possessed by some comparatively ignorant preachers in secluded districts. They tell their own experience freely and do not shrink from mentioning persons even in an adjoining neighborhood whose cases they can make instructive.

2. Pure Invention. It is perfectly acceptable to invent an illustration, even in the form of a story, provided that it possesses verisimilitude and provided that it is said to be imaginary or that nothing depends upon the idea that it is real. Some of our Lord's parables are in this sense fictitious. It is shown, in one case, by the very form of the expression, "The sower went forth to sow." When an imagined illustration is used for argument, great care must be taken to make it fair. It is very common for controversial speakers or writers to "suppose a case" and suppose it of such a kind as just to suit their purpose, without due regard to fairness. "If lions were the sculptors, the lion would be uppermost." Imagined illustrations for explanation or ornamentation are frequently too formal or elaborate. Nevertheless, one may use his imagination to create materials.

3. Science. Besides what is derived from observation of nature and of human life, there is an immense fund of illustration in science, which collects the results of a far wider observation, classifies and seeks to explain them. With the vast growth of physical science in this day and the extensive diffusion of scientific knowledge, it becomes increasingly appropriate that preachers should draw illustration from that source. In this way, too, they will most effectually counteract the efforts of some scientists and some unwise teachers of religion to bring Christianity and science into an appearance of hostility. It is much better, both for this purpose and for others, that preachers should strive to be well acquainted with one or a few fields of physical science than be slightly knowledgeable in many.

Preachers have drawn upon almost every branch of science —astrology, geology, zoology, botany, physics, chemistry, all the social sciences, etc.—for illustrative material. Recent space exploration has provided new material in many scientific areas. Science still provides an abundant source of illustration.

4. History. Preachers have always made much use of illustration from history. The field is in itself boundless but is in practice greatly limited by the average person's lack of historical knowledge. As in the case of science, the preacher may sometimes skillfully introduce what is familiar to but a few and may often give, briefly, without ostentation and in a interesting manner, the requisite information. Great as is the value of science, the pastor must not forget that history, from its narrative and descriptive character and its human interest, has a peculiar and almost unrivaled charm. And in some respects this is especially true of biography, both general and religious. Here there is the interest in a person, an individual human life. And biographical facts can often be more easily stated than those of general history. Early English preachers drew nearly all their historical and biographical illustration from ancient history. Jeremy Taylor, for example, does this often. In our day more modern sources are, of course, more popular, and ancient writers are again comparatively a fresh resource, particularly if one will read about them firsthand and not simply borrow from other preachers or from recent works on ancient history. Herodotus and Plutarch, even in a translation, can be used with great advantage, and also Josephus, whose works are now by most preachers unwisely neglected. Spurgeon often used illustration from the lives of devout men; and Richard Fuller used all manner of historical and biographical material, both secular and religious, with unusual ability.

All preachers derive illustration from the news of the day. Some carry this too far, warranting the reproach that they "get the text from the Bible, and the sermon from the newspapers." But it is a grave mistake if any avoid such a source of interesting illustration—one much more generally familiar to the audience than either science or history. By judiciously alluding to all suitable recent occurrences, whether recorded in the newspapers or happening in the community, the preacher may make the sermon more interesting and may at the same time have opportunity to add useful practical remarks about many questions of right and wrong.

Anecdotes, literally things unpublished, originally denoted interesting historical and biographical incidents gathered from unpublished manuscripts of ancient authors and thrown into a miscellaneous collection. Though now more widely used, the term is still most properly applied to stories of single interesting incidents that one has observed or has heard from someone else. These are a valuable means of illustration, which some preachers use excessively or in bad taste but which others ought to use much more than they do. He who feels that his style would be degraded by introducing an anecdote may profitably question whether or not his style is too stilted or, at any rate, too monotonous in its sustained elevation for popular discourse. Anecdotes should certainly be true if presented as true, and they should be told without exaggeration or embellishment. They should not be ludicrous—though a tinge of pleasant humor is sometimes acceptable—nor trivial, and especially not tedious. Because illustration is in general a subordinate thing in preaching and that which is subordinate should rarely be allowed to become prominent, a preacher should avoid such a multiplication of anecdotes in the same sermon or in successive sermons that would attract very special attention. A greater freedom, both as to amount and kind, is admissible in platform-speaking than in those more serious discourses which are usually called sermons.

5. Literature and Art. Even when science and history have been excluded, ancient and modern literature in prose and in verse covers an immense field and offers a vast store of illustrative material. Suggestive, pleasing, or impressive sentiments and expressions may be quoted, and allusion made to well-known literary works and characters whenever it will really help to make the discourse interesting and useful. Quotations of poetry, though made by some men in offensive excess, are used by many with admirable effect. While a few need to limit this practise, most ministers should try to read and retain more poetry and to use it more freely. No one can have failed to

notice how often quotations from hymns, particularly when they are familiar, add greatly to the interest and effect of a sermon. Spurgeon often uses these very effectively. The *Pilgrim's Progress,* with its strength and homely simplicity, its poetic charm and devotional sweetness, is so rich in choice illustration that every preacher ought to make himself thoroughly familiar with it and to review it again and again through life. Fables are so often alluded to in common conversation that we scarcely notice them, and the occasions are numerous in which they might be usefully used in preaching. An author of distinction and of many accomplishments and experience of life remarked some years ago that, in his judgment, next to the Bible and Shakespeare, the most instructive book in the world was Aesop's *Fables.* Even nursery rhymes, though not often exactly appropriate in regular sermons, have been used well in speaking to children.

Proverbs are an especially valuable means of stating truth forcibly and impressively. True, they usually represent an imperfect generalization and are one-sided so that almost any proverb can be matched by an opposite one. Yet in exhibiting particular aspects of truth, in impressing particular points, they have great power, especially with the popular mind. "Great preachers for the people, such as have found their way to the universal heart of their fellows, have been ever great employers of proverbs."[6] Our Lord repeatedly uses expressions which appear to have been proverbial. This was one of the many ways he tried to impress the heart and mind of common people. The preacher should study the Proverbs of Solomon and often quote them. The proverbs of our own country and language are especially forceful. Besides proverbs proper, there are many sage maxims which are often repeated in conversation, and many wise sayings which can be quoted from the Fathers, the Old English divines, and others.

Illustration is also frequently drawn from works of art, especially from pictures. These are constantly used in books under the name of "illustrations" of the narrative or treatise and never fail, when good, to interest every class of readers. Similarly, the description of pictures and statues may be effectively used in a sermon. Such a description should be brief and free from any appearance of ostentation.

6. Scripture. The Bible is one of the best sources of illustration. The Scriptures present materials of illustration suited to every legitimate subject of preaching and belonging to almost every one of the above-mentioned classes, especially history and biography, poetry and proverbs, and all kinds of wise sayings. Several causes combine to make this the best of all the sources of illustration. The material is to some extent familiar to all, and thus the illustration will be easily understood. Again, this material will be much more impressive than any other because of its sacredness and its known and felt relation to ourselves. Besides, the frequent use of scriptural illustration serves to revive and extend the knowledge of Scripture among the hearers. Dean Brown of Yale declared,

The Bible is the greatest picturebook in print. The preacher may well "search the Scriptures" for illustrations as well as for the promises of eternal life. He will never exhaust their rich content and the illustrations from that source will have all the more value because of the sacred associations which cluster around them.[7]

Every preacher should most diligently draw from this source. And to this end, preachers should continue regular, attentive reading of the whole Bible.

4. BUILDING THE ILLUSTRATION INTO THE SERMON

After illustrations have been found, then the primary task begins. They must be fitted into the sermon. Just as windows must be set into the framing of a house, illustrations must be built into a sermon. Consider some general suggestions for building the illustration into the sermon.

1. Do not be in a hurry to use an illustration. The preacher follows the wrong order when he finds an illustration and looks for an idea. Discover an idea and then seek for an illustration which will illuminate it. Keep your illustrations until the right

occasion arises. "It will always be a temptation to strain a favorite illustration in an effort to make it fit into next Sunday's sermon. This never works; unless the illustration is right, it is worse than none at all."[8]

2. Be certain an illustration really illustrates. Be sure an illustration fits. An illustration must add something to the idea under discussion. When the preacher needs to build a bridge from illustration to idea, he has failed. J. H. Jowett asserted, "An illustration that requires explanation is worthless."[9]

3. Carefully avoid turning attention away from the subject illustrated to the illustration itself. This is obviously a grave mistake which is often committed. Illustrations stated at great length with elaborate imagery will almost inevitably have this effect. A candle should be held beside a picture in order to see the picture. Likewise, an illustration should illumine an idea.

4. Do not over-illustrate. A house with too many windows will have too much light. Too much light causes glare. A sermon may also have too many windows. Illustrations are to add luster to ideas; they should not obliterate ideas. It is a mistake to construct a sermon with one small idea and several big illustrations.

5. Be certain of the accuracy of every illustration. If a preacher cannot verify the details of an incident, he should not use it for illustrative material. Truth is often stranger than fiction, but a preacher should not get a reputation for telling tall stories. For example, a student talked about Chrysostom, "that great eighteenth century preacher." But the professor knew that he had missed the dating by 1400 years. The facts of an illustration should be the subject of research and not the product of imagination.

6. Seek for variety of illustration. Choose material from many areas. Also select material from many different periods in history. Above all, do not use the same illustration again and again. Ideas may be forgotten, but illustrations are remembered. A preacher's illustrations should be even more varied than his texts and subjects.

While these general suggestions may help, specific suggestions are needed for the actual building of the illustration into the sermon. This is a big task that requires real skill. This kind of skill may be attained by giving attention to the four essential elements of an illustration—the beginning, the action, the climax, and the conclusion.

1. Climax. Climax is considered first because it is the most important part of an illustration. The preacher must give careful attention to the climax or the point of the story. In the use of humor, the climax is often called the punch line. The question should be raised, What is the real point of the incident? Once a decision is made about the climax, then the other parts of the illustration are arranged around it.

2. Beginning or introduction. The illustration needs to be introduced into the sermon. It should be woven into the sermon so there will be no jerk or jar as the preacher moves from idea to illustration. The introduction will always be brief. Generally, just a few words will be sufficient. Here also, attention should be given to variety. The lack of variety may result in dullness. John Nicholls Booth suggests the use of imagination in illustration introductions.

It is easy to summon each quotation with: Roosevelt says, the Bible states, Shakespeare wrote, Byron sings. It is less easy, but vastly more pleasing and effective, to rearrange them picturesquely: into the microphone Roosevelt repeated . . . , written boldly into the Bible is this phrase . . . , Shakespeare felt keenly that . . . , that flaunter of convention, Lord Byron, passes this thought to us across the years. . . .[10]

Some advice concerning illustration introduction may help. In the first place, do not talk about illustrating, just do it. Do not say, "I shall illustrate the point in this manner," or "Now to illustrate." These are really illustration beginnings which should be avoided. Whenever a preacher really illustrates an idea, the people will know it. If he says he is going to illustrate an idea and does not do it, he has made a promise which he does not keep. Then, the preacher should not ask permission to illustrate. Do not introduce illustrations by saying, "Now let me illustrate," or "Please let me use this example." Such a request is not sincere. The preacher has decided to use the material and could not be stopped. Moreover, do not promise what an illustration will do. It is not uncommon to hear this kind of illustration introduction: "Here is a story which will show you exactly what I mean." The meaning may be clear, but then it may not be. An illustration should never be introduced with a promise.

3. Action or movement. The third part of an illustration is action or movement. This is the material which comes between the introduction and the climax. Generally, this is highly interesting material. However, extraneous material should be omitted. Many long, detailed illustrations could be presented much more briefly. In rural America when lighting was provided by the kerosene lamp, it was often necessary to trim the wick in order for the light to burn more brightly. Likewise, many sermon illustrations should be trimmed so that they will create more light.

Occasionally better action may be created by the use of dialogue. Preachers have a tendency to take dialogue material and turn it into expository accounts. This should not be done. Rather, the opposite should be true. Expository accounts should be turned into dialogue whenever possible. Whether by dialogue or by some other means, the story should move quickly from introduction to climax.

4. The last part of a sermon illustration is conclusion. It comes after the climax, and it may or may not be stated. If the point being illustrated is clearly before the congregation, the conclusion may be understood. However, it is often stated as a form of application. In a sermon entitled, "What Do You Say to Yourself?" Dr. Harry Emerson Fosdick uses an illustration which clearly presents all four parts of the illustration.

Consider an incident during the great war: A young French soldier, very weak and white, lay on a hospital cot. The surgeon who had just amputated his shattered arm stood looking sympathetically at his drawn face. "I am very sorry," he said, "that you had to lose your arm." Then the soldier's eyes opened, and with an accent of protest he said, "I did not lose it, I gave it."

The soldier was wise enough to see that his whole attitude toward the necessity that confronted him depended on what word he used. He might go on saying, "I lost it," or he might say, "I gave it," and the way he chose to talk to himself about the event would ultimately determine its meaning for him.

No happening in life is the whole of itself; the rest of it is what we make of it by the way we talk to ourselves about it.[11]

The introduction to this illustration is clear. The action is terse and interesting. The conclusion is longer than usual, but nonetheless enforces the point of the sermon.

5. The illustration in delivery. Sermon delivery will be considered in a later chapter, but because the delivery of illustration is so important, certain advice is offered here. First, be thoroughly acquainted with all illustrative material. Occasionally preachers will give attention to ideas and assume knowledge of the sermon's illustration. Then in the midst of delivery, the illustrative material is not well handled because the preacher is not familiar with it. Therefore, the preacher should practice delivering an illustration. He should get on his feet and talk through the illustration just as he would do in actual delivery. This will help him both to know the illustration and to deliver it well. In the next place, the preacher should try to recreate the illustration at the moment of delivery. He should seek to enter into it and to feel the emotions which may be expressed in the illustration. Preachers have often felt deeply when illustrations were practiced, only to discover that they do not have the same feelings in the act of delivery. In practice, the illustration was real; in actual delivery, the illustration was secondhand. Therefore, it is important to recreate an illustration in the moment of delivery. Also, the preacher should not reveal the mood or climax of an illustration. If the people sense the climax or the mood of the climax, much of the effectiveness of the illustration is destroyed. For example, most of the material in an illustration is matter-of-fact until the climax is reached. Therefore, it should be handled in a matter-of-fact manner. To reveal humor, sadness, or any other mood before the climax is reached will undercut its effectiveness. Above all, an illustration should be delivered in tones which capture the spirit of the

original experience. If the experience was conversation, it should be delivered as conversation. If an incident originally called for force and volume, then it should be told in the same manner. Some preachers "declaim" all material. Generally, narrative material should be presented in a direct, straightforward way. This is one way to bring about variety in sermon delivery.

NOTES

1. Dawson, Bryan, *The Art of Illustrating Sermons* (New York: Abingdon-Cokesbury Press, 1938), p. 17. One of the many values of this book is that it shows the significant relation of illustration to every part of the sermon.
2. Ian Macpherson, *The Art of Illustrating Sermons* (New York: Abingdon Press, 1964), lists seventeen uses of illustration. W. E. Sangster, *The Craft of Sermon Illustration* (London: Epworth Press, 1946), gives seven uses of illustration.
3. Compare Phillips Brooks, *Lectures on Preaching* (New York: E. P. Dutton & Co., 1907), p. 175.
4. Ibid., pp. 156, 160.
5. Alan H. Monroe, *Principles and Types of Speech* (Chicago: Scott, Foresman, 1955), p. 160.
6. See Richard Trench, *On the Lessons in Proverbs* (New York: Redfield, 1855). There is a good deal about both fables and parables in C. H. Spurgeon's *Art of Illustration* (New York: Wilbur B. Ketcham, 1894), and quite a collection in his *Salt Cellars* (New York: A. C. Armstrong & Son, 1889).
7. C. R. Brown, *The Art of Preaching* (New York: Macmillan Co., 1948), pp. 132–33.
8. Gerald Kennedy, *His Word through Preaching* (New York: Harper & Bros., 1947), p. 145.
9. J. H. Jowett, *The Preacher, His Life and Work* (New York: Harper & Bros., 1912), p. 141.
10. John Nicholls Booth, *The Quest for Preaching Power* (New York: Macmillan Co., 1943), p. 147.
11. Quoted in Booth, pp. 138–39.

For Further Reading:
Functional Elements of the Sermon

Breed, David R. *Preparing to Preach.* New York: George H. Doran Co., 1911.

Brown, H. C., Jr. *A Quest for Reformation in Preaching.* Waco, Tex.: Word Books, 1968.

Cleland, James T. *Preaching to Be Understood.* New York: Abingdon Press, 1965.

Macpherson, Ian. *The Art of Illustrating Sermons.* New York: Abingdon Press, 1964.

Muehl, William. *The Road to Persuasion.* New York: Oxford University Press, 1956.

Oliver, Robert T. *The Psychology of Persuasive Speech.* New York: Longmans, Green & Co., 1957.

Sangster, W. E. *The Craft of Sermon Illustration.* London: Epworth Press, 1946.

Part V

THE STYLE OF THE SERMON

CHAPTER 22

General Observations
on Style

1. NATURE AND IMPORTANCE OF STYLE

It is frequently said of a writer that he wields a ready, an elegant, or a caustic pen. Similarly, the stylus, the pointed iron instrument with which the Romans wrote on their tablets covered with wax, is often used by Cicero to describe the manner of writing, the manner of expressing one's thoughts in writing and at a later period was very naturally extended by analogy to the fine arts, to dress, and a great variety of matters. A person's style, then, is his characteristic manner of expressing his thoughts, whether in writing or in speech.

Everyone has his own handwriting if he writes at all easily and well. Everyone also has his own style. The most slavish imitation could not be perfect; the individual's own character will sometimes, in spite of him, modify his style. No writer on the subject fails to quote the saying of Buffon, "The style is the man." This saying Buffon himself curiously illustrated, for his style is marked by a stately and elaborate elegance, and it is said that he could not write well unless he was in full dress! To the same effect Landor said, "Language is a part of a man's character";[1] and Lessing, "Every man should have his own style as he has his own nose."[2] But here, as everywhere else, that which is most characteristic in a person may be disciplined and indefinitely improved without losing individuality.

It is not surprising that the term *style,* as figuratively denoting one's manner of expressing his thoughts, should be used in different cases with a very different meaning. It is sometimes taken to include arrangement, even that of an entire treatise or discourse; and there can certainly be no absolute distinction made between the arrangement of sentences and paragraphs and that of the discourse. Commonly, however, the general arrangement is not included in the term. On the other hand, style is sometimes distinguished from diction, the latter then denoting one's vocabulary, the character of the words and particular phrases which he uses, while the former would include everything else belonging to his mode of expressing thought. But it is best, according to the usual practice, to include diction as a part of style.

Thus understood, style is obviously a matter of very great importance. A person's style cannot be separated from his modes of thought, from his whole mental character. The natural and common image by which it is called the "dress" of thought is very apt to mislead; for style, as Wordsworth forcibly says, is not the mere dress, it is the incarnation of thought. Another's thoughts are known only as thus revealed, thus incarnate.[3] Aristotle, it is true, speaks slightingly of style as a subject recently introduced into treatises of rhetoric which is somewhat necessary to consider in every system of instruction, though the proof is the main thing.[4] His practice accords with this opinion, for his own style is not only careless and harsh but often vexatiously obscure. And yet there were already in his language many noble examples of style in poetry, history, and oratory which have never been surpassed; so true is it in rhetoric that just theory follows excellent practice. It is only a few people whose writing is so surpassingly valuable as to be highly prized, like Aristotle's, in spite of great faults of style. The speakers and writers who have been widely and permanently influential have usually accomplished it by good thoughts, well expressed. Often, indeed, excellence of style has given a wide and lasting popularity to works which had little other merit. Gold-smith's *Histories* long held their place in many schools because they were so charmingly written, though they were inaccurate and very poorly represented the historical accomplishments of their own age. The widespread, though short-lived popularity gained by Renan's fanciful *Life of Jesus* was due not merely to the sensational character of its contents but very largely also to the extreme beauty of the style, particularly in the original French. When a student at a Jesuit College, Renan paid great attention to the cultivation of his style and afterwards devoted himself mainly to the study of language and literature. In like manner, science has in many cases gained a just appreciation only when represented in a pleasing style. This was what Buffon did for natural history. The popularity of geology was immensely increased among the English speaking peoples by Hugh Miller through his marvelous powers of description and the general freshness and animation of his style. And so it was later with Agassiz, Huxley, and Tyndall. Such facts go to show that style is not merely ornamental. Style is the glitter and polish of the warrior's sword but is also its keen edge. It can make mediocrity acceptable and even attractive, and power more powerful still. It can make error seductive, while truth may lie unnoticed for lack of it. Shall religious teachers neglect so powerful a means of usefulness? True, Paul says, "My message and my preaching were not with persuasive words of man's wisdom" (1 Cor. 2:4). He refused to deal in the would-be philosophy and the sensational and meretricious rhetoric which were so popular in that rapidly growing commercial city; but his style is a model of passionate energy and rises upon occasion into a real and exquisite beauty.[5]

The traditional English university training, with all its defects, produced good style, as could be seen not only in the great Parliamentary orators and the admirable newspaper writing which England boasted but also in preachers. The famous *Oxford Tracts* would not have been so influential but for their admirable style. The sermons of J. H. Newman, Robertson, Liddon, and Bishop Wilberforce were in this respect greatly admirable. And in that tradition, the public speakers of England, both in the pulpit and in Parliament, maintained for the most part a high standard.

In America a growing number of writers and speakers, both secular and religious, can be held up as models. But a negligence and looseness of style is observable in many otherwise capable ministers. And the great American fault in speaking and writing is an excessive vehemence, a constant effort to be impressive. Such style, as well as its delivery, too often lacks the calmness of conscious strength, the repose of sincerity, the quiet earnestness which only now and then becomes impassioned.

There is the full and yet rounded style of oratory, the plain style that is not devoid of vigour and force, and the style which combines elements of either class and whose merit is to steer a middle course.[6]

One cause of this neglect of style among us is the failure to understand its inseparable connection with the thought conveyed and the dependence of truth upon the clarity of the manner in which it is expressed. The best style attracts least attention to itself, and only the critical observer is apt to appreciate its excellence, most people giving credit solely to the matter and having no idea how much the manner has contributed to attract and impress them. The thought is certainly the main thing; but the style also is important.

The experience of all times, and the testimony of all teachers, present to us as inseparable, these two propositions: (1) That we must not flatter ourselves that we shall have a good style, without an interesting fund of ideas. (2) That even with an interesting and substantial supply of ideas, we must not flatter ourselves that style will come of itself.[7]

2. STYLES AND STYLE

To say that every writer or speaker has his own characteristic manner of expressing thought and feeling does not mean that every person is a law into himself. In music Handel, Bach, and Chopin each had his own characteristic style, but their compositions were great music because in each case genius allied itself with, or rather found itself in, the basic laws of music. So in preaching, effective style is achieved by observing the fundamental requirements of language and the whole context of circumstance. Indeed, the nature of preaching makes it doubly imperative that great care should be given to every factor and condition that might help or hinder the power of speech, for preaching is more than art for art's sake, more than self-expression; it is speaking for God.

1. Individual style, then, moves properly within boundaries. First, it is under obligation to the laws of language. There are grammatical principles which ought to be observed for both moral and practical reasons.

> Grammar discovers the facts of language, from which it formulates the laws of correct expression; and these laws rhetoric must observe, because correctness lies necessarily at the foundation of all intelligible utterance, rhetorical or other.[8]

Grammatical processes are the working tools of rhetoric, too useful, too necessary, to be neglected. Again, style must have regard for the times. It is not bound by tradition. As Christianity moved out into the gentile world, the style of preaching changed. It followed the customs and tastes of different peoples and different ages.[9] No age, no school furnished a "sacred rhetoric" which could ignore or transgress the best methods of public speech in current use. To be sure, Christian preaching, by its very excellence, has been an influential factor in creating standards of style; but its excellence has been its ability to sense the intellectual and emotional dispositions and tastes of a given age and relate itself to them effectively. Whenever preaching has failed to do this and become merely imitative of another age or some prophetic hero like Chrysostom, Bernard, Jeremy Taylor, Liddon, Beecher, or Spurgeon, it has lost in power. And history's road is strewn with the bones of ineffective imitators. Concerning the limitations set in more recent times, Patton pointed out that

> the tempo of our life is fast, not to say jerky. The entire religious service takes less time than the sermon used to have for itself. The shortness

of the sermon reacts upon its vocabulary and style, as well as upon the mood of the listeners. People today will hardly have patience or know how to listen to a preacher whose leisurely, orotund, well-balanced periods suggest that he is in no hurry to get through.[10]

Yet, again, style must adapt to the sermon, the character of the audience, and the nature of the subject. A street corner and a nursing home call for quite different things; so do children's sermons, baccalaureate addresses, and revival sermons. As to appropriate styles for different subjects and purposes, compare the Sermon on the Mount with the twenty-third chapter of Matthew.

2. Certain qualities or properties of style are indispensable: grammatical qualities concerning correctness and purity of language, and rhetorical qualities concerning more particularly the impression or effect of discourse. The latter may be classified as clearness, energy, and elegance.

Precise and perspicuous expression, being the staple, the backbone of composition, is to be cultivated first and most conscientiously of all; but the cases in which mere clearness is enough, without the aid of other qualities, belong to the comparatively elementary forms of literature, those works in which the bare thought is all-sufficient to supply the interest. But when the idea comes home more closely to reader and writer—when on the one hand it must gain lodgment in dull minds or stimulate a laggard attention, or when on the other its importance arouses the writer's enthusiasm or stirs his deep convictions—there is or must be imported to it greater life than its merely intelligible statement would demand. . . . An idea (however) may be stated with perfect clearness, may make also a strong impression on the reader's mind and heart; and yet many of the details may be an offense to his taste; or a crude expression and harsh combinations of sound may impair the desired effect by compelling attention to defective form. Any such disturbing element is a blemish in the style. Nor is it an offense to the cultured reader alone. Everyone may be aware that a style is crude, though he may not be able to locate or explain the cause; and when an idea is expressed with supreme felicity, everyone may appreciate it. There is needed, therefore, in every well-formed style, an element of beauty to make the style a satisfaction to the reader's taste as well as to his thought and conviction.[11]

What Genung says here concerning writing is equally true of preaching and is of such importance that these qualities will be discussed at length later.

3. It is necessary to warn against giving way completely to one's natural bent and thus falling into faulty styles. One's personal dispositions must be under discipline, not smothered, but corrected and supplemented. Among the faulty styles observable in preachers are those that result from too exclusive attention to the fact that the sermon is something to be heard. They are too conscious of sound. Among the kinds of style discussed by Oman,[12] four can be traced to this cause. First is the *spacious style* in which grandeur is the goal, which is pursued by solemn, resonant, impressive tone and expanded statement. Oman gives this example:

"The sun never sets on the king's dominions" might seem to be spacious enough, but this style would expand it to: "As I have had occasion to remark before, the celestial luminary is never at any time wholly below the horizon of the imperial dominions of our most gracious sovereign."

A second variety is the *polished style* in which the conspicuous thing is that the sermon is well tailored and well kempt. Its best compliment is neatness and finesse. A third variety is the *fine style* which "concerns itself with words and phrases for their own sake, and mostly for their mellifluousness." It specializes in prettiness of sound. There may be distinguished, also, the *flowery style* which is highly ornamental, often hiding the truth in beautiful words or making conviction of truth appear less important to the preacher than his oratory. It is over-dressed speech.

Other faults of style result from too exclusive attention to the fact that the sermon is concerned with truth. One of the dangers of theological and literary studies is that the materials and forms of the classroom will be transferred to the pulpit. It is very easy to introduce into one's sermons the style of the professor in the classroom and to write in the style of a paper on theology or ethics. The style of an abstract, an essay, or a lecture may be excellent from the purely intellectual and literary standpoint. But a sermon must be understood, must be interesting, must come to grips with life and its problems, must be moving. True preaching is not truth centered; it is truth, truth centered on life. The preacher must always be conscious that a sermon is prepared to be spoken. But, again, too much attention to this fact may result in faulty style. Some preachers thus fall into a casual, not to say careless, conversational style. Properly defined, the conversational style is highly appropriate in the pulpit. Preaching must be audience-conscious, person-to-person; it is something told. But there are levels of conversation, and the pulpit is not a park bench, nor is the subject the weather. The place is the house of God and the issue is critical. The sermon is properly conversational in its familiarity, directness, and simplicity, but it is more; it is a prophet's message, it is truth. Too exclusive attention to the persons addressed has the further danger of leading a preacher, according to his disposition, into a dogmatic or combative or else ingratiating style, in which language as well as manner will be either too harsh or too pleasing.

Be careful to observe that these styles are faulty only when they are developed without regard for all the demands of a sermon. In combination and proper proportion they become the instruments of effectiveness. A sermon is something to be heard, it is concerned with truth, it is addressed to individuals; it needs not one but all three qualities of beauty, clearness, and force.

NOTES

1. James M. Hoppin, *Homiletics* (New York: Funk & Wagnalls, 1893), p. 585.
2. Erastus Otis Haven, *Rhetoric* (New York: Harper & Bros., 1869), p. 241.
3. See also Henry N. Day, *Art of Discourse* (New York: Charles Scribner & Co., 1867), p. 213.
4. Lane Cooper, *The Rhetoric of Aristotle* (New York: D. Appleton-Century Co., 1932), p. 185.
5. Notice chapters 13 and 15 of this same epistle.

6. Cicero, *De Oratore* (London: William Heinemann, 1942), III, 52, p. 199.
7. Alexander Vinet, *Homiletics,* 3rd ed. (New York: Ivison, Blakeman, Taylor, 1871), p. 353.
8. John Genung, *The Practical Elements of Rhetoric* (Boston: Ginn & Co., 1886), pp. 108–9.
9. E. C. Dargan, *The Art of Preaching in the Light of Its History* (Nashville, Tenn.: Sunday School Board of the Southern Baptist Convention, 1922).
10. Carl S. Patton, *The Preparation and Delivery of Sermons* (Chicago: Willett, Clark & Co., 1938), p. 67.
11. Genung, pp. 21 and 23.
12. John Oman, *Concerning the Ministry* (New York: Harper & Bros., 1937), pp. 85–89.

CHAPTER 23

Attaining the Qualities of Style

AS was noted in a part of the discussion of the last chapter, the three principal qualities of style are clarity, energy, and elegance, or clearness, force, and beauty. These three qualities are listed in the order of their importance. While some authors give a much longer list of qualities, these three seem to be basic and sufficient.

The first of these is clarity. By clarity is meant that the preacher speaks or writes in such a way that his congregation understands what he says or writes. Or clearness is writing or speaking in such a way that no reader or hearer can misunderstand. In other words, the message is transparently clear.

Some speakers and congregations seem to equate obscurity with brilliance. Just the opposite is true. A grand style often obscures the truth. A. J. Gossip cites an example of a preacher who thought he was improving the crystal clear story of the Prodigal Son.

Not "I will arise and go to my father"; but "I am determined to go to my dear aged parent, and try to excite his tenderness and compassion for me. I will kneel before him, and accost him in those penitent and pathetic terms, 'Best of parents, I acknowledge myself an ungrateful creature to heaven and to you. Condescend to hire me into your family in the capacity of the meanest slave.' " Stuff such as that will save no souls. And that is what kills many a sermon, and the truths they blur and smudge! In much preaching the great Christian verities fall dully on bored ears, largely because the language used is so opaque, so colorless, so unarresting.[1]

It is the preacher's primary task to reveal the truth, not to conceal it.

Clarity of style is important for several reasons. Henry Ward Beecher gives one facetious reason.

I know that some men . . . justify the obscurities of their style, saying that it is a good practice for men to be obliged to dig for the ideas which they get. But I submit to you that working on Sunday is not proper for ordinary people in church, and obliging your parishioners to dig and delve for ideas in your sermons is making them do the very work you are paid a salary to do for them.[2]

One of the reasons for clarity in preaching is of ultimate importance. The success of a message depends on its being understood. If the message is not grasped, then all else is lost. Clarity has to be the beginning point and the most important point of style. Matthew Arnold once exclaimed, "Have something to say, and say it as clearly as you can. That is the only secret of style."[3] The preacher's message should be as clear as sunlight. One of the highest compliments a preacher can receive is to have a hearer say, "I understand you."

A second quality of style is energy or force. Force refers to the impact the message makes upon those who hear it. Energy is a combination of liveliness, passion, and power. Energy is a quality of style that impresses and stimulates. Sue Nichols has a concise definition of energy. "Energy means communicating with force. It means propelling our thoughts into the minds of others. It means girding our message in strong, vivid language so that what we say 'registers.' "[4]

Energy is closely related to both subject matter and to delivery. The preacher needs to believe in his subject. He must feel that what he is saying is important. It is difficult to speak forcefully concerning an idea about which the speaker has little enthusiasm. On the other hand, a consuming subject will defy languid expression. Also some people have more forceful, passionate natures than others. Energy is a part of some personalities. For these people, forceful expression is easy. When a person is not naturally energetic, he must give attention to the way he expresses ideas. By such attention he may develop a pattern of forceful presentation.

A third quality of style is elegance or beauty. Elegance is a quality of style which "conveys a sense of order, harmony, and loveliness."[5] Elegance has been defined as the elimination of stylistic blemishes and the obedience to laws of good taste and imagination. Quite simply, elegance may be defined as the quality of style which satisfies the listener's desire for the beautiful. Within every listener there is an innate craving for the beautiful. Beauty is a reminder of God and the loveliness of his creation.

Elegance is a quality of style which should not usually be sought for its own sake. It should be a derivative quality.

Beauty in sermons does not usually come from adornment. It can be found in clarity, in the apt word and moving thought. The experience of the aesthetic in a sermon can open the way to what is good and right. Beauty is a delight that should be one of the sources of the joy of worship.[6]

When a sincere effort is made to attain these qualities of style, the way will be essentially the same for each preacher. Those people who were endowed with a facility in expression will still need to work on their style; likewise those who have limited gifts must also work hard to improve their abilities. Let both work with the assurance that work will bring reward. O. S. Davis insisted that the secret of success in the cultivation of style is "work and practice; then work and practice; then still more work and practice."[7]

How may these qualities of style be attained? Actually, many factors will enter into the attainment of these qualities. Some factors will help fulfill one or more of these qualities, or even all three at the same time.

Since style cannot be separated from thought, perhaps the place to begin is with the preacher's own thinking. Practice in clear thinking begins in the preacher's mind. He must work with his own understanding first. He may well raise questions like these: Do I fully understand the idea I am developing? Do I see its ramifications clearly? These questions are exceedingly important because style belongs more in thought as it is expressed than in the words used in expressing it.

A second factor which will help achieve the qualities of style is a clear subject. The preacher who is thinking clearly can arrive at his focal idea, his subject. The preacher must reach the point where he can answer the question, What am I talking about? A well-defined subject is the key to clarity. When a preacher's focal idea is identified, he is then in position to make clear statements about it. In turn, clear ideas tend to march, and thereby add force to a message.

Another means of attaining the qualities of style closely related to the two just considered is arrangement. Strunk and White have reiterated that the writer should work from a "suitable design."[8] The value of logical arrangement has been considered in Chapter 13. A careful plan contributes to clarity. While it is difficult to understand an unorganized mass of material, it is easy to comprehend a well-organized message. The progressive movement of good plan also adds energy. Moreover, a plan that has good order is more pleasing.

These qualities of style may be greatly enhanced by giving special attention to the paragraphs which develop the plan just discussed. Ideas are broken into smaller units of thought or paragraphs. Sue Nichols has said:

A paragraph is like a rodeo. The first sentence forms a fence around the whole topic. It causes onlookers to focus their attention on a given area. As the paragraph proceeds, individual thoughts leap out into the ring one at a time to perform.... The last sentence in a paragraph may attempt a summary or prepare for the next topic or both.[9]

A. W. Blackwood declared, "A good paragraph starts with clarity and ends with force."[10] It should begin with a clear key sentence that charts the way, and close with a sentence that prepares the way for that which follows.

Still another factor which will help attain these qualities of style is the sentence. Within each paragraph, consider the sentences. For not only are paragraphs important, but the sentences which make up the paragraphs are also important. These suggestions may help the preacher to write clearly and forcibly.

The sentences should be kept fairly short. Rudolf Flesch in *The Art of Plain Talk* uses a table to show that brief sentences aid understanding.

Average Sentence Length in Words[11]

Very Easy	8 or fewer
Easy	11
Fairly Easy	14
Standard	17
Fairly Difficult	21
Difficult	25
Very Difficult	29 or more

The short sentences will also contribute to energy. "I came, I saw, I conquered" is the classic example of brevity and force.

Also, the subject and predicate should be kept close together. When the word acting and the word expressing the action are close together, the ideas they are conveying will more likely be clear.

Then, "use the active voice. The active voice is usually more direct and vigorous than the passive."[12] The active voice is likely to be more lively and emphatic.

"Avoid making a detour within a sentence."[13] Just as the main road is often lost on a detour, so is the primary thought.

Sentences should be positive statements. Make assertions. Be declarative. Since the preacher is a herald, declaration should be easy.

Give attention to the location of words and phrases in the sentence. Generally, the best place for words or groups of words which the speaker wants to emphasize is at the end of the sentence. The beginning, however, is also a prominent place. Emphatic words should be put at the beginning or the end, not in the middle.

Since style is often equated with word choice, it is often especially important to give attention to words. The observance of several elemental rules will assist in attaining the primary qualities of style.

First, use plain words. These plain words need not necessarily be of Anglo-Saxon derivations. They do need to be short and simple. Again Flesch has a table showing that longer words (those with more prefixes and suffixes) are more difficult to understand.

Number of Affixes per 100 Words[14]

Very Easy	22 or fewer
Easy	26
Fairly Easy	31
Standard	37
Fairly Difficult	42
Difficult	46
Very Difficult	54 or more

Then choose concrete, specific words. Whenever possible use a definite word rather than a general word. Do not say, "A catastrophe occurred; there was a dreadful loss of life." Rather the speaker should choose the specific; he should say, "A mine caved in; twenty men were killed and eighty were injured." Concrete and definite words add to clarity and interest.

Select live words, words of action. This means that the speaker should choose verbs. Use active verbs which express action.

The verbs you want to use are those that are in active business doing verb work; if you use a verb in the passive voice or make a participle or noun out of it, you have lost the most valuable part in the process: it's like cooking vegetables and throwing away the water with all the vitamins in it.[15]

Finally, the speaker should use words that suggest more than they say. He should choose words that paint large pictures, that will activate the imagination. Examples of words such as "bloody" revolution or "bruising" battle were noted in Chapter 21. These suggestive words create energy or interest.

Style cannot be taught. Principles of style can be learned, but style must be developed, and that development will come slowly and painstakingly. An incident from the life of Henry Van Dyke makes the point and needs no application.

The autumn of 1892 was a time of sickness and sorrow for Henry Van Dyke.... One anguished, sleepless night, there came to him "suddenly and without labor" *The Story of the Other Wise Man.* Patiently, in the following months, he gathered the detailed knowledge that the telling of the tale required, and wrote it down with meekness and joy. In a letter to Cleland B. McAfee, Henry Van Dyke wrote: "If the story itself came without effort, the writing of the story was a serious piece of labor. I cared for it so much and felt so grateful that I should have been ashamed to put it off with cheap and easy work. I wanted to find the exact words, if I could, for every sentence. A clumsy phrase, a cloudy adjective, seemed intolerable—there are pages in the book that have been re-written ten times. For the brief description of the ride to Babylon I read nine books of travel, ancient and modern, in German, Greek and Latin.... I am not ashamed to confess these things because I think that a man ought to respect his work enough to be willing to try hard to make it as good as he can, and always to regret that it is not better."[16]

The writing of sermons is one of the primary ways to improve style. It will be considered in a larger context in the next chapter.

NOTES

1. A. J. Gossip, "An Appreciation," in W. M. Macgregor, *The Making of a Preacher* (Philadelphia: Westminster Press, 1946), p. 12.
2. Henry Ward Beecher, *Lectures on Preaching,* First Series (New York: Fords, Howard, & Hulbert, 1900), p. 158.
3. Quoted in George E. Sweazey, *Preaching the Good News* (Englewood Cliffs, N.J.: Prentice-Hall, 1976), p. 130.
4. Sue Nichols, *Words on Target* (Atlanta: John Knox Press, 1946), p. 19.
5. O. S. Davis, *Principles of Preaching* (Chicago: University of Chicago Press, 1924), p. 258.
6. Sweazey, pp. 142–43.
7. Davis, p. 260.
8. William Strunk and E. B. White, *The Elements of Style* (New York: Macmillan Co., 1959), pp. 10, 57.
9. Nichols, p. 50.
10. A. W. Blackwood, *The Preparation of Sermons* (New York: Abingdon-Cokesbury Press, 1948), p. 185.
11. Rudolf Flesch, *The Art of Plain Talk* (New York: Harper & Bros., 1946), p. 38.
12. Strunk and White, p. 13.
13. Blackwood, p. 186.
14. Flesch, p. 43.
15. Ibid., p. 67.
16. Cited in A. W. Blackwood, *The Fine Art of Preaching* (New York: Macmillan Co., 1937), p. 139.

CHAPTER 24

The Writing of Sermons

THE habit of writing sermons should be carefully considered. Many preachers never write any sermons; few write all their sermons. In general, the writing of sermons has been gravely neglected. The advantages of writing sermons, however, far outweigh disadvantages. These advantages should be evaluated.

1. Writing greatly assists the work of preparation by making it easier to concentrate on the subject. Mental application is facilitated by any appropriate bodily action. Writing involves a high degree of that control of body which so contributes to control of the mind; at the same time it has the advantage of possessing a closer natural relation to thought than any other act except speaking itself. Indeed, everyone knows how much writing helps to keep the thoughts from wandering.

2. Writing a sermon also requires more thorough preparation. He who prepares without writing may follow out all the developments and expansions of his thoughts as far as the discourse is to carry them; but he who writes must do this, is compelled to it.

3. Still further, writing aids the development of better style. As a general thing, unwritten speech cannot equal written speech in grammatical correctness, in precision, conciseness, smoothness, and rhetorical finish. These are highly important

properties of style, and particularly with respect to the demands of some audiences, occasions, or subjects. Thus, if one is discussing a controversial point of doctrine in the presence of persons ready to misunderstand or misrepresent him, it is even more than usually desirable that his language should be precise and unmistakable, an achievement greatly facilitated by having written it out beforehand. Some hearers are very fastidious about the preacher's finish of style. His language, as well as his manner of delivery and his dress, must be *comme il faut,* or they will have nothing to do with him.

4. Writing sermons tends to help the preacher in several other ways. The written discourse can be used on subsequent occasions without the necessity of renewed preparation and thus frequently saves a good deal of time and labor. The sermons remain for publication, if ever that should be desirable. Many a truly great preacher, widely useful in his day, has left but a fading, vanishing name. The successful preacher has now many opportunities to publish, and he can increase his influence by using these opportunities.

Therefore, writing has a number of advantages. What, then, are its disadvantages?

1. If writing aids in thinking, it is likely to make one largely dependent on such assistance. Especially objectionable is the fact that this practice accustoms the preacher to think logically only as fast as he can write, when it is more natural and more convenient that one should think as fast as he can talk.

2. And if writing compels the preacher to go over the material more completely, it is not always done more thoroughly. The thinking is more extensive but may be less intensive. Being obliged to run over the surface everywhere, the preacher may go beneath it nowhere. If many sermons are spoken with very superficial preparation, so with very superficial preparation are many sermons written, particularly if they are not to be read or published. There is an immense amount of strictly extemporaneous writing.

3. Similar to this last disadvantage is the consumption of so much time in the merely mechanical effort of writing—time

which might often be more profitably spent upon the thoughts of the discourse or upon the preacher's general improvement. The pastors of large churches in this country are often, indeed commonly, expected to do the work of several people. Their pastoral and social work, the various demands of their position as community leaders, the calls for denominational service, and the imperative need of constant self-improvement, all press very heavily upon overburdened pastors. It is doubtful that a pastor who preaches three times each week can write all three sermons in full.

The wise conclusion for the pastor would seem to be that he should not attempt to write all sermons, but that he should discipline himself to write often, perhaps at least one sermon a week. And the written sermon should not always be the Sunday morning sermon. It may be the evening sermon or the Wednesday night message.

If a pastor does not write a sermon in full, he should prepare a sermon brief. He should write the introduction in full, write the outline in sentence form, and then write the conclusion in full.

If a pastor does not write his sermons, he should choose some substitute for writing. For example, he may record sermons and listen to the recordings. He may have manuscripts typed from the recording. Then he can revise and improve his material. He could also do some other kind of writing to improve style.

Writing should always be done with a congregation in mind. The sermon is written to be heard. The preacher does not want to develop an essay style but an oral style. He should write as he speaks.

After the preacher has written his sermon, he should revise and rewrite. Revision is a part of writing. To examine what one has written is to discover flaws and to see the need for correction. To make these necessary revisions is to pave the way for improvement in writing.

CHAPTER 25

Imagination in Preaching

THE foregoing chapters of this study have dealt with the sermon in respect to its basic materials, its forms, functions, and style. The concluding chapters will be on methods of preparation and delivery. This chapter on Imagination lies in between as an essential consideration, for without imagination the principles of preaching cannot be utilized in effective practice. The invention of materials, the construction of discourse, the style of expression in language and delivery are equally dependent upon it. Joseph Addison ranked a sound imagination with correct judgment and a good conscience as life's three best endowments.[1] And Henry Ward Beecher regarded it as "the most important of all the elements that go to make the preacher,"[2] that is, to make the minister in whom genuine faith, character, and consideration are taken for granted, an effective interpreter and herald. Apart from the insight and inspiration and power of a consecrated imagination, the highest intellectual and moral attainments are insufficient. It is highly necessary, therefore, for the preacher to give particular attention to the nature of imagination, its service in preaching, and the means of its cultivation.

1. THE NATURE OF IMAGINATION

Imagination is the imagining function of the mind. It is thinking by seeing, as contrasted with reasoning.

The imagination sees. Out of the material stored in the mind it creates a living world. By its forces the Parthenon is no longer a ruin, and all the Greeks yet live. The imagination gives atmosphere and stimulates individual ideas. Mere facts may make a wrong impression, but imagination clothes facts with living scenes and situations and presents the hidden truth. Imagination is the basis of all figurative language. It compares object with object, identifies the unknown and the known, and creates a new whole.[3]

The popular conception of imagination connects it with the unreal, as seeing what is not there, its product being imaginary rather than an imaginative representation of reality. In this conception it is indulgence in exaggeration and caricature and assists the orator only by producing elaborate imagery, such as sophomores affect and half-educated people admire. But modern psychology considers imagination very important because of its various influences. It is recognized as giving indispensable aid in scientific research and philosophical abstraction, in the formation of geometrical and ethical as well as artistic ideals, in the varied tasks of practical invention, and even in the comprehension and conduct of practical life.

In an excellent chapter on imagination Woodworth distinguishes it from such other mental processes as attention, perception, and reasoning.[4] These are explorative; they seek to discover facts; their concern is simply to find out what is there. Imagination, on the other hand, is manipulative; it uses facts that have already been discovered. It begins with the accumulated elements of experience, observation, and knowledge. They are the materials of imagination. The first step in the imaginative process is the recall to consciousness of material from memory; but whereas memory only seeks simple and literal reproduction, comparable to taking old photographs out of a drawer to look at, imagination proceeds to compare the recollected facts, to observe their relations, and to set them in new relationships. To quote Woodworth directly:

Sometimes it has been said that imagination consists in putting together material from different sources, but this leaves the matter in mid-air; recall can bring together facts from different sources and so afford the stimulus for an imaginative response, but the response goes beyond the mere togetherness of the stimuli. Thinking of a man and also of a horse is not inventing a centaur; there is a big jump from the juxtaposition of the data to the specific arrangement that imagination gives them. The man plus the horse may give no response at all or may give many other responses besides that of a centaur, for example, the picture of the man and the horse politely bowing to each other. The particular manipulation, or imaginative response, that is made varies widely; sometimes it consists in taking things apart rather than putting them together, as when you imagine how a house would look with the evergreen tree beside it cut down; always it consists in putting the data into new relationships.[5]

In this respect, imagination also differs from reasoning, although they are closely parallel. The first stage of each is getting data together—premises, facts. The final responses are similar,

but imagination is freer and more variable. Reason is governed by a very precise aim, to see the actual meaning of the combined premises, that is, it is exploratory; while imagination, though it is usually more or less steered either by a definite aim, or by some bias in the direction of agreeable results, has after all much more latitude. It is seeking not a relationship that is there but one that can be put there.[6]

In this meaning imagination is thus closely bound to reality.

It is creative in that it originates meritorious ideas, embodying them in poetry, prose, the material works of inventive genius, and the numberless hypotheses of science. There are, however, limitations to the creative activity of this type of imagination. The man who would visualize anything both new and valuable must bind his supposed novelty to reality by bonds which cannot break. The region of reality may itself be whatever one pleases to select, ranging from the Dismal Swamp in Virginia to the Sistine Madonna. Once adopted, far-reaching variations may be imposed upon it. But no imaginative strength can overcome those fixed barriers which inhere in the nature of things as they are; a new combination of colors may be imagined, but not a new color.[7]

Imagination, that is to say, is under the control of reality. Mental manipulation, however, always moves at this high level. It is sometimes free and at play, as, for example, when a child plays with its toys, and in daydreams (including reverie and worry) and dreams.[8] In these there is no control, either by objective fact or intelligent criticism and purpose. The mind simply plays along in the instinctive desire for mastery over circumstance or some other gratification and so fabricates all sorts of fanciful and absurd mental pictures. For this ungoverned, unprincipled process is reserved the term *fancy*. Ruskin and others have made a sharp distinction between fancy and imagination as representing two distinct mental faculties. But the proper distinction is not between faculties, but between principles of operation in the mental process. The one is free; the other is controlled.

Fancy is the inventive power of the mind working without reference to fact and eliciting from it more than it yields to observation. The artists are always careful to make and to keep this distinction. An artist may endow a sunrise or a sunset with the light that never was on land or sea. But he may not make his sun rise in the west and set in the east.[9]

Mental manipulation is called *fancy* when playing on the mere surface of things, *imagination* when penetrating to the heart, the essence; *fancy* when sportive or cold, *imagination* when passionate, or at least serious; *fancy* when it is careless of facts and ends, *imagination* when it gives facts a new radiance and vital significance.

Imagination should be thought of not simply as the imaging function of the mind, but that function controlled by facts, with the end result of placing facts in new combinations and relationships. Cadman called it "the power to evoke the prophetically new from material which is familiarly old."[10] It is at once reproductive or descriptive, constructive or synthesizing, and creative or analogical. For example, it sees the familiar picture, often repeated in experience, of a farmer sowing in a field; it constructs in kaleidoscopic fashion a whole series of pictures portraying the drama of the field from planting to harvest, making a fresh synthesis of facts; and then it proceeds to show the analogy between that drama and the experience of the evangelist and teacher in the field of life. Or in the worshipful mood of the poet, it contemplates a sunset, and sings:

> Hills, wrapped in gray, standing along the west;
> Clouds, dimly lighted, gathering slowly;
> The star of peace at watch above the crest—
> Oh, holy, holy, holy!
>
> We know, O Lord, so little what is best;
> Wingless, we move so lowly;
> But in thy calm all-knowledge let us rest—
> Oh, holy, holy, holy![11]

2. THE ROLE OF IMAGINATION IN PREACHING

1. Beginning at the point of technique it may be said that imagination is of indispensable value in the construction of discourse. To give familiar materials any fresh interest, they must be brought into new combination; and to form a discourse at all, the materials must be made into a complete and symmetrical structure. Piles of bricks and lumber and sand are as much a house as the mere piling up of thoughts will constitute a discourse. The builder of palace or cabin works by constructive imagination; and it is the same faculty that builds a speech. In fact imagination, the wonder-worker, does much more than this. It is only a lower imagination that takes fragments of material and builds them, each fragment preserving its individuality, into a new structure; high, intense imagination fuses the materials, reduces them to their natural elements, and makes them into a structure possessing complete unity. The one process is a new composition of fragments; the other is a new organization of elements. The one cements the materials together, or at best welds them together; the other makes them grow together by

furnishing a principle of vitality which takes up the analyzed material and organizes it according to new laws. Imagination does not create thought in the primary sense, but it organizes thought into forms as new as the equestrian statue of bronze is unlike the metallic ores when they lay in the mine. This constructing, fashioning, organizing function of the imagination is exercised in forming a poem or a story but still more in forming a discourse, where there is far greater need of unity, symmetry, and adaptation to a specific design.

And not only is it needed in constructing discourses, but every paragraph, every sentence are properly a work of imagination, a work of art. The painter, sculptor, or architect does not design merely the general outline of his work and leave the details to chance. The whole is but the parts taken together. Each part must have a certain completeness in itself and yet must be in itself incomplete, being but a fragment of one whole. So must it be in the construction of discourse.

The precise functions of imagination in the invention of thought have not yet been settled by psychologists. There can be no doubt that it does somehow aid in penetrating to the heart of a subject and developing it from within, that it thus assists the work of original analysis, as well as that of exposition.

2. Imagination also enables the preacher to clothe ideas in familiar and revealing imagery. It gives thought a definite shape, concrete expression. This excites the imagination of another and thus affects his feelings. Real objects affect the feelings most powerfully, and images more closely resemble real objects than do mere ideas. If, instead of dwelling upon the idea of benevolence, we present the image of a benevolent man or a benevolent action, it is much more affecting. And a picture of reality is often more convincing than an argument.

> The poets, the dramatists, the prophets move us more strongly than the logicians, because they bring facts, situations, problems alive for us as our own concern.[12]

And whether the particular idea can or cannot be converted into an image, the preacher may group around it, by resemblance or analogy or by contrast, some other idea or ideas which can be formed into images and which will reflect their sensations upon the main idea. This is illustration, with all its power not only to please but to assist comprehension, to carry conviction, and to awaken emotion.

Therefore, it is mainly through imagination that preachers touch the feelings and so make truth affect the will, which is the end and the very essence of eloquence. And, on the other hand, emotion kindles imagination. Love, for instance, will give the dullest mind some sparks of imagination. Anger, overwhelming grief, passionate supplication, will often struggle to express itself by the boldest images. Thus imagination and feeling continually act and react, giving each other more intensity.

3. Another use of imagination, though not wholly distinct from the last, is in realizing and depicting what the Scriptures reveal. It has already been noted that much of the Bible consists of narrative and that the preacher should be able vividly to describe its scenes and events.

One can only make history real by an imaginative revival in his own mind of the scenes, persons, and events of the past, by thinking oneself back into a period, or bringing it forward to our own time, and mentally observing and participating in what transpires. This is true, for example, of the life of our Lord himself, as C. R. Brown so well says:

The bare events even of that matchless life which has come to be the light of the world have little power to change and to move the hearts of men until they are interpreted and related to the immediate interests of these lives of ours. It is for us, every man in his own order and according to the grace given him, to repeat and realize in our own experiences the majestic truths suggested by the incarnation, the transfiguration, the crucifixion, the resurrection. We are set not only to revere, but according to the measure of our ability to reproduce the life which was in him. And the minds of men can only be inspired to these high endeavors as the sacred, significant events which lie in the remote past are made to live before their eyes.[13]

"Historical imagination," in reproducing the past, is one of the most powerful allies of preaching. In its exercise one must take great care to direct and control it by thorough knowledge of the times reproduced and true sympathy with their spirit, or the preacher will carry back his own experiences and modern conceptions and make, as historical description often has done, an utterly erroneous representation. But with this caution, historical imagination is indispensable, not only to description of biblical history but to the correct comprehension of the whole system of doctrine and duty, for all rests upon a basis of fact.

And not only is imagination needed for the past, it is requisite if pastors are to conceive correctly and realize vividly the scriptural revelations concerning the unseen world and the eternal future. Faith believes these revelations, and imagination, aroused and used by faith, makes the things unseen and eternal a definite reality to the mind, so that they affect the feelings almost like real objects and become an influence in our earthly life. It may also to some extent fill out the biblical pictures of the unseen world by following the analogies of this world; but here there is demanded a moderation and reserve, a care in distinguishing between the revealed and the supposed, which in some books and many sermons are sadly needed.

4. Of equal value is what may be called "sympathetic imagination." It has been said of George Eliot that

she had the secret not only of reading the diverse hearts of men but of creeping into their skins, watching the world with their eyes, feeling the latent background of conviction, discerning theory and habit.[14]

It is that sympathetic visualization of the experiences and problems of others that makes any writer or preacher interesting and challenging. Imaginative participation in the fortunes and feelings of his people enables the preacher, as nothing else can, to make the healing and guiding connections between life and truth which alone make his preaching worthwhile. Ezekiel set an example for prophets of all time. He said in a critical time, "I sat where they sat, and remained there astonished among them seven days" (Ezek. 3:15). He put himself in their place. He contemplated the whole situation until their doom became his own sorrow. The preacher who sits where young people are until he knows their hearts, their motives, and temptations and aspirations, until he is young with them, will be heard by them. The same is true in respect to all persons and classes and groups.

Sympathetic imagination lends appropriateness to preaching. For the pastor to put himself in the place of others will give their needs a new importance and urgency. It helps solve the problems of freshness and of holding attention. When a preacher touches a personal problem or interest, shows knowledge and just appreciation of a person's point of view, he will not need to ask for that person's attention or catch the person by subtle artistry. Such a preacher speaks with authority. He has the secret of power. On the other hand, if the preacher is mentally lazy or selfish and will not take time and trouble to get into the life of people, if he chooses to live in a world pleasant to himself and is content to generalize about truth, he will inevitably be academic, conventional, and dull—and futile. George Fox's prayer is properly every preacher's prayer: "I have prayed to be baptized into a sense of all conditions, that I might be able to know the needs and feel the sorrows of all."

3. MEANS OF CULTIVATING THE IMAGINATION

In some degree all people possess the power of imagination. Like all mental processes, its qualities depend on natural endowments and cultural development. Some people seem to have what may be called imaginative genius. Poets, it is said, are born not made. But even poets, artists, and inventive geniuses have to cultivate their native gifts. And average men, subjecting themselves to an equal discipline with a Shakespeare, a Michelangelo, an Edison, always make progress. Imagination, whatever its original promise, depends upon and responds to cultivation.

How it may be cultivated becomes apparent when the nature of imagination is recalled, namely, that it is the mental process by which facts of experience are brought together, set in their true or actual relations to one another, and rearranged in new combinations and relationships. Facts, reality, recollection, discrimination, inventive manipulation—these are the elements of a sound imagination. It follows that imagination suffers in quality when it lacks facts, and its possibilities increase with the acquisition of facts. But facts are so much lumber if there is no architect, no artist, in the soul. The principles of reproductive, constructive, creative imagination must be learned from men of imaginative genius. It should be observed, also, that the practical value to others of a preacher's imaginative power depends upon the imagery by which he expresses what he sees. An unfamiliar picture may mean as little as an abstract idea and be even more misleading. Many a preacher wonders why his vision of truth, which stirs him so profoundly, falls flat, not realizing that his words gave no familiar pictures. His hearers were farmers, perhaps, while his pictures were of city life, problems, scenery. It is, accordingly, necessary to the cultivation of effective imagination for the preacher to see with his people's eyes and imagery. Still further, in preaching it is the task of imagination to relate the seen to the unseen, the actual to the ideal, the present to the future, the transient to the eternal. That suggests the need of something beyond rhetoric and logic; it calls for what Isaiah did in the year that King Uzziah died, and what the psalmist did when by reasoning he could find no harmony between human fortune and human character—it calls for worship, prayer, spiritual meditation. Jesus had his wilderness and lonely mountain, Paul had his Arabia, and every man has his closet.

As practical disciplines of the imagination, then, the following may be suggested:

1. Study nature and art in order to gain a rich factual knowledge of the world, together with its treasure of aesthetic and spiritual values. A certain indefinable sympathy exists, by a law of our being, between external nature and man. Its forms and colors have a meaning more subtle than language conveys and excite in us strange longings of soul. The thoughtful observation of nature may be aided by science. The systematic study of the

natural world reveals new and wonderful things and teaches us to read the handwriting of God. Geology acquaints us with earth's past; astronomy introduces us to the glories of the wonder-crowded universe till the "music of the spheres" attains for us a sublime, orchestral grandeur, an unearthly sweetness, a wealth of precious meaning. If the pastor wishes for power of imagination, let him commune with nature.

Nature, however, is by most people imperfectly understood and appreciated until properly interpreted by an artist. It is possible for a person to grow up among glorious mountains or beside the sea and yet know little of their meaning or of their inspiration, until some high priest of nature teaches him how to see and comprehend and sympathize.

Sculpture, painting, architecture, and music have a strange power to develop the imagination in general and sometimes to stimulate it for particular efforts, and they can be devoid of interest to none who possess imagination in even a moderate degree. When Andrew Fuller stopped suddenly among the architectural glories of Cambridge and proposed that his guide go home and discuss the doctrine of justification with him, he betrayed that deficiency of imagination which is conspicuous in the structure and the style of his otherwise admirable sermons. There is many a preacher who could tell how some picture, perhaps casually looked at, has helped him in making a sermon: there is many a one utterly unable to tell how much the general study of works of art has contributed to develop his imagination.

2. Study imaginative literature (drama, poetry, fiction) in order to learn not only what people of imagination are able to see, but where they see it and how they portray their vision in vivid scenes and gripping imagery.

To be sure, all literature is the servant of imagination in the degree that it makes knowledge more accurate, leads us into wider ranges of truth, and sets facts in their organic relationships. But poetry and drama and certain types of fiction express truth in picturesque and emotional language, in moving scenes and episodes that challenge the reader's imagination more than his reason, and so inspire his own powers of pictorial realization and inventiveness. The poets are accessible to all, and they are excellent teachers. They see the analogies of external nature to moral and religious truth as most people cannot. From them the preacher may learn how to observe and compare, how to depict and interpret. And it is not necessarily those poets who seem to the average reader to show most imagination, but those who most kindle the imagination that will be most useful. In this respect, the poems of Wordsworth and the Brownings are much more profitable than those of Moore and Scott. The best poet awakens the imagination, gives it general direction, stimulates it by some of the most suggestive details, and leaves it to do all the rest for itself. In order to receive this benefit, one must study poetry.

There is much highly imaginative prose which has a similar value. Fiction would, if properly managed, be to some preachers exceedingly profitable in respect to imagination and literary taste. As a rule, one should read only the very best works of the very best novelists; and he should never read two novels in succession but always put between them several works of a very different kind. The danger in reading fiction is that it may leave the reader too passive, giving him passive enjoyment without rousing him, as the poet does, to exercise his own imagination in order to see and utilize fully what is said. This, however, is a matter of lassitude or alertness and purpose in the reader.

Become at home in this imaginary world (of the fiction-writer); know it as if you were an observer on the scene; become a member of its population, willing to befriend its characters and able to participate in its happenings by sympathetic insight, as you would do in the actions and sufferings of a friend. If you can do this, the elements of fiction will cease to be so many isolated pawns moved about mechanically on a chessboard. You will have found the connections which vitalize them into the members of a living society.[15]

Moreover, the great orators and preachers give examples of a proper use of imagination. If one wishes to stimulate in himself the desire for affluence of imaginative thought and diction, let him read Plato, Cicero, Chrysostom, Jeremy Taylor, Milton,

Burke, Chalmers; if he wishes to discipline himself into a more serious and controlled use of imagination, so that it is appropriately subordinated to other faculties, let him read Demosthenes, Tacitus, Daniel Webster, Robert Hall. In general, it must be remembered that here, as elsewhere, appetite is not always a sure guide.

3. Keep close to the people of your time, particularly the people of your congregation. Sympathetic imagination is not possible otherwise. In his chapters on mental imagery and mental systems, C. S. Gardner shows the importance of intimate fellowship with and close observation of people and their ways of life.

There is laid upon the preacher the necessity of entering, as far as is humanly possible, into the mental systems of his hearers and of limiting himself as closely as practicable to the use of meanings that are common to his own and the various minds of his auditors. Before him are represented mental divergences arising from organic differences, differences of occupation, various types and stages of culture, and usually also divergences arising from various mental environments in which the hearers have lived. . . . And his disadvantage is increased by the fact that he has usually had special training in an order of ideas and terms which in recent times seem to be becoming less and less familiar to the people. This does not mean that he should quit studying theology, but that he needs more and more to study the daily life of the people as well. It is obvious to one who closely studies preaching today how comparatively few preachers realize the extent to which they are not understood or are positively misunderstood, in their solemn deliverances. They simply do not know how seriously they are insulated mentally from the masses of the people.[16]

This insulation can be broken by pastoral interest and association that will supply the factual and emotional materials of a sympathetic imagination. If the preacher would know how to interest his people and make those connections between the actual and the ideal in terms that catch and grip them, he should go among them and learn their attitudes, their words and meanings, their work and play, their morals and religion. He can then give himself to the unselfish task of finding in

God's eternal truth a definite word for definite need.

4. Keep close to the eternal source of spiritual vision. Imagination finds its inspiration and power in the upper room today as on that wonderful day of Pentecost; expectant waiting, continuing prayer, reflection upon the Word of the gospel, faith—these were the background. And what happened? Tongues of fire and a rushing sound were its open symbols, and the coming of the Holy Spirit its explanation. By the power of the Spirit these things happened: a great realization, an overwhelming spiritual energy, and power of utterance. The eyes of their faith were opened and they saw Reality as they had never seen before. The invisible spiritual world became more real than the upper room; it was no longer remote or future. They were even now under the ruling authority of God more than under Caesar or the Sanhedrin. From that time on their imaginations—power to see and to relate facts—were given unclouded vision, their wills the strength of a rushing wind, and their speech the glow and energy of fire. That is how the spirit of God always responds to the open heart. Rhetoric, logic, psychology are the channels and instruments of preaching; the spirit of God is the source of power, as his word is the message of life.

5. Practice should be added as a constant practical necessity. The preacher must begin where he is and always do the best he can, undeterred by what others do.

The excessive display of second-rate imagination which some preachers make so offensive drives others to the opposite extreme, so that they shrink from illustration and imagery where they are really needed and never stop to consider how numerous and varied and extremely important are the functions of this much abused faculty. A person should freely exercise imagination in constructing and inventing, in picturing and illustrating, in reproducing the past and giving vivid reality to the unseen world; but one should always exercise it under the control of sound judgment and good taste, and above all of devout feeling and a solemn sense of responsibility to God. The imaginative reproduction of scenes witnessed, read, or heard of, and the imaginative construction of new scenes may be helpful or harmful to the moral nature depending upon whether these scenes are good or bad, elevating or degrading. It is impossible to estimate what a profound influence a person's imagination has upon his moral and spiritual life; and thus through these channels, as well as more directly, it has a momentous importance for the preacher in his preaching.

NOTES

1. Cited by S. Parker Cadman, *Imagination and Religion* (New York: Macmillan Co., 1926), p. 18.
2. Henry Ward Beecher, *Lectures on Preaching,* First Series (New York: Fords, Howard, & Hulbert, 1900), p. 109.
3. S. S. Curry, *Foundations of Expression* (Boston: The Expression Co., 1920), p. 145.
4. Robert S. Woodworth, *Psychology* (New York: Holt, 1921), Chapter 19.
5. Ibid., p. 520.
6. Ibid.
7. Cadman, pp. 33–34.
8. See Woodworth, pp. 485–509, for a good discussion.
9. Willard A. Sperry, *We Prophesy in Part* (New York: Harper & Bros., 1938), p. 147.
10. Cadman, p. 66.
11. John Charles McNeill, quoted in Jerome Stockard's *A Study in Southern Poetry* (New York: Neale Publishing Company, 1911).
12. Sperry, p. 76.
13. C. R. Brown, *The Art of Preaching* (New York: Macmillan Co., 1948), p. 147.
14. Lord Acton, quoted in James Reid, *In Quest of Reality* (London: Hodder & Stoughton, 1924), p. 181.
15. Mortimer J. Adler, *How to Read a Book* (New York: Simon & Schuster, 1940), p. 310.
16. C. S. Gardner, *Psychology and Preaching* (New York: Macmillan Co., 1919), p. 57.

For Further Reading:
The Style of the Sermon

Blankenship, Jane. *A Sense of Style.* Belmont, Ca.: Dickenson Publishing Co., 1968.

Buechner, Frederick. *Telling the Truth.* San Francisco: Harper & Row, 1977.

Flesch, Rudolf. *The Art of Readable Writing.* New York: Collier, 1962.

Garrison, Webb. *Creative Imagination in Preaching.* New York: Abingdon Press, 1960.

Jones, E. Winston. *Preaching and the Dramatic Arts.* New York: Macmillan Co., 1948.

Knoche, H. Gerard. *The Creative Task: Writing the Sermon.* St. Louis: Concordia, 1977.

Morris, Colin. *The Word and the Words.* Nashville, Tenn.: Abingdon Press, 1975.

Nichols, Sue. *Words on Target.* Atlanta: John Knox Press, 1963.

White, R.E.O. *A Guide to Preaching.* Grand Rapids, Mich.: Wm. B. Eerdmans, 1973.

Part VI

THE PREPARATION OF SERMONS

CHAPTER 26

General Preparation

THOSE persons who have had no experience in preaching often ask how much time is required for the preparation of a sermon. No definite answer is possible, because all of a minister's past study, all of his reading, meditation, prayer, all pastoral ministration, all observant contacts with the world of people and things contribute something to the groundwork and superstructure of every sermon. Experience warrants only the general statement that the time required in immediate preparation is in inverse ratio to the time spent in general preparation. The sermons that require least time in immediate preparation are frequently better than sermons laboriously created through long hours of intense study. This is true because they have used materials accumulated in the mind through months and years and now remembered in favorable circumstances. To both kinds of preparation, therefore, the preacher must give serious attention.

More than once in previous chapters it has been pointed out that preaching requires constant study. Such study will have both immediate and continuing value. For one thing, regular study is necessary if a person's Sunday by Sunday preaching is to be effective. Each sermon needs the keen edge of good preparation. Jowett declared, "Cases are won in the chambers."[1] Spiritual victories are won in the study. Also, study is essential if the preacher is to grow in ability and in knowledge. Successful farmers are constantly building their soil. The effective preacher must add to his spiritual and mental resources. The mind will produce a good "harvest" only when it is improved.

In order for a preacher to do continuing study, he must have a place to work. His study should be a definite place that belongs solely to him. It should not be a part of an office or a part of a living room. It must be a place where the minister can be alone, where he can work at his books. Often a study will be provided by the church. Occasionally it will be necessary for a person to provide his own study. An extra classroom may become the study. The spare bedroom may also become a study. One man developed the storage space in his carport as a study. The room was just four feet by twenty feet; therefore, he had room only for shelves and a desk. But there was no telephone in the small room, and he could work without interruptions. When one pastor could not find a definite place to study either at the church building or at home, he rented an office for his study.

The location of the study will depend upon the immediate circumstances in each pastorate. At one period in a pastor's life it may be better for him to have a study in the church building. At another period, when his children are away from home, it may be best for him to have a study at home. The primary thing is that a minister have a place set aside for his private use. The study is most important, for the study is where he will meditate upon the Scriptures, pray for his people and their needs, dream dreams, and have visions of what can be done for God.

If a pastor's time in the study is to be most meaningful, it must be carefully organized. It should be study according to a plan. Every pastor will need certain hours each day to give to uninterrupted study. Generally, a pastor will study in the morning, four hours a day, five days a week. This will give him twenty hours for uninterrupted work. A preacher should not hesitate to ask his congregation for this time. If a preacher tells them that he desires certain hours each day for uninterrupted study and then proves on the succeeding Sundays that he has really studied and not done something else, they will not only be glad to let him have his mornings, but they will be proud that they have a minister who can preach.[2]

Pastors organize such study time differently. Many study different things each day, allowing time for sermon preparation. Others will study only one subject each day, leaving some time for sermon preparation. The actual plan is not as important as the fact of some plan. Any plan is much better than none.

There will be other hours in the day when a pastor can study. He may reserve all of his "news reading" for times when he is waiting for appointments or for meals. He may also have times in the afternoon that he can set aside for study. The pastor's schedule may allow him to have time for additional study in the evening. Both Saturday and Sunday will give him hours that he can use for final preparation of sermons. Generally speaking, the minister will need forty hours each week for study, and then he will need perhaps an additional forty hours to do all of the other work a pastor must do. While an eighty-hour week may sound unrealistic, it is the kind of work load many pastors face.

NOTES

1. J. H. Jowett, *The Preacher: His Life and Work* (New York: Harper & Bros., 1912), p. 113.
2. Charles Edward Jefferson, *The Minister as Prophet* (New York: Thomas Y. Crowell & Co., 1905), p. 83.

CHAPTER 27

Special Preparation

NO matter how widely read and full of general knowledge and thought a preacher may be, he must yet make special accumulation of materials for each sermon. Many a preacher, particularly after he has had long years of experience and has accumulated a considerable amount of sermon stock, has failed at this point. He depends on general instead of special preparation. No person can keep fresh who does not put fresh material in every sermon—something which particularly belongs to that sermon and occasion and fits no others so well. It is imperative, therefore, that the preacher should also give his very careful thought not only to his general stock but to what could be called "materials provided at the time."

Probably no two preachers have exactly the same method of procedure in immediate preparation. But a review of the self-reported habits of outstanding preachers reveals several constants.[1] Dr. George A. Buttrick, out of his own practice, suggested the following:[2] (1) Choose your subject and text. The order of choice will vary. (2) Study the text in its context until you get its meaning and its mood. (3) Study the text in commentaries. (4) Pass the text through your own experience, jotting down any ideas that occur, any reminders of relevant happenings, quotations, passages in books. Often in a day or two an amorphous mass of material, more than can be used, will be at hand. (5) Brood over the material in mind. "Let the sun go down a day or two upon a sermon: the subconscious mind must do its part." (6) "Let the imagination have large liberty." (7) Then write the sermon—not as an essay is written, with only the subject in mind, but as a sermon—with the eyes of the congregation looking at the writer over his desk. "Let the sermon be written. If not written on paper, it must be written just as scrupulously on the tablet of the mind." The procedure of Dr. Henry Sloane Coffin was as follows: (1) Decide upon a pressing need of the congregation. (2) Select the aspect of the gospel which meets that need. (3) Look for a text that embodies the message. (4) Study the text for its full meaning. (5) Make an outline with a few notes as to illustrations. (6) Write it out whether it is to be read or delivered extemporaneously. (7) Correct and polish it. Dr. S. Parkes Cadman's practice was (1) to choose a suitable theme and a text that fits; (2) to assemble all the literature available on the subject; (3) to mull it over; (4) to write the sermon; (5) to revise it carefully; (6) to make an abstract for pulpit use. Dr. H. A. Prichard[3] began with a theme, "suggested usually by some conversation that had been held in the recent past, by some episode or observation or experience or sentence in a book." He then found a text, preferably one that lended itself to illustration and elaboration. His next step was "to think of all references, historical, biographical, scientific, theological, personal, that may bear on it, with a view to weaving these somewhere into the fabric of the sermon. Gradually, by a process of mental digestion, this matter begins to assume a systematic shape." On Friday, he noted down the main sequence of thought, with illustrations, and on Saturday evening wrote down on a small sheet of paper the essential points for pulpit use. "No thought is given to any verbal form of expression."

In his inspiring volume *The Preacher: His Life and Work,* Dr. J. H. Jowett emphasized several things as having great value to himself. (1) Preachers ought to prepare and preach their own sermons. "You will find that the freshness of your own originality will give new flavor and zest to the feast which you set before your people."[4] (2) One ought not to preach on a theme too soon after it occurs to him.

I think it frequently happens that we go into the pulpit with truth that is undigested and with messages that are immature. Our minds have not done their work thoroughly, and, when we present our work to the public, there is a good deal of floating sediment in our thought, and a consequent cloudiness about our words. It is a good thing to put a subject away to mature and clarify.[5]

(3) "Let the preacher bind himself to the pursuit of clear conceptions, and let him aid his pursuit by demanding that every sermon he preaches shall express its theme and purpose in a sentence as lucid as his powers can command."[6] It was Dr. Jowett's conviction that "no sermon is ready for preaching, ready for writing out, until we can express it in a short, pregnant sentence as clear as a crystal."[7] (4) Very suggestive is Dr. Jowett's habit of imagining how other preachers might deal with his theme.

I ask, —how would Newman regard this subject? How would Spurgeon approach it? How would Dale deal with it? By what road would Bushnell come up to it? Where would Alexander Whyte lay hold of it? . . . I have looked at the theme through many windows, and some things appear which I should never have seen had I confined myself to the windows of my own heart and mind.[8]

(5) Another practice of his was to think of at least a dozen men and women he knew as he sat down to prepare his exposition and to ask constantly how he might help one or another:

What relation has this teaching to that barrister? How can the truth be related to that doctor? What have I here for that keenly nervous man with the artistic temperament? And there is that poor body upon whom the floods of sorrow have been rolling their billows for many years—what about her?[9]

So he kept his touch with life and sought to relate truth to actual experience. (6) Dr. Jowett wrote his sermons, taking great care to make his expression fresh and free from the much-worn phraseology that has lost its significance. His advice on this point is, "Do not foolishly attach value to carelessness and disorder. Pay sacred heed to the ministry of style. When you have discovered a jewel give it the most appropriate setting."[10] (7) Finally, he put great emphasis upon the prayerful attitude of the preacher as he seeks to interpret the Scriptures. "Unless our study is also our oratory, we shall have no visions. . . . Even hard work is fruitless unless we have 'the fellowship of the Spirit.' "[11]

Most preachers follow a similar procedure in immediate preparation. The following steps represent a synthesis of these methods.

1. The first step is to have many texts which have grown and developed in the preacher's mind. They have grown in his "homiletical garden." Preachers speak of "getting up" sermons, but no one can "get up" a sermon. A rose grows; an ear of corn grows; so, a sermon grows.

Henry Ward Beecher said that his sermons were like apples in a drawer. He would go each week and pick the two ripest.

But Gerald Kennedy was right in declaring, "There is a kind of preaching which seems like a new house—too new, and still in the process of construction."[12] It is essential for the preacher to have many ideas "incubating" in his mind.

2. The second step in immediate preparation is to choose two specific texts and/or ideas for next Sunday. (Only one text or idea need be chosen by the pastor who preaches only on Sunday morning.) These should be chosen early in the week. If the preacher has no special inspiration, he should choose two worthy texts and begin to study. Inspiration often follows hard work.

3. Having decided upon two texts and their corresponding subjects, then the preacher should write down everything he can about these subjects. He should record his own interpretations, thoughts, impressions, and illustrations. For the preacher to draw upon his own materials first will have at least two values. For one thing, this process will develop his own originality. For a second thing, this recording of ideas and materials will make them easier to remember.

4. The fourth step in immediate preparation is for the

preacher to gather materials from every available source. He should consult commentaries, Bible dictionaries, and related books. Sermons on the same theme will be helpful. The preacher should locate all the material which will help him develop the subject.

5. The next step which many ministers follow is to make a tentative plan or outline. The text may have provided a natural outline, a plan may have come from previous study, or a plan may need to be developed. However, it is important for the preacher to make a tentative arrangement of the material under the subject which he has chosen. While this particular plan may not be final, it will prove to be very helpful.

6. Some few ministers then take an additional step in immediate preparation. They speak through their material. They may do this quietly to themselves, or they may get on their feet and speak in the same manner that they would before a congregation. Often this process will help the preacher to gather additional material. New material comes to him as he speaks through the sermon. Also, this process will help the preacher to develop an "oral" style. This is essential because a sermon is prepared to be heard.

7. The next step in immediate preparation is to make any necessary changes in the plan of the sermon. In speaking through the sermon the preacher may have discovered that it was poorly arranged and did not flow easily. Now is the time for the preacher to refine the organization of the sermon.

8. Finally, the preacher is ready for the last step—the writing of the sermon. Ideally, every sermon should be written in full. Certainly one sermon should be written in full each week. The minimum writing for each sermon would be to write the introduction in full, to write a detailed outline of the body of the sermon, and to write the conclusion in full.

Every preacher must find the procedure that suits him best. But there is no easy way. Self-discipline is necessary, and method must be improved until the product represents one's best effort and can stand the essential tests of good preaching. The student preacher needs to be warned against the peril of falling into careless and unworthy habits of sermon-making. Occupied principally with his theological studies, it is easy for him to take other ministers' outlines or entire sermons and otherwise to deal superficially and even immorally with his subjects. He should remember that it is easier to form a habit than to break one. At the cost of time and great difficulty, therefore, he should find and incorporate in his early methods what will not need to be abandoned later. It would be of immense value to the young preacher to examine critically the habits of others and mark out for himself a procedure to which he can give himself wholeheartedly.

NOTES

1. For many examples of immediate preparation see H. C. Brown Jr., *Southern Baptist Preaching* (Nashville, Tenn.: Broadman Press, 1959) and *More Southern Baptist Preaching* (Nashville, Tenn.: Broadman Press, 1964); see also Donald Macleod, *Here is My Method* (Westwood, N.J.: Fleming H. Revell, 1952).
2. George A. Buttrick, *Jesus Came Preaching* (New York: Charles Scribner's Sons, 1931), pp. 152–62.
3. H. A. Prichard, *The Minister, the Method, and the Message* (New York: Charles Scribner's Sons, 1932), p. 181. The reports on Dr. Coffin, Dr. Cadman, and others also are given in Dr. Prichard's book, pp. 147–83.
4. J. H. Jowett, *The Preacher: His Life and Work* (New York: Harper & Bros., 1912), p. 129.
5. Ibid., p. 130.
6. Ibid., pp. 133–34.
7. Ibid., p. 133.
8. Ibid., p. 127.
9. Ibid., p. 136.
10. Ibid., p. 139.
11. Ibid., p. 141.
12. Gerald Kennedy, *His Word Through Preaching* (New York: Harper & Bros., 1947), p. 41.

CHAPTER 28

Preparation of Special Types of Sermons

A SIGNIFICANT segment of the preaching which a pastor must do is occasional preaching. In this chapter some suggestions are offered for sermons on particular occasions, or for sermons addressed to particular groups.

1. FUNERAL SERMONS

In some places, especially though not exclusively in the cities, the current demand for brevity in religious services, with perhaps other causes also, has induced some decline in the practice of preaching set funeral sermons. People often prefer a simple religious service with sometimes a brief memorial address or several addresses in cases of special interest. Yet, there is still in many areas a powerful sentiment in favor of funeral sermons. The average pastor will have more calls for funeral sermons than for any other special type. The preacher should know how to meet this demand. Besides, much that needs to be said about funeral sermons will apply as well to the short personal address as to the more elaborate and formal discourse.

When people are bereaved, they feel a special need of God's

mercy and grace. The pastor should gladly take the opportunity to recommend the gospel of consolation and to impress the need of personal faith so that people may be ready to live and ready to die. Some regular hearers will be then better prepared to receive the word. Also, those persons who rarely attend worship services may be open to the Christian message. It is highly important, therefore, that funeral sermons should clearly point out the way of life to people and tenderly invite them to Jesus Christ.

Moreover, in the freshness of grief people instinctively desire to give, or at least to hear, some eulogy for the departed. All nations have had some method, by speech or song or broken lament, of satisfying the desire. That Christian ministers are expected to perform this function, while it sometimes places them in a difficult position, is yet a sign of their influence and a means of using that influence to good purpose. Yet the preacher must remember that he is not a mere eulogist of the dead, but that his task is to preach the gospel to the living. Accordingly, his words about the departed must be only a part of what he says, usually but a small part, and must be scrupulously true, though not necessarily all the truth. When the departed was a Christian, he should speak chiefly of that fact, bringing out anything in the character or course of life which he knows and which others will recognize to be worthy of imitation. When the departed was not a Christian, he may sometimes lawfully speak comforting words concerning those things which especially endeared the deceased to his friends. But this must be done without exaggeration. It is a solemn duty to avoid saying anything which suggests that these good points of character afford any ground of hope for eternity. In general, the preacher ought to exercise reserve in what he says of the departed; and in the case of wicked people, it is frequently in the best taste and shows the most real kindness to say nothing.

On those occasions when the funeral message is a part of the funeral service, that message should be characterized by several qualities. First of all, it should be biblical in content. It should have the spirit of "Thus saith the Lord." In times of sorrow people want to hear some sure word from God. Then the funeral message should be brief. Since the entire funeral service will probably be not more than thirty minutes in length, the message should be about eight to twelve minutes. Also a preacher's funeral messages should be marked by variety. Some ministers use only a few ideas for their funeral preaching. Others try to prepare for each service and thereby develop a wholesome variety. Service books for ministers will have suggestions. Dr. A. W. Blackwood's *The Funeral* has a section of sermon suggestions, giving texts and ideas.[1] The preacher should develop his own collection of ideas.

2. ACADEMIC AND ANNIVERSARY SERMONS

Sermons at institutions of learning or on occasions of literary interest are often not well managed. The preacher imagines that he must not give a regular gospel sermon but must deal with matters highly erudite or metaphysical. It is really desirable on such occasions to preach upon eminently evangelical topics, the very heart of the gospel. Science and erudition are the everyday work of these professors and students; from the preacher they had much rather hear something else. Even those who care nothing for religion will feel, as persons of taste, that it is congruous, is becoming, for a preacher to preach the gospel; while the truly pious, worrying about their unconverted associates, will long to have the preacher offer saving truth to them in the most earnest and practical way. Of course, the sermon should have point, force, freshness; and the associations of the occasion may sometimes suggest slight peculiarities of allusion, illustration, and style; but it ought to be a sermon full of Christ.

Preachers are often called on to deliver sermons at various kinds of anniversaries. In general, such sermons are never so acceptable to devout hearts and never so appropriate to the goals sought on these occasions as when they are filled with the very essence of the gospel. For example, the "annual sermon" before an association, convention, or other religious body should not be soaring, philosophic, ambitious, but should seek by earnest, direct, and moving presentation of gospel truths and motives to arouse a deep religious feeling. It is a wise minister who prayerfully avoids making a show on such occasions but sincerely endeavors to bring his colleagues with himself nearer to his Master. Even where some particular doctrine or topic, historical, memorial, or other, is assigned him, the preacher should strive so to present his theme so as to awaken and encourage devout sentiments.

And the same principles hold true in regard to other anniversary sermons. It sometimes occurs that a society, religious or benevolent, celebrates its anniversary by having a sermon preached. Besides the sermon, it may be remarked in passing, the minister should look well to the other services of the occasion and see that they are not only suitable and impressive but solemn and spiritually profitable. Occasions of this kind often give the preacher an opportunity to reach people who seldom go to church, or to his church, and whom he may never meet again. It will be profitable both for him and for them, if by skillful and deeply earnest handling of his theme and his opportunity, he might be able to win and edify the souls of his hearers. The preacher cannot afford to be merely the head man of the parade at such time; he must be the devout and inspiring soul of the occasion.

3. REVIVAL SERMONS

The phrase *revival sermons* is not altogether a suitable one; yet, it is readily understood to mean those sermons which are especially appropriate in revival meetings where the principal object is to arouse those who are not Christians and win converts.[2] It is obvious that in their general conduct and treatment discourses for these occasions should not materially differ from other sermons. Yet in the choice of topics for successive presentation, there are some points of special interest which make these discourses somewhat peculiar and warrant particular discussion. Sometimes the pastor may have to conduct his own revial services, and this is an exceedingly desirable thing for him to do. At other times he may be called on to aid a fellow pastor in a series of meetings. In these meetings he will preach once, and sometimes, two or three times each day. Thus the selection, order, and treatment of his subjects are matters of importance and sometimes of difficulty. So varied are these occasions of revival and so different their demands that it would be impossible to make rules to cover all cases; and yet a few practical suggestions concerning the general character and management of revival sermons may be useful.

1. They should be short. Since the preacher has just a few days and an abundance of material, he may be tempted to increase the length of the sermons. This is always a mistake. The people may be exhausted by coming often to successive meetings. Also, there are other elements of the service besides the sermons, such as the songs, the prayers, the Scripture, and the appeals.

2. They should be greatly varied in character and contents. Monotony is harmful to the best effects. In the congregation which usually gathers for these special services, there is every variety of people with every variety of attitude and opinion, and at no time is the preacher more solemnly bound to be all things to all men so that he might by all means save some. This variety of adaptation will be necessary both in the selection and the treatment of the topics of discourse. Sometimes the sermon must edify, comfort, and encourage the saints and faithful workers; at others it must rebuke the lax and cold church members whose worldliness and inconsistencies are a hindrance to the success of the gospel; now it must proclaim in no uncertain voice the fearfulness of the Lord's judgment upon sin; and again, it must gently win and urge the hesitating by presenting the inestimable love and mercy of God. With some the preacher must argue, to some he must dogmatize, others he must touch with tender anecdote and pathetic appeal; some he must rebuke with sharp attack on the conscience, others he must encourage with patient persuasion to accept now the Lord's promises. This variety is important in revival discourses.

3. They should generally follow some law of sequence. What

that order shall be will depend upon such a variety of circumstances that it would be impossible to make any general rule cover all cases; the exceptions would be likely to be more important than the rule. Yet, partly for the sake of the preacher's own mind in its logical, and therefore more efficient, working and partly for the sake of continuity of effect on the minds of others, some orderly arrangement in the series of discourses is usually desirable in revival preaching. A general sequence like the following is often useful: First address the church, seeking to arouse a more active spiritual life, to win back the worldly and inspire the pious, awakening in all the spirit of prayer and of intense concern for the salvation of others. Then present for several meetings the terrors of the law, searching the conscience, arousing concern for sin, the fear of judgment, and the consequent imperative need of a Savior. Then present the mercy and love of God as displayed in the gospel of his Son, the certainty and completeness of the divine forgiveness of sin upon repentance and faith; and finally urge immediate decision and acceptance of the gospel terms, with public confession of Christ. Whatever order is observed, none of these topics can be safely omitted from a series of revival sermons. Several of them may be combined in the same discourse, and very often the earnest presentation of one will incidentally and powerfully enforce another. Grave mistakes are often made by insisting too exclusively upon one or another of these parts of the gospel message. Especially is this true in regard to the last—the duty of immediate confession of Christ. Some take this up at once and insist upon it all through the meetings to the slighting of the topics which naturally and logically precede it. It is to be feared that many superficial persons are thus persuaded to make a public confession of religion who have had no true conviction of sin, no real sense of their real need of the Savior, and consequently no sound scriptural conversion.

4. They should preeminently exemplify a sound, thoroughgoing, and complete gospel preaching. There is much so-called revival preaching which sadly lacks this character. That which is called revival preaching is mere claptrap and sensationalism,

tirades of cheap wit, vulgar denunciation, extreme and one-sided statements, half-truths, and specious errors. An earnest and loving, but at the same time faithful and strong, presentation of pure biblical truth on the great matters of sin, judgment, atonement, salvation, regeneration, grace, repentance, and faith is the distinctive and emphatic need of the revival preaching of this age. Revival preaching should not be primarily bad news about people; it should be good news about what God has done in Jesus Christ.

4. SERMONS TO CHILDREN

Work for the children and young people is one of the current movements in the church. It is necessary to give particular attention to the subject of preaching to children. Suggestions on this subject will also relate to the less formal addresses to children in the Sunday school, in Bible school, and other occasions. There is likely to be too broad a difference in style and tone between sermons to children and speeches to them. If the sermons could be a little more familiar and the speeches a good deal more serious than is commonly the case, then suggestions for the one could, without any appearance of incongruity, apply to the other.

Everyone notices how few persons succeed decidedly well in speaking to children. But many preachers possess greater power in this respect than they have ever exercised, because they have never devoted to the subject much reflection, observation, or careful practice. These powers can be developed by giving attention to certain facts and principles.

In general, in preaching to children the three primary things to do are to interest, to instruct, to impress. Speaking is in vain unless the children are interested. Grown people may pay attention to what does not deeply interest them, but children do not, perhaps they cannot. In order to interest them, there must be clarity both in plan and style; they must understand. Two favorite words with children are *pretty* and *funny*. It is well, therefore, in seeking to interest children, to use freely the beautiful and the humorous; yet, neither must be overdone. In all sermons to children there should be instruction by illustrations that will appeal to the childish mind. The themes may be the fundamental verities of religion, sin, atonement, repentance, faith, or moral virtues, such as courage, honesty, purity, unselfishness, industry, reverence. In impressing children with religious truth, care should be taken to appeal to their affections rather than to their fears. The preacher should not frighten children, but rather he should instruct them and lead them to acceptance of truth. One might add that children are not to be addressed as pious, but as needing to become so; and that they have to become Christians in essentially the same way as adults —by repentance and faith, through the renewing of the Holy Ghost. Many mistakes result from the fact that so many who speak to children seem not to understand clearly this unquestionable truth.

A few remarks concerning the occasions or services in which it is proper to preach to the children might be helpful. Naturally there is considerable diversity of practice in regard to this. It was a custom of Whitefield to address himself to the children sometimes in the midst of his sermons to the general congregation. This is an excellent method and should be often used in our regular ministry, but it is scarcely sufficient. The children should sometimes have a whole sermon to themselves. Others have had a brief address to the children before or after the regular sermon to adults. This might be good sometimes, but it would hardly be suitable or desirable every Sunday. Some preachers take the Sunday school hour for an occasional sermon to the children. Short addresses are generally better on these occasions, better both for the children and the preacher. Sometimes the method has been tried of having a separate service for the children at the same hour as the stated service for the congregation; but because it is necessary to have different preachers and rooms, it is usually inconvenient. In large churches where there are several pastors or assistants, and suitable auditoriums, this might do very well. Another method is that of having stated or occasional services for the children in the afternoon in addition to the regular services. But some have objected that separate services for children set them apart in worship when it would be better for the whole family to worship together. Another way is to devote some morning service to the children. Let the whole service be theirs. Make it shorter than usual, and let them feel that it is their special occasion. The adults—mostly parents or others interested in children—will usually gladly cooperate with this arrangement. In fact, some have been known to prefer the children's sermon to their own because they understood it better!

5. SERMONS FOR OTHER SPECIAL CLASSES

For various reasons the preacher may find it desirable, and sometimes even necessary, to preach to many special groups. Sometimes this will be in connection with an anniversary, a celebration, a banquet, a convention, or a club meeting. Thus, the pastor might sometimes preach especially to the aged, to the bereaved, to young men or women, to mothers or fathers, to merchants, to lawyers, to doctors, to teachers, to laborers, or to businessmen. It is easy to see how occasions for this kind of preaching will frequently arise. It will be the pastor's privilege and duty to make the best of such opportunities.

It is not necessary to discuss each of these groups of hearers and the best ways of preaching to them; but a few general suggestions, applicable more or less in all cases, are offered: (1) Be careful in the selection of text and subject. Try to have those which will be fresh, striking, and appropriate; but avoid ostentation, and particularly avoid what is forced and improbable in the application of subject to occasion. (2) Do not be too pointed and personal in address and application. The occasion itself will do much in applying what the preacher says to a particular group of people. There is danger of repelling the very persons the pastor wishes to reach if he singles them out too pointedly. Yet, sensitive personal appeal is natural and may be highly effective. (3) As always—preach the gospel. Do not be betrayed or enticed into mere sensationalism. These special occasions easily degenerate in the hands of worldly preachers into means of airing themselves before the community and in the newspapers. Let the grand truths of the Bible find clear and unmistakable expression and earnest, prayerful application.

NOTES

1. Andrew Watterson Blackwood, *The Funeral* (Philadelphia: Westminster Press, 1942), pp. 146–49.
2. The terms *revival sermons* and *evangelistic sermons* are both used in this sense.

CHAPTER 29

Planning a Preaching Program

BOTH general and immediate preparation will be easier if there is an overall plan for a pastor's preaching program. Far too many preachers plan one sermon at a time or for one Sunday at a time.

Pastors give many reasons for a lack of systematic planning: community demands, administrative duties, and pastoral responsibilities. While the demands made upon the pastor cannot be minimized, the real reasons for unplanned preaching are closely related to a lack of discipline and a failure to establish priorities.

Moreover, reasons for planned preaching are numerous and important. For example, preaching is supremely worth planning. To speak for God is the most exalted task given to man. Surely, preaching should rate the most careful planning.

Planning will give purpose and direction to preaching. The preacher is forced to keep his objectives before him. Moreover, planning also helps the preacher with sermon preparation. Because a text or topic is already chosen, he does not wait for inspiration; he goes to work. Recurring ideas can be eliminated thus giving his preaching a greater variety.

Planning removes much of the stress and strain of lack of

preparation. The preacher can work rather than worry. Planned preaching means a growing preacher and an edified congregation. His planning and related study bring spiritual and intellectual maturity. The comprehensive program of preaching builds up the congregation.

For the pastor to plan his preaching will also help him to plan worship. As sermons are projected on different themes, the pastor may have more variety in his choice of hymns, prayers, and other parts of the worship service.[1]

What methods can be used as a basis for planning? Here are some methods that can be used.

One of the easiest methods to plan but perhaps the most difficult to fulfill is consecutive exposition of the Scriptures. The pastor chooses a book of the Bible and then passage by passage "exposes" it to his people. John Calvin used this method. When he completed one book, he began another.

A few pastors have tried consecutive exposition of the entire Bible. As has been noted previously, W. A. Criswell spent more than eighteen years preaching through the Bible to his congregation. Consecutive exposition gives the pastor a specific work plan.

A second method of planning is using the objectives of preaching. According to J. B. Weatherspoon, the primary objectives or needs of the congregation are evangelistic, theological, ethical, devotional, inspirational, and actional. Since these are the main needs to be met in the lives of people, sermons in each area can be planned during the year. In a given year, one objective might be magnified.

Messages related to emphases in the church and denominational calendar is a third method of planning. What special days and weeks will the local church observe? What is the denominational emphasis? These emphases augment an overall plan.

A fourth method utilizes the national holidays. Sermons related to Labor Day, Veterans Day, Thanksgiving, Christmas, New Year's, Easter, Mother's Day, and Father's Day will make relevant additions to a preaching plan.

Planning sermons related to the Christian year is a fifth

method. Specific Scripture passages are used to present the life of Christ and the life of the church. Properly done, to follow the Christian year is to give a New Testament basis to preaching. The main emphases of the Christian year could be used as the foundation for evangelical preaching.

Each of these methods will contribute to an annual preaching plan. But the question remains, how can a plan be projected?

First, determine the year to be planned. Is the year to run from January to December, or for another period? September through August seems to be the best planning year for many pastors. Vacations are generally over in August, and the fall program is about to begin. The pastor can construct a plan that moves from the preparation for the new church year, to its beginning, through its major emphases, on to the end of summer.

Second, determine the Sundays and Wednesdays to be considered in the plan. Are there vacation Sundays? Will there be pulpit guests? How many Sundays will be revival Sundays? These and other factors determine the number of sermons to be prepared in a given year. It is important to know whether the plan is for forty-eight Sundays or for forty-two Sundays.

Third, use a file folder for each sermon to be prepared. Some pastors label these: first Sunday, A.M., first Sunday, P.M., first Wednesday, and on through the year. A few preachers use a large looseleaf notebook with a page for each sermon. The folder is preferable because it is easy to remove from the file, and material to be used in final preparation can be placed in the folder.

Fourth, prepare a general plan. From the synthesis of methods, list occasions, themes, and texts for each Sunday and Wednesday. For example, the consecutive exposition of a book will provide a general plan for many Sundays. A short series will fill in from four to eight morning or evening services. Special emphases and days will offer a plan for other Sundays. This general plan will chart the course for the year.

Fifth, fill in specific texts and subjects whenever possible. Last year's general preparation should have provided sermon ideas which are ready for development. Regular study gives a back-log of texts and outlines which can now be used.

Some additional advice might prove helpful to the pastor who is planning a year's pulpit work.

Try to begin the preaching year with a general plan complete. If possible have a specific plan, texts, subjects, and outlines for the first three months. Some preachers have specific plans for a year, but they often preach only once each Sunday for ten months of the year. Those who preach three sermons per week for at least forty-eight weeks per year will find that detailed planning for a quarter is demanding enough.

Plan for next year while fulfilling this year's plan. While preparing a specific sermon, ideas will often come for a sermon on a similar theme. While studying one book of the Bible, interest may develop in another. A pastor might well keep a notebook for two years ahead. He can jot down ideas for future use.

Vary the preaching plan each year. The determining factor is always the needs of the congregation. A year with an unusual doctrinal emphasis might be followed by a year with a strong ethical emphasis. One year might emphasize biblical characters and personalities, while the next year might consider great texts.

Moreover, any preaching plan is subject to change. A plan is not an end in itself; it is a means to a greater objective. Some specific need, some crisis, or some catastrophe can demand change. Since the plan is for the pastor and need not be announced, a change in the plan will not usually create a problem.

While planning saves work, it also requires work. Real diligence is demanded of the preacher. But this work contributes to the spiritual maturity of the pastor and his people.

NOTE

1. J. Winston Pearce, *Planning Your Preaching* (Nashville, Tenn.: Broadman Press, 1967), pp. 15–16.

For Further Reading:
The Preparation of Sermons

Asquith, Glenn H. *Preaching According to Plan.* Valley Forge, Penn.: Judson Press, 1968.

Blackwood, Andrew W. *Planning a Year's Pulpit Work.* New York: Abingdon-Cokesbury Press, 1942.

_____. *The Funeral.* Philadelphia: Westminster Press, 1942.

Crum, Milton, Jr. *Manual on Preaching.* Valley Forge, Penn.: Judson Press, 1977.

Erdahl, Lowell O. *Preaching for the People.* Nashville, Tenn.: Abingdon Press, 1976.

Gibson, George Miles. *Planned Preaching.* Philadelphia: Westminster Press, 1954.

Pearce, J. Winston. *Planning Your Preaching.* Nashville, Tenn.: Broadman Press, 1967.

Perry, Lloyd Merle. *A Manual for Biblical Preaching.* Grand Rapids, Mich.: Baker Book House, 1965.

Stidger, William L. *Planning Your Preaching.* New York: Harper & Bros., 1932.

Wiseman, Neil B., comp. *Biblical Preaching for Contemporary Man.* Grand Rapids, Mich.: Baker Book House, 1976.

Part VII

THE DELIVERY OF SERMONS

CHAPTER 30

The Methods of Delivery

A SERMON, in the strict sense of the term, exists only in the act of preaching. All that precedes is preparation for a sermon; all that remains afterwards is a report of what was spoken. Yet it is exceedingly important not to think of the speech and the delivery as things existing apart. Whatever be the method of preparing, what has been done should be regarded as but preparation; the sermon must be cherished and kept alive in the mind, must be vitally a part of itself, and then as living, breathing thought it will be delivered.

And as the preparation is not a speech till it is spoken, so the mere manner of speaking should not at the time receive separate attention. It should be the spontaneous product of the speaker's peculiar personality, as acted on by the subject which now fills his mind and heart. The idea of becoming eloquent merely by the study of structure, of voice, and of gesture is essentially absurd. Delivery does not consist merely, or even chiefly, in vocalization and gesticulation, but it implies that one is possessed with the subject, that he is completely in sympathy with it and fully alive to its importance, that he is not repeating remembered words but setting free the thoughts shut up in his mind. Even acting is good only in proportion to the actor's identification with the person represented—he must really think and really feel what he is saying. The speaker is not undertaking to represent another person, to appropriate another's thoughts and feelings, but aims simply to be himself, to speak what his own mind has produced.

Why then do speakers so often and so sadly fail in respect to this chief element of delivery? One reason is that many of the thoughts they present are borrowed and have never been digested by reflection and incorporated into the substance of their own thinking. Another reason is that they so frequently don't say what they really feel, but what they think they should feel. And another is that they are reproducing the product of a former mental activity, namely, at the time of preparation.

It is important for the preacher to choose the method of delivery which is best suited to his personality, which will allow him to express himself. Which is the best method—reading, reciting, extemporaneous speaking, or free delivery? Though often discussed, this question constantly recurs, not merely for the young preachers who must choose a method, but for many more mature preachers who are not satisfied that they have been pursuing the wisest course. It is surely a matter of great importance to one whose best energies in life are devoted to preaching that he should speak in the most effective way.

1. READING

One method is the reading method. A sermon is written, and the manuscript is taken to the pulpit and read. Some notable examples of effective readers were Jonathan Edwards, Thomas Chalmers, Horace Bushnell, and Peter Marshall.

This method has certain advantages. One is that it places the preacher more at his ease, both before and during the delivery. Having the sermon written, he will be safe from complete and mortifying failure. It is a great relief to escape the distressing anxiety which one may otherwise feel. The preacher who reads has a far better chance to sleep soundly on Saturday night. It is also an advantage to be collected and confident while delivering the sermon, rather than oppressed by anxiety or over-stimulated by uncontrollable excitement. Some preachers find that reading saves them from an excessive volubility or an extreme vehemence.

On the other hand, reading the sermon has several disadvantages. 1. It deprives the preacher's thinking of the benefit of all that mental inspiration which is produced by the presence of the congregation. As for thoughts which suddenly occur during the sermon, it is true that preachers of rare flexibility, tact, and grace can often introduce them effectively in connection with their reading. But such preachers are the exception, and most of those who read have to lose such thoughts altogether or introduce them awkwardly and with comparatively poor effect.

2. Reading is of necessity less effective than speaking, for all the great purposes of oratory. Greater coldness of manner is almost inevitable. If one attempts to be very animated, it will look unnatural. The tones of voice may be monotonous or have a forced variety. The gestures are nearly always unnatural because it is not natural to gesticulate much in reading. The mere turning of the pages, however skillfully done, breaks the continuity of delivery.

In a word, reading is an essentially different thing from speaking. When well executed, reading has a power of its own, but it is unnatural to substitute it for speaking, and it can at best only approximate, never fully attain, the same effect.

3. It should be added that reading is more harmful to the voice. Anyone who is so unfortunate as to have become subject to laryngitis will soon find that he can speak with much less fatigue than he can read. This shows a natural difference.

4. That the habit of reading should make one afraid to attempt speaking without a manuscript is not a necessary consequence. Every enlightened defender of reading would urge that the preacher ought to practice unwritten speech also and thus be able to speak when suddenly called on; and certainly there are people who habitually read and yet upon occasion can extemporize effectively. Yet, the tendency, the common result, of habitual reading is to make one dependent and timid; and such preachers often miss opportunities of doing good and are sometimes made ridiculous by their inability to preach by not

having "brought along any sermons." For this and other reasons, habitual reading is seldom advocated, though still often practiced.

The advantages and disadvantages of reading sermons having been considered, a few suggestions are now offered to those who adopt this method.

If you read, do not try to disguise the fact. Coquerel remarked that all the artifices practiced for this purpose

> have bad grace and little success. If one reads in the pulpit, it is better to read openly and boldly, taking no other pains than to have a manuscript easily legible and properly smoothed down on the front of the pulpit; then, to turn the leaves without affecting disguise, which is useless and unbecoming. We may be certain that the hearers are not deceived in this respect; they always know when an orator is reading.[1]

Do not attempt to convert the reading into speaking. The two are, as already said, essentially different. Is it possible for someone to speak as if he were reading? If a preacher tries this and nearly succeeds, he will effectually spoil his speaking. The person who reads must become a master of the art of reading.

Anyone who reads must give special attention to content. The sermon must be worth reading. The content must augment any deficiency in delivery.

2. RECITATION

Recitation, or repeating from memory what has been written and learned, is another method of preaching. It has been defended by even so acute and sensible a writer as Coquerel.[2] On the other hand, Phillips Brooks speaks of it as "a method which some men practice, but which I hope nobody commends."[3] It has had more general use in Europe than in this country; but a few things concerning it should be said.

1. This has all the advantages of the first method, as regards more complete and finished preparation, practice in writing, and possession of the sermon for subsequent use and for publication. There is here, however, no safeguard against utter fail-

ure and from the dread of failure. It has two advantages which the former method does not possess. To recite one's own composition is really one kind of speaking. To recite is speaking under difficulties and disadvantages, but it is speaking. It is not unnatural to treat it as such or impossible to make it approximate somewhat closely the excellence and power of well-prepared free speech. The other advantage is that recitation develops the memory. Any real improvement of the memory is certainly a matter of great value; people who habitually recite must always receive this benefit, and with some the results are remarkable. It must not be forgotten, however, that while recitation is, in this way, superior to reading, it is not superior to free delivery; for the power of verbal memorizing is really less valuable than the ability to retain ideas and to share them with words that come in the act of delivery.

2. Concerning disadvantages, recitation has many of those related to reading. There is here still less opportunity for correcting errors observed at the moment of delivery, for interpolating thoughts which then occur for the first time, or for giving new dimensions to the thoughts and new force to the expressions, than under the excitement of actual speaking.

This method requires still more time in preparation. He who adopts it must not only prepare the materials and form the plan of the discourse, as must be done in any method, and not only spend many hours in writing it out in full, as the reader also must do, but he must spend hours, and with most men not a few, in the task of memorizing. For one who preaches two or three times a week to write and memorize all his sermons is certainly incompatible with the proper performance of a pastor's other duties. The painful dread of failure is also a very serious objection to recitation, a dread from which the preacher cannot escape till the delivery begins, and which is then only heightened. For the extemporaneous speaker, anxiety about failure sometimes causes a helpful excitement; but to him who recites, it brings no benefit but only distress.

Furthermore, the delivery of what is recited must always be more or less artificial. It is doubtful whether anyone could so recite an entire and extended discourse in verbatim recitation without the audience detecting something unnatural. He who recites must be full of indignation and fervor, or else the delivery of these will be more or less artificial. Affectation cannot be tolerated by a preacher or by a congregation who properly appreciates and deeply feels the reality of preaching and hearing. Of course, there might be so much genuine earnestness in a really great preacher that a deep impression is made in spite of the inevitable artificiality of manner.

This method, then, may suffice, if skillfully managed, for college addresses, for public lectures, for extraordinary orations, for any speaking in which art properly forms an important element. It should be remembered, however, that to make the delivery as free and unconstrained as possible for recitation, a preacher needs to have ample time for becoming thoroughly familiar with the discourse—unless he is one of the few who possess a wonderful memory.

3. EXTEMPORANEOUS PREACHING

Still another method of delivery is the extemporaneous. The technical meaning of this expression needs to be defined. Primarily, of course, it denotes speaking without preparation, simply from the inspiration of the moment. The colloquial expression for this is speaking "off the top of the head," meaning speaking without much mental preparation. This popular phraseology is suggestive. By a natural extension, the phrase "extemporaneous speaking" is applied to cases in which there has been preparation of thought, however thorough, but the language is left to be suggested at the moment. Still further, when notes are made as a help to preparation, when the plan of the discourse is drawn out on paper and all the principal points are stated or suggested, it is called extemporaneous speaking because all this is regarded only as means of arranging and recalling the thoughts and the language is extemporized. Extemporaneous preaching is best understood as preaching after limited preparation.

1. Consider then, the advantages.

a. This method teaches one to think more rapidly and with less dependence on external aids than if he habitually depended on a manuscript.

b. Again, this method saves time for general study and for other pastoral work. At first, to be sure, the inexperienced preacher often needs more time to make thorough preparation for preaching extemporaneously than he would use in writing; but after he has learned to be at ease and self-reliant, much time is saved. Beecher and Spurgeon could never have done as much other work as they did, and at the same time have preached so well, if they had taken time to write out their sermons beforehand.

c. In the act of delivery, the extemporaneous speaker has immense advantages. With far greater ease and effectiveness than if reading or reciting, he can use ideas which occur at the time. Any man who possesses the fervid oratorical nature, even in a humble degree, will find that after careful preparation some of the best and most inspiring thoughts he ever has will come while he is speaking. If, involved in his theme and impressed with its importance, he gets the interested and sympathetic attention of even a few good listeners and the fire of his eyes comes reflected back from theirs until the electricity passes to and fro between them and his very soul glows, he cannot fail sometimes to conceive thoughts more splendid and more valuable than ever come to him in solitary study.

d. Another advantage is that the whole mass of prepared material may become illuminated, animated, sometimes transfigured by this inspiration of delivery. The preacher's language rises, without conscious effort, to suit the heightened grandeur and beauty of his conceptions. This exaltation of soul, rising at times to rapture, can never be fully described; but the speaker who does not know what it means in some measure was not born to be a speaker. And great stress should be given the fact that, besides the thoughts which occur during delivery, the delivery itself changes the dimensions and incalculably augments the power of the thoughts previously prepared.

e. Moreover, the preacher can watch the congregation's response as he proceeds and purposely change the ideas expressed, as well as the manner of delivery, according to his own feeling and that of the congregation. Especially in the hortatory parts of a sermon, which are often the most important parts, this adaptation is desirable.

f. Moreover, in extemporaneous speaking, delivery is usually more natural. In this method, the voice, the action, the eye will be natural and attain their full power. And while with painstaking practice the preacher vainly strives to read or recite precisely like speaking, the extemporaneous speaker can with comparative ease give the best delivery of which he is capable. However, if one preaches an unwritten sermon so many times that it becomes a mere recitation, then it loses power. If the preacher is not interested in the sermon, if he is not expressing living thought, then he should lay it aside until it becomes real again.

g. This method also has the advantage of giving facility in speaking without immediate preparation. The preacher who cannot do this upon occasion misses many opportunities of usefulness and loses influence with the people by an incapacity which they consider a reproach.

h. This leads to what is really among the most important advantages of extemporaneous preaching. With most of the people to whom one ministers, it is a popular method. People like for the minister to look at them and to share directly with them. It is difficult to overestimate the importance of eye contact.

2. But extemporaneous preaching also has disadvantages, some of which require not only careful consideration but watchful attention in practice.

a. Perhaps the gravest disadvantage of all consists in the tendency to neglect preparation, after one has gained facility in unaided thinking and extemporized expression.

b. Still another serious disadvantage of this method is its tendency to prevent one's forming the habit of writing. As fluency increases, the contrast between winged, glorious speech and slow, toilsome writing becomes to many preachers too great for their patience. Writing promotes accuracy of thought as well as exactness of statement; the thought becomes objective and can thus be more carefully scrutinized. Habits of writing and of speaking will maintain an equilibrium in our methods of thinking and style of expression when each is practiced according to its own essential and distinctive character.

c. The style of an extemporaneous sermon is apt to be less condensed and less finished than if it were written out and read or recited. But this is not necessarily a fault. The style might be all the better adapted to speaking, as distinguished from the essay style. While, however, a condensed and highly finished style is not generally appropriate in speaking which aims to make any practical impression, there is danger of boring repetition, of "linked dullness long drawn out," especially of what someone calls "conclusions which never conclude." This danger can be prevented by careful preparation and speaking, and by the constant practice of careful writing.

d. A more serious disadvantage is the danger of making mistakes in statement. In the ardor of the moment the extemporaneous speaker is likely to say some things that are irrelevent, ill-considered, improper, and sometimes, inaccurate. Some men more than others run this risk, but all are more or less liable to the danger. Some hints are given as safeguards: Make thorough preparation and thus greatly diminish the danger. Keep a cool head, no matter how warm the heart becomes, while preaching. If the slip is serious, correct it on the spot and go on; if very serious and not observed at the time, correct it on another occasion. But for the most part, leave these mistakes alone. If you have real merits and enjoy the confidence of the people, it will be one of your most blessed privileges to live down many blunders.

e. Then the success of an extemporaneous sermon is too largely dependent upon the preacher's feelings at the time of delivery. If he is not physically well, he may not be mentally alert. If he is depressed in spirit, he may not be able to preach with warmth and enthusiasm. When these things happen, the preacher's limited preparation may not be sufficient.

4. FREE DELIVERY

Another method is free delivery or preaching without notes or manuscript.

At least three elements are involved in free delivery. The first is careful preparation. When the preacher stands up to preach, he is carefully prepared. This usually means that the completed sermon will be a full manuscript or at least in detailed outline form. Or one could prepare adequately, as Alexander Maclaren often did, by constant and deep meditation upon the Scripture. But regardless of the means of preparation, there is nothing "impromptu" about the sermon: the preacher is fully prepared.

After this preparation, the preacher goes into the pulpit without notes or manuscript. Notes should be left in the study. To put them in the Bible may leave temptation too near at hand. The preacher stands before the people, looks directly at them, and shares with them God's message which has become a part of him. The sermon which he has been led to preach is carried in his mind and heart.

At the same time there should be no conscious effort to memorize the sermon. To be sure, if a preacher has gathered material, has organized it into a sermon, has then thought through it, he will reproduce much of it verbatim. But he is not to do this consciously; he is not concentrating on words, but on the sharing of thoughts and ideas. In a practice preaching class, J. B. Weatherspoon said to a student, "Many of the words which you used in your sermon are not in the manuscript, but the words you used are just as well chosen as those in the manuscript." The student had grasped the idea of free delivery. He was sharing ideas and letting the words come as they would in the act of delivery.

What are the advantages of free delivery? It has all the advantages of other methods of sermon delivery without their disadvantages. It takes the best from all the others.

1. As in the recitation method, free delivery will develop the memory. Though one does not consciously memorize, the memory is used, and constant use means a strengthened and more effective instrument. *Memoria* was one of the elements of ancient rhetoric, and a good memory has always been an asset to any speaker. The practice of free delivery will make the memory more usable and dependable.

2. Like the recitation and reading methods, free delivery has all the advantages of writing. A manuscript or detailed outline will preserve the preacher's work, make it available for future reference, give him a basis to improve his style, help him to see if there is a wholesome variety of emphasis, etc.

3. Moreover, free delivery has all the oratorical advantages which come with extemporaneous speaking. One has eye contact with his audience, can profit from their reactions, and can use the opportunities and inspirations of the moment. Gerald Kennedy, in comparing the methods of sermon delivery has said, "Other things being equal, the man who stands without written support finds his way to the wills of his hearers with more directness and welcome than any of the others."[4] Also, because of his adequate preparation, the preacher who uses free delivery is not likely to make many of the blunders and slips of tongue which the extemporaneous speaker often makes.

4. Again, the most popular method of preaching is free delivery. As has been noted, people like directness. They want the preacher to look at them. Listeners, however, also want a preacher to have something to say. The minister who prepares adequately and then speaks freely will thus fulfill the layperson's ideas of the way a preacher should preach.

5. Free delivery is the method which best suits the minister's office and calling. Preachers have been called to proclaim a message, a message which has been revealed. The preacher is a herald of the *Gospel.* It seems rather strange that a herald should read a message which has been given to him and which he has spent years studying to understand, interpret, and illustrate. One cannot imagine Simon Peter and the apostles dragging out their notes before they preached Jesus. In fact, the use

of manuscripts and the reading of sermons came later in Christian history when preaching was in a period of decline. It seems fitting that one called to proclaim a message should do it without written support in the pulpit.

6. In addition to the other advantages, free delivery after careful preparation will give the preacher the fullest joy and satisfaction in his preaching. The highest privilege given to us is to proclaim God's message to others! To stand before others with a message in mind and heart, to have the barrier of notes or manuscript removed, to share with them a God-inspired and directed message—that is to know the deepest satisfaction which can come to a preacher. The minister realizes a sense of fulfillment—he is doing what God called him to do.

A fair question would be, "If the free delivery method has all of these advantages, why do not more ministers use it?" It must be frankly admitted that there are some objections to this method.

Some people object to preaching without notes because they might leave out bits of their sermons—a choice phrase, an epigrammatic sentence, an excellent illustration, or even a principal idea. When someone begins to use free delivery, he will omit some material, but most sermons are long enough even with omissions. Then there is this especially comforting thought —because of the similarity of ideas in one's sermons, that "really good" illustration will probably be more useful the next Sunday or the next.

Another objection is the danger of forgetting. This is a real danger. The preacher may have a mental block, or a disconcerting incident may cause him to forget the next idea. Preachers have forgotten sermons in the past and will in the future. But embarrassing moments come with all methods of delivery. The reciter may also forget. Actually his danger is greater than his who practices free delivery because he does not have the same sense of freedom and cannot respond to audience reaction or response. The sermon reader might have the pages of his manuscript scattered by a vigorous gesture. What could be more embarrassing than a preacher's having to gather the scattered pages of his manuscript from the floor before he continues to speak! The person who uses notes may discover that he has gone to church, but that his notes have not. It is terribly embarrassing to have to send one of the deacons or one of the children after the little slip of paper on the desk in the parsonage. The extemporizer is constantly shamed by his errors of grammer or slips of tongue. Though there is the danger of forgetting, those uncomfortable moments will come regardless of method. Moreover, if anyone can learn to think on his feet and become the master of every situation, the preacher who speaks from one to many times each week (more often than almost any other speaker) should be able to master the technique.

Still another objection, though rarely voiced, is that preaching without notes requires real work. And it does! It demands more work than extemporizing, or using notes, or perhaps even than reading. A person who uses free delivery not only has to prepare his sermon, but he also has to prepare himself to preach the sermon. This kind of preparation necessitates strenuous study. But then, if a person has heard the call of God, he is ready to work and undergo any discipline that will make him a more effective preacher.

Perhaps the most common objection is that some pastors feel that they do not have the mental capacity or the kind of memory needed to preach without notes. The answer to this objection is that free delivery requires only average intelligence and does not require an exceptional memory. Free delivery is a technique; it is something which can be developed. Gerald Kennedy has declared, "Any man can learn to stand on his feet and preach with freedom."[5] Any man can master this technique providing he is willing to undergo the necessary self-discipline.

If free delivery can be learned, what then is the technique? How can the art of preaching without notes be developed? Giving attention to certain basic steps will insure the mastery of this method.

1. Careful attention must be given to elements of immediate preparation. First, the preacher must use ideas which have grown and developed in his own mind. As a result of regular

and systematic study, the minister will use ideas which have become a part of him. Some ministers cannot preach without the aid of notes because their material is "too new." Perhaps they found it on Wednesday or even as late as Saturday. Such material is exceedingly difficult to remember because it is not really their own; it is not a part of them. On the other hand, it is easy to remember and share material which comes out of one's own inventive processes. Second, the plan of the sermon should be simple and logical. If the ideas of a sermon follow a good order, they are easy to recall. Some sermons are hard to reproduce because they lack a skeleton. It is almost impossible to retain a mass of unorganized material. No matter how profound may be the thought within the sermon, the organization should be simple and logical. Next, transitions from part to part of the sermon and from idea to idea should be carefully planned. If attention has been given to the transitions, the next idea appears before the mind. Also, the sermon material must be concrete. This does not mean that the sermon is to lack worthwhile thought, but it does mean that specific and clear words will be chosen instead of the abstract and cloudy. Moreover, difficult ideas must be illustrated. Concrete material is a desirable characteristic of any effective sermonizing, but it is an absolute necessity if one is to preach without notes. Therefore, the first step in learning the technique of free delivery is in these elements of sermon preparation.

2. The next step is rehearsal, or preparing to preach the sermon after it has been prepared. Even the person experienced in this method will find it necessary to spend from thirty minutes to an hour getting ready to preach a sermon. Some do this by reading through a sermon and meditating upon it. Some do it by getting on their feet and going over the sermon orally. In developing this technique, one preacher prepares a tentative outline and then goes over it orally (without referring to the outline). He then makes a final detailed outline or writes the sermon in full. Finally, just before preaching, he thinks through the sermon again, trying to fasten the sermon in his mind and to prepare himself to preach it. Such a rehearsal or

getting ready to preach is essential. However, a word of caution might be helpful. It is possible that the feeling which one experiences in rehearsal may be completely missing in actual delivery. This is true because the preacher is recalling something that was real to him, but is now second hand. Each part of the sermon must be relived at the moment of delivery.[6] The preacher must actually feel the emotions which he expresses.

3. The next step in learning to preach without notes is using and depending on the memory. Some ministers do not know how useful and reliable their memories are because they have never trusted them. John Oman has aptly said, "Memory, like other servants, is most reliable when most trusted."[7] Dawson Bryan added to this idea when he stated, "Few, if any, of us ever trust our memory enough. It will prove as faithful a servant as we have faith that it will be. It is surprising how an outline or even an entire written sermon appears before the mind if it is given a chance."[8] Young preachers often make the mistake of saying, "I will use notes now, but as my knowledge increases and my experience broadens, then I can throw them away." This is rarely true. If memory is not used, it becomes an ineffective instrument. The time to begin its use is now. To preach without notes one has to depend upon the memory.

4. Another step which will aid in mastering free delivery is physical fitness. Physical well-being contributes to mental acuteness. In order to think clearly one must feel well. This means that rest and relaxation before preaching are very helpful. Henry Ward Beecher, one of the great pulpit orators of the last century and a man with a rugged physique, devoted his Saturdays to rest and recreation so that he would be physically prepared to preach to his congregation on Sunday. Many sermons have been ineffective, not because they were poor sermons or poorly prepared, but rather because the preacher was not physically able to be at his mental and spiritual best. Rest before preaching is even more important than rest after preaching. In fact, proper physical and spiritual preparation will do much to eliminate the nervous exhaustion that many

people have after having preached. Good physical condition will help the preacher think clearly as he stands before an audience.

5. Perhaps the most important step in preaching without notes can be called a risk of faith. A preacher prays for leadership in choosing a sermon topic, he asks God's guidance in its preparation, then he takes an additional step—he also prays for his help in delivering it. In a real sense the preacher asks for and depends upon the Holy Spirit. Not only does the preacher depend upon the Holy Spirit for power to convince, but also he depends upon him for liberty and freedom in preaching. It is not unreasonable to assume that the preachers who say constantly to their people, "Trust God! Depend upon the Holy Spirit!" should exercise the same implicit faith for the twenty-five or thirty minutes it takes to deliver a sermon. Some persons who preach without notes testify that they remember sermons more easily than anything else. They know that this is true because they ask for the Spirit's help; and because they ask believing, they receive it. So preaching without notes is ultimately a risk of faith. The preacher prepares well—he does not presume—but then he launches out in faith, trusting the Holy Spirit to help him speak well.

Because of the advantages of free delivery, every preacher, especially every young preacher, should give this method a fair trial. It will certainly help every person attain his maximum effectiveness, and it is not beyond the ability of anyone with average ability. James Stewart has asserted, "Any preacher, even the most tongue-tied and diffident, can achieve freedom of utterance—on two conditions: he must be willing to face the necessary self-discipline, and he must begin early enough."[9]

NOTES

1. Athanase Coquerel, *Observations on Preaching* (Paris: J. Cherbuliez, 1860), p. 177.

2. Ibid., p. 181 ff.
3. Phillips Brooks, *Lectures on Preaching* (New York: E. P. Dutton & Co., 1907), p. 171.
4. Gerald Kennedy, *His Word Through Preaching* (New York: Harper & Bros., 1947), p. 88.
5. Ibid., p. 89.
6. See Robert Kirkpatrick, *The Creative Delivery of Sermons* (New York: Macmillan Co., 1944) for helpful suggestions on this point.
7. John Oman, *Concerning the Ministry* (New York: Harper & Bros., 1937), p. 130.
8. Dawson Bryan, *The Art of Illustrating Sermons* (New York: Abingdon-Cokesbury Press, 1938), p. 247.
9. James S. Stewart, *The Heralds of God* (New York: Charles Scribner's Sons, 1946), p. 182.

CHAPTER 31

The Voice in Delivery

IT is never necessary to urge the importance of delivery upon persons who correctly understand its nature and who appreciate the objectives of public speaking.

The famous saying of Demosthenes, repeatedly mentioned by Cicero, is sometimes completely misrepresented. He did not say that the first thing, second thing, third thing in oratory are "action," in the present English sense of that term, but "delivery," for this, as is well known, is what the Latin *actio* signifies.

The voice is the speaker's great instrument. Nothing else in a person's physical constitution is nearly so important. ". . . For effectiveness and distinction in delivery the greatest share undoubtedly belongs to the voice," says Cicero.[1] Not every eminent orator has possessed a commanding person, but every one of great eminence has had an effective voice. The faults that result from lack of training, such as drawling, feebleness, and defective articulation, can often be partially corrected by judicious and patient effort: witness Demosthenes. And a voice extremely faulty in some respects might in other respects have great power and be precisely suited to the mental character of the person. For example, Robert Hall had a comparatively weak voice; but he made it effective by speaking rapidly; and when he was excited, it would swell into power. The vocal gifts of

Chrysostom, Whitefield, Spurgeon are well known. From all this it appears that while one cannot be an orator of the highest class without an unusually gifted voice, one can be a highly effective speaker in spite of serious defects, so everyone should be encouraged to make the best of the vocal powers that he possesses.

An extensive knowledge of the anatomy and physiology of the organs of speech is not necessary to the orator. Even a general knowledge of them is more useful in avoiding disease than in positively improving delivery.

1. THE VOICE—ITS DISTINCT ABILITIES

It is important to consider certain vocal abilities with reference to public speaking.

1. Compass is the range of pitch over which the voice extends. The difference between voices in this respect is very obvious in the case of singers, but it is also a factor in speaking and is a matter of great consequence in expressing the wide variety of emotions which a speaker will feel even in the progress of the same discourse.

2. Volume, the quantity of sound produced, is entirely distinct from pitch, though frequently confused with it in the popular use of such terms as *loud* and *strong*. Ample volume, properly regulated, will make the voice audible to a greater distance, and will make it more commanding.

3. Penetrating power, the distance to which one can be heard, does not depend simply on volume and pitch or on distinct articulation; there is a difference between voices in their power of penetration. A similar difference exists in the case of many other sounds, natural and artificial. The physiology of it has not been satisfactorily explained, and the fact is scarcely noticed in treatises on elocution, but a very little observation will convince one that the difference is real.

4. Melody depends on both sweetness and flexibility of voice. The single sounds must be sweet, and the constant transitions in pitch required by changing emotions must be made with

promptness, precision, and smoothness. A voice is not melodious if deficient in either.

2. GENERAL IMPROVEMENT OF THE VOICE

Cicero tells us that Caius Gracchus, when speaking, kept near him and out of sight a servant with a flute. Its note would now and then bring up the orator's voice when flagging or recall it when overstrained; and he judiciously adds that it would be better to leave the flautist at home and carry to the forum the habit acquired.[2] This is true with all vocal improvement, in fact with all that pertains to delivery. The preacher must seek by general practice and care to form such habits of speech and of bearing that there will be little need to give them attention when actually engaged in public speaking.

Whatever improves the general health will improve the voice, especially muscular exercise which develops the chest and promotes good posture. Singing develops the voice in almost every way, probably to a greater extent than anything else except actual speaking. There are many reasons that make it desirable that a minister be able to sing and to read music; and young ministers and those preparing for the ministry should learn to sing. If it should take as much time and effort to learn to sight-read church music as it takes to learn a modern language or a branch of science, it would be fully as profitable, and almost any person who is still young can learn to sing moderately well by disciplined and continuing effort. Reading aloud is a good way of developing the voice. It is, however, more tiring than speaking and should be promptly stopped when it becomes decidedly fatiguing. A proper management of the voice in all ordinary conversation is very important. As in politeness and as in style, so in the use of the voice (and also in action), it is impossible for one who is habitually careless to do really well on special occasions. This has already been noted in relation to style and extemporaneous preaching, but it deserves to be repeated. Take care that speech in conversation always be audible, agreeable, and at the same time easy and natural. Then in public speaking, speaking will almost take care of itself. Vocal exercises may be quite useful for certain purposes. If excessive or incorrectly done, they may seriously injure the vocal organs; and there is still greater danger that they will produce artificiality. When conducted in private, under the direction of a really judicious speech teacher, they might be of great service in correcting special faults. However, some teachers of public speaking, even intelligent ones, are prone to attempt too much, to be dissatisfied with the simple task of correcting faults; they undertake to superinduce some artificial excellence. After all, next to care in conversation, practice in actual speaking is the main thing. But it must be thoughtful practice, with observation of the faults and effort to avoid them, or it will only confirm one's natural or accidental defects. Someone has said: "Practice makes perfect; and bad practice makes perfectly bad."

One must be careful not to destroy individuality of voice. A person's voice is a part of himself, a part of his power; he must keep it essentially unaltered, while improved as far as possible.

A few suggestions can be given concerning means of improving particular vocal abilities.

1. Compass, or range, will be improved most by singing. It might be helpful to repeat a short sentence on a key successively elevated or lowered to the full limit of one's voice, being careful to be speaking at every pitch and not half singing. In such exercises it is necessary to remember that it is best to speak slowly on a low key, and to speak swiftly on a high key. The difference is clearly seen in comparing the lower and upper tones of a piano or violin. In actual speaking, nature at once prompts the swifter or slower speech, if we only follow nature.

2. Concerning volume, the speaker improves mainly by habitual good posture and physical exercise that expands and strengthens the lungs. Running, swimming, and certain gymnastic exercises have this effect, as soon appears from increased breadth of chest. Taking a series of long breaths every morning before breakfast or at any time of day when the stomach is not full will exercise the lungs and, if regularly practiced, accomplish much more than might be supposed. The habit of talking

with the mouth well opened to give full and free speech is quite important. Occasional loud singing (not on a high pitch) and actual speaking steadily increase the volume of one's voice in youth.

3. Penetrating power may be increased by giving the matter distinct attention in vocal exercises and sometimes in speaking. The effort should be to project the voice, to make it reach farther, without elevating the pitch or increasing the quantity of sound. By calling to a friend on an opposite hill or by fixing the eye on a distant person in a large audience and trying to make him hear, the preacher naturally develops this power. Great care must be taken not to change pitch or tone. It is found by physical experiments of different kinds that pure tones, tones full, clear, steady, are heard at a greater distance than others. This is even a more important reason for cultivating purity of tone than its melodious effect.

Purity of tone applies chiefly to vowel sounds. But penetrating power of voice is also greatly assisted by the distinct articulation of consonants.

In distinct articulation, great faults are very common, and there is ample room for improvement by simple means. In conversation, reading, speaking, especially in singing (because there it is most difficult), one should constantly articulate every letter according to its true sound, and particularly every consonant. Special exercises can be used, containing often neglected consonants, such as the strong *r* and the nasal sound of *ing*, or difficult combinations of two or three consonants, such as "shrink," "expects," "fifth and sixth verses." Where a consonant or combination of consonants ends one word and begins the next, there is often special difficulty. For example, consider "take care," "sit down." Not one in five of educated ministers will correctly articulate the words, "in the evening it is cut down and withereth." An excellent example is the saying, "It is the first step that costs."

Distinct articulation cannot be neglected by the preacher. At the same time, one must beware of extremes. The rolling Scotch *r,* for instance, is contrary to the established usage of

America and should not be imitated. The preacher who grew up with a regional accent might try to develop a cosmopolitan speech which will be accepted in each section of the country.

He who wishes to be heard at a great distance must speak rather slowly. There is thus a clear interval between the sound waves, and even when they have come a long way and are growing faint, they will still be distinct.

This penetrating power of voice, with the distinct articulation which aids it, deserves the special attention of all public speakers.

4. Concerning melody, it has been noted that it depends on sweetness and flexibility of voice. The former is chiefly a natural quality, but it may be improved by singing, in conversation by attention to purity of tone, and in general by keeping the organs of speech in a healthy condition. The vowel sounds are most important, the prolongation of these making the sweet tones. The consonants, while distinctly articulated for other purposes, must be spoken with smoothness and ease for melody. There is a marked tendency in this country to omit or disguise many unaccented vowel sounds, thereby greatly impairing the melody of the words and sometimes making them indistinct. Take, for example, the shortening of "absolute," "tolerable," "immensity."[3] This tendency ought to be studiously avoided by all who desire to speak melodiously. But many preachers go to the opposite extreme and exhibit an affected precision.

Flexibility is necessary for the exact expression of different emotions as well as for melody. It will improve by practice if one speaks with sincere feeling, and it can be cultivated by any exercises involving quick transitions from one pitch to a much higher or lower one.

Probably the best exercise is that of reading aloud . . . dialogues, in which the reader represents alternately a number of interlocutors. The animation which is characteristic of this species of discourse, and the frequent and rapid changes of the voice which are requisite to maintain the distinction of persons and characters, afford the most effective aids to the development of this power. Humorous selections also are good for this purpose.[4]

Melody is very desirable, but without possessing it in a great degree a speaker's voice can be, on other accounts, very effective. And it is a serious fault to "play tunes" on the voice, to give a sort of musical accompaniment, distinct from the feelings expressed, as appears to be quite common in England and is sometimes seen in America in the pulpit tone of even educated people.

3. MANAGEMENT OF THE VOICE WHEN PREACHING

A few simple hints can be profitably remembered.

1. Do not begin on too high a key. One is particularly apt to do this in the open air, or in a large and unfamiliar church, or when much excited. If the preacher begins on too high a level, when impassioned passages come in which the voice must rise, it will rise to a scream! Everyone has often witnessed this process. It is, of course, not impossible to change the key, and this should be carefully attempted when necessary. But one should avoid beginning wrong. Tenor voices, it is obvious, are especially apt to begin too high.

If one becomes impassioned in the early part of the discourse, he should not then use his voice in its full force but reserve its highest power for some later and culminating point, as is done with the more powerful instruments in an oratorio. In fact, the voice should very rarely go to its highest pitch or to its fullest volume; there should always be a reserve force, except in some moment of the most exalted passion.

It was speaking long on a high key in the open air, with unrestrained passion, that led many of the early Baptist preachers of this country into that singsong, or "holy whine," which is still heard in some parts of the country. The voice, strained and fatigued, instinctively sought relief in a rhythmical rise and fall, as was also the case in the loud cries of street peddlers. They were commonly zealous and sometimes great men who fell into this fault, and it was often imitated by those who followed them, after the usual superficial fashion of imitators, mistaking the obvious fault for the hidden power. To some people this peculiar whine is connected by a lifelong association with the most impressive truths and the most solemn occasions; and so it touches their feelings independently of what is said and sometimes when the preacher's words are not heard—like the revival tunes or those familiar to us from childhood.

The preacher must not begin on a high key, and yet the text should be distinctly heard. The difficulty thus arising with a large audience can be overcome by stating the text slowly, distinctly, and, if necessary, a second time, and by projecting the voice, instead of elevating it.

2. Do not let the voice drop in the last words of a sentence. Though it must often sink, returning to the general pitch of the discourse, it must not fall too suddenly or too low. It is not unusual for the last words to be quite inaudible.

3. Never fail to take a breath before the lungs are entirely empty, and usually keep them well filled. This is generally done effortlessly in extemporaneous speaking, but in recitation and reading it requires special attention.

A speaker must not gasp in his breath through the mouth but breathe through the nostrils, regularly and steadily. He must keep the head and neck in an upright posture for the sake of breathing freely as well as for other reasons, and there must be nothing tight around his throat.

4. Look frequently at the remotest hearers, and see to it that they hear you. If particular persons anywhere in the room have grown inattentive, they can often be aroused by unobtrusively aiming the voice at them for a moment.

5. There should be variety—of pitch, of force, and of speed. Monotony utterly destroys eloquence. But variety must be gained by taking care to have a real and obvious variety of emotions, and then simply expressing each particular feeling in the most natural manner. Emphasis requires much attention. In speaking, a correct emphasis will be spontaneous whenever one is fully in sympathy with his subject.

Think about the subject and those who hear it, not the voice.

NOTES

1. Cicero, *De Oratore* (London: William Heinemann, 1960), III, 60, p. 224.
2. Ibid.
3. Compare Robert Lewis Dabney's *Sacred Rhetoric* (Richmond: Presbyterian Committee of Publishing, 1870), p. 305.
4. Joshua Hall McIlvaine, *Elocution* (New York: Charles Scribner & Co., 1870), p. 320.

CHAPTER 32

The Body in Delivery

THE term *action* is now usually restricted to what Cicero calls the *sermo corporis,* or speech of the body, including facial expression, posture, and gesture, but not including the use of the voice.

The freedom and variety of action exhibited by children when talking to each other show that it is perfectly natural. Its wonderful expressiveness, even apart from language, is sometimes displayed by the deaf mute and by others skilled in pantomime. There is a familiar story of a dispute between Cicero and Roscius, an actor famous for pantomime, concerning which could express a thought more eloquently, the one by words or the other by signs. In many cases a gesture is much more expressive than any number of words.

How truly language must be regarded as a hindrance to thought, though the necessary instrument of it, we shall clearly perceive on remembering the comparative force with which simple ideas are communicated by signs. To say, "Leave the room," is less expressive than to point to the door. Placing a finger on the lips is more forcible than whispering, "Do not speak." A beck of the hand is better than "Come here." No phrase can convey the idea of surprise so vividly as opening the eyes and raising the eyebrows. A shrug of the shoulders would lose much by translation into words.[1]

He who is master of this sign-language has, indeed, an almost magic power. When the orator can combine it with the spoken language, he acquires thereby exceeding vivacity of expression. Not only his mouth but his eyes, his features, his fingers speak. The hearers read the coming sentiment upon his countenance and limbs almost before his voice reaches their ears: they are both spectators and listeners; every sense is absorbed in charmed attention.[2]

It was said of Cicero that there was eloquence even in the tips of his fingers, and of Garrick that by merely moving his elbow he could produce an effect that no words could achieve.[3]

How has the adult so often lost this wonderful power which the child possessed? In some cases he has been hardened, even in early adulthood, by the unpleasant realities of life and has lost the fresh and lively feeling of childhood. In most cases he has become constrained and self-conscious, no longer forgetting himself as the child did in the subject he speaks of, and whether he is timid or vain, his manner is of necessity unnatural and awkward. Action is natural only when it is spontaneous and for the moment almost unconscious. Even the child becomes constrained as soon as he is aware of being observed; and, on the other hand, the most shy or most conceited person, if his whole being is absorbed in his subject and himself for the time forgotten, again becomes free and expressive in action. And besides all this, there has sometimes been the influence of incorrect ideas about action learned from poor teachers or from hearsay.

How then can the preacher "be as the little children" in this respect? He must cultivate his religious sensibilities and a growing faith. He must prayerfully try to care more for his sacred themes and less for himself—to keep the thought of self habitually and thoroughly subordinate to the thought of saving souls and glorifying the Redeemer. He must remember that he himself, as the Creator made him, is called to preach the gospel, and that, with his individuality unimpaired, he is to do the work appointed to him while faculties are developed and faults corrected. Then, thoroughly possessed with his subject, lifted above fearing men and inspired into zeal for usefulness, he should speak what he thinks and feels. No doubt he will make some mistakes, but what of that? A child can never learn to walk without sometimes falling. But the child will not keep on falling the same way, and so the speaker's mistakes can teach him something. Though probably not aware of them at the time because too busy with more important things, he may afterwards remember his awkward actions or may be told of them by some kindly or perhaps some unkind critic, and next time he will notice a little and correct or avoid them.

Some people have naturally much more action than others. And the same person will have more or less action, according to his physical condition and mood, as well as according to the subject and the circumstances. Trust, then, to spontaneous impulse. Do not repress nature except where particular faults present themselves. And never force nature because action is not indispensable, while unnatural action would be harmful. Robert Hall did not use many gestures, though his facial expression was remarkable. Spurgeon had nothing very striking in his action, but he had an extraordinary voice. On the other hand, "there is an oaken desk shown at Eisenach, which Luther broke with his fist in preaching"[4]; and the apostle Paul appears to have had a peculiar and impressive manner of stretching out his hand. The preacher, then, should do what is natural for him at the time.

It has been remarked above that action, the "speech of the body," includes several distinct things.

1. Facial expression has great power.

The glance is a great factor, for it expresses all our feelings and rivets men's gaze even before we speak.[5]

With the exception, however, of one feature, facial expression is almost involuntary, and little can be done to improve it beyond the correction of faults. When a preacher is involved in the subject and thoroughly subordinates all thought of self, his countenance will spontaneously assume the appropriate expressions.

But the exception is notable. Cicero says: "But everything

depends on the countenance, while the countenance itself is entirely dominated by the eyes."[6]

The expressive power of the human eye is so great that it determines, in a manner, the expression of the whole countenance. It is almost impossible to disguise it. It is said that gamblers rely more upon the study of the eye, to discover the state of their opponents' game, than upon any other means. Even animals are susceptible of its power. The dog watches the eyes of his master and discovers from them, before a word is spoken, whether he is to expect a caress, or apprehend chastisement. It is said that the lion cannot attack a man so long as the man looks him steadily in the eyes. . . . All the passions and emotions of the human heart, in all their degrees and interworkings with each other, express themselves, with the utmost fullness and power, in the eyes.[7]

Now the eyes can in some respects be controlled. The preacher can look at his hearers. And the importance of this would be difficult to overstate. Besides the direct power which the speaker's eye has over the audience, it is by looking that he sees their expressions and empathizes with them. He who does not feel helped by this and does not greatly miss it in circumstances without it was not born to be a public speaker, or has distorted his natural responses by incorrect ideas and methods. And in addition to the involuntary effect upon the speaker of seeing the faces of his hearers, he can watch the effect produced by his sermon and purposely adapt his thoughts, style, and manner to the present situation.

If a preacher feels as he should, his expression at the outset will be respectful without timidity, independent without defiance or conceit, and solemn without sanctimoniousness, and then will spontaneously change its character with every variation of feeling.

2. Posture also is important. In walking, standing, sitting, one should try to acquire habitual good posture and ease; and then in public speaking there will be little danger of assuming any other than an appropriate posture. But many persons exhibit

various faults through lack of such habits or from mistaken views of oratory or inappropriate feelings at the time of speaking. Quintilian and later writers warn against these and some of them ought to be mentioned.

Among the most common faults of preachers is leaning on the pulpit. All inexperienced speakers, feeling ill at ease, are apt to be unsteady and to look for something to lean against. The pulpit is so convenient for this purpose that it is not surprising if a habit of leaning on it is often formed. When a young preacher finds himself inclined to do this, he should not only resist the tendency while in the pulpit, but should try to stand with nothing before him in social meetings, Sunday school speaking, etc. A few early experiences will rapidly form a habit, good or bad.

The body should be simply erect. A slight inclination of the head at the beginning of the sermon is with most persons a natural expression of deference for the audience, but it must be very slight and should disappear as the preacher grows more animated. A habitual stoop is a serious fault, since it is both unattractive and harmful to the vocal organs, and should be corrected if possible; with a few people it is natural and incurable. To "rear back" as some do suggests, sometimes unjustly, the idea of arrogance or conceit.

The arms should at first hang quietly by the side. To fold them on the chest is rarely appropriate. To place the hands on the hips, with the fingers forward, seems to indicate defiance; if the fingers are backward, it suggests weakness in the back. To clasp the hands over the abdomen is offensive; and to clasp the hands behind the back, though not offensive, is scarcely graceful. To put them in the coat pockets is inelegant, and in the trousers' pockets is too casual. To stand, as many do, with one hand in the coat or playing with a button is undesirable. It is natural for the arms to hang at first easily by the side until there is occasion to move one or both in gesticulation, and after any gesture they should return to the same position, though in many cases they remain for a while in some intermediate position of comparative repose.

The feet should neither be far apart nor in immediate contact. Their precise position will be determined by the preacher's form and habits, and rules laying down one particular posture should be rejected. The Roman orator commonly stood with the left foot forward because he carried the toga on his left arm, and the ancient soldier advanced the left foot because his left arm carried the shield. No similar causes now exist for regularly advancing the left foot. The reason for choice would seem to be that, if one hand is at any time actively used in gesticulating, it seems natural and easier to have the corresponding foot moved somewhat forward. How often a speaker changes posture will depend on his temperament and his excitement at the time; one need not worry about that unless he happens to be inclined to a restless, fidgety movement, which should be avoided.

Anyone inclined to any of these faults should resolutely correct them. The only real difficulty about correcting such comparatively trifling faults is that preachers will not think them worth the trouble. But nothing that affects a preacher's usefulness is really trifling. Young people have little trouble in curing these bad habits; for those of middle age it will be more difficult. Resolute determination, perseverance, and the development of good habits when out of the pulpit will usually succeed. If such defects really cannot be remedied, one must try not to be worried about them but to do his best in spite of them.

3. Gesture—when posture has been excluded—denotes movement, whether of the whole person, the feet, the body, the head, or the hands. It is not natural for a speaker, if at all animated, to stand perfectly still; but it is important not to fidget about or to walk the platform like a tiger in his cage. Between these extremes, a person will change place more or less freely according to temperament, circumstances, and his own judgment. Stamping the foot may sometimes naturally express indignation or certain other vehement feelings, but it is apt to suggest an impotent rage; and, at any rate, it is scarcely ever becoming in a preacher. Movements of the body, such as rocking to and fro or swaying from side to side, should almost always

be avoided, and bending far forward is rarely proper. The head has a variety of appropriate and expressive movements, but one must beware of awkwardness, extreme vehemence, and monotony.

The arms and hands have to be considered together because in public speaking there can be scarcely any gesture with the hand that is not naturally accompanied by some movement of the arm. The Greeks described the whole art of elocution with the term *chironomy,* or management of the hands. Certainly gestures of the hands and arms are very important. Quintilian says:

The variety of motions possible for the hands is vastly important, for hands almost speak. With them we demand, promise, call, dismiss, threaten, beg, scorn, fear, ask, deny; with them we show a dozen emotions.[8]

It would be tedious to catalogue the faults observed in gestures with the hand and arm. Among the most common are a fluttering of the hands, which with some persons becomes a marked habit; a shoving motion, which is appropriate to express abhorrence or repulsion; and a sort of boxing movement. Some work the arm up and down like a pump handle, and others flap the forearm only, instead of moving the arm from the shoulder with free action. Angular movements are appropriate to certain sentiments but, in general, are very awkward. The palm of the hand, as its most expressive part, should in general be turned towards the audience and somewhat expanded. The clenched hand and the pointed forefinger are very effective when their particular meaning is needed, and otherwise are proportionally inappropriate and damaging.

In all situations, the speaker's bearing should be free, uninhibited, and graceful. Then in speaking he will have little reason to think about posture or gesture and may, without fear, move naturally. In general, one should never repress a movement because he is afraid it might not be graceful. After all, life and power are far more important than social grace; and, in fact, timid inhibition destroys such grace itself. On the other hand, never make any gesture from calculation. It must be the spontaneous product of present feeling or it is unnatural. He who practices or even thinks over his address beforehand and arranges that here or there he will make a certain gesture will inevitably mar his delivery at that point. It is completely unwise to begin gesticulating at any point with the idea that it is now time to begin. The time to begin is when one feels like beginning, neither sooner nor later. A sermon or other speech usually ought to begin quietly, and therefore there will usually be no gestures at the outset.

4. A few simple rules should be added with regard to action of any kind.

a. Action should be suggestive rather than imitative. Closely imitative gestures, except in the case of certain dignified actions, are unsuitable to serious discourse and belong rather to comedy. In saying, "he stabbed him to the heart," one will make some vehement movement of the hand, suggestive of the mortal blow; a movement imitating it would be ridiculous, comic. Even lifting the eyes toward heaven or pointing the finger toward it, or pressing the hand upon the heart, etc., though permissible, are sometimes carried too far or too often repeated.

b. Gesture must never follow, and commonly must slightly precede, the emphatic word of the sentence.[9] It seems to be natural that deep feeling would be more promptly expressed in the instinctive movement than in speech, which is the product of reflection. In argumentative speaking, the gesture will naturally come with the emphatic word.

c. Action must not be excessive in frequency or in vehemence. To some subjects, occasions, or states of feeling in the speaker, it is natural that the action should be rare and slight. Too frequent gesture, like italics in writing and emphasis in speaking, gradually weakens its own effect. Extreme vehemence repulses the hearer, a tendency to just the opposite of what the speaker desires. Hamlet says to the players:

Do not saw the air too much with your hand thus, but use all gently: for in the very torrent, tempest, and (as I may say) whirlwind of your passion, you must acquire and beget a temperance that may give it smoothness.

d. Avoid monotony. Unvarying postures and gestures, again and again repeated, are a somewhat common and very serious fault. Similar to it, though not yet so offensive, is the habitual use of some favorite gesture when the emotion felt would be better expressed by some other. The noticeably frequent recurrence of a word, a tone, or a gesture is always a fault and, as soon as one becomes aware of it, should be carefully avoided.

In conclusion, it is proper to repeat that in all situations there must be life, freedom, power. Do not repress nature, though it must be controlled; and do not force nature. Do not aim at positive improvement in action, but negative—the correction of faults as they appear. Look out for such faults. Now and then ask some true and judicious friend to give an appraisal of both voice and action. Speak out freely and boldly what is felt. A person can never learn to perform any movement gracefully except by performing it frequently without inhibition. Some of a person's faults, in action and in voice, might be a part of himself. Correct them wherever possible; but it is better to let them remain than to replace them either by artificiality or by insipidity.

NOTES

1. Herbert Spencer, *Essays: Moral, Political, and Aesthetic* (New York: D. Appleton and Co., 1865), p. 11.
2. Robert Lewis Dabney, *Sacred Rhetoric* (Richmond: Presbyterian Committee of Publishing, 1870), p. 323.
3. William G. Blaikie, *For the Work of the Ministry* (London: Daldey, Isbister & Co., 1878), p. 234.
4. James M. Hoppin, *Homiletics* (New York: Funk & Wagnalls, 1893), p. 667.
5. Marcus Fabius Quintilianus, *The Institutio Oratoria* (Nashville, Tenn.: George Peabody College for Teachers, 1951), XI, 3, p. 72.

6. Cicero, III, 59, p. 221.
7. Joshua Hall McIlvaine, *Elocution* (New York: Charles Scribner & Co., 1870), p. 409.
8. Quintilian, XI, 3, p. 85.
9. Richard Whately, *Elements of Rhetoric* (New York: Harper & Bros., 1853), p. 445.

CHAPTER 33

Contemporary Approaches to Sermon Delivery

UP to this point, the methods of preparation and delivery presented have been traditional. While variety has been stressed, "the secure old positions and rationales of Broadus and Sangster"[1] have been reexamined without apology. This conventional preaching has its critics. It has been called dying, dead, and decaying; it has been blamed for the failures of the church; it has been called irrelevant and dull. Yet " 'conventional preaching' has been written off too soon. It might be sick or even dead in some areas, but a twenty-minute sermon delivered by the pastor is the most significant communication some persons have all week, even in this day of cool multimedia."[2] For there is a renewed interest in preaching, and many eager worshipers are hearing the preacher's message. Perhaps David H. C. Read was right when he insisted that

. . . it is not the sermon that is obsolete, but many of the methods of those who still believe in it, and all the theories of those who have written it off. For the Word of God is alive in Jesus Christ; the biblical record is alive through the Holy Spirit; and there will still be men and women "sent from God" who are called to declare that Word in the living accents of today and tomorrow.[3]

Nonetheless, it should be helpful to examine the contemporary approaches to sermon delivery. Most of these methods are not really new. They are rediscoveries of approaches that have been used now and again throughout Christian history.

One approach is the letter sermon. The sermon is prepared and presented as a letter or letters to the congregation. This is a recovery of an early church practice. The letters of Paul were read in the context of New Testament worship. "Letter" sermons may be shared with great effectiveness today. Letters from missionaries are highly inspirational. "A Christmas Eve Letter" presented in *Experimental Preaching* is an excellent example of this approach.[4] The letter may also be used as an introduction to the sermon or as a part of the sermon.

Another approach is the short story sermon. The sermon is a short story or is based on a short story. The book of Esther has often been considered a short story. Robert E. Luccock wrote *The Lost Gospel and Other Sermons Based on Short Stories,* a book of sermons drawn from short stories and appropriate texts. Probably the best example of the short story preacher was Jesus. Jesus presented great spiritual truths in story form. The short story may also serve as a highly effective introduction to a sermon.

Another contemporary approach is the parable sermon. This method is closely related to the short story sermon. Again, the parables of Jesus provide the best and most beautiful examples of this method. The world will never forget "A certain man had two sons. . . ." One man preached a sermon entitled, "A Parable That Might Have Been." He took the parable of the rich fool and had him acting wisely instead of foolishly. The man did all the right things. Present-day parables can be used to convey eternal truth.

Still another contemporary approach is the interview sermon. The sermon is an interview between two or more participants. The interview has become a technique used in a big segment of radio and television programming. Consequently, some ministers are using this method as a pattern for sermons. This is an exciting variation of the "old testimony" as the pastor interviews persons who both illustrate and demonstrate some great Christian truths.

Another contemporary approach is to use audio-visual aids in the sermon or as the sermon. The preacher can use records, tape recordings, slides, overhead projectors, filmstrips, or films. These aids can be the vehicle of the sermon, be a part of the sermon, or be the entire message. The Billy Graham Evangelistic Association has produced many films which are used to present Christian truth. In this way, drama is presented as a motion picture.

Yet another approach is the object lesson sermon. This method is most frequently used in children's sermons. In this kind of sermon some object is the central illustration; and the list of objects is endless—a chart, a graph, a map, a book, a placard, clothing, vegetables, or fruit. For example, a plumb line was fastened to the front of a pulpit and hung in full view while a pastor preached on the text concerning the plumb line. Another minister "built" a "diagrammed sentence" and placed the subject, predicate, and object in the sentence at the proper point in the sermon. Others have used a cross or crosses as they preached on the subject of the cross. Some pastors regularly use charts to present programs or budgets. News headlines and magazine articles are used as objects which provide the central lesson of the sermon. Perhaps the most effective object sermon is the "chalk talk"; a picture, depicting the theme of the sermon, is drawn as the preacher talks.

Some form of dramatic presentation is another approach to the sermon. Many plays with a spiritual message have been published. An example of this kind of drama is Phillip William Turner's *Christ and the Concrete City.* Often ministers will write a drama based on some biblical character or event. The drama not only gives the message; it also involves the participation of many people, both in acting and staging.

A variation of this type of presentation is to combine drama and preaching. W. A. Poovey has provided excellent examples of this in two books, *Cross Words* and *Banquets and Beggars.* The first book has seven plays and seven sermons. Both the play and the sermon are based on one of the seven last words of Christ and are presented as a unit. The second book also combines drama and sermon. The six couplets are based on the parables of Jesus and are sermons for some Sunday of the Christian Year. Professor Poovey has written of *Cross Words,*

This book is the result of an experiment which blended drama and preaching in the context of congregational worship. . . . The combination of play and sermon was intended to make real to the contemporary world the truth of the biblical words.

The plays were deliberately made easy to stage and to grasp, so that members of the congregations could participate in the worship service through drama.[5]

Some real possibilities for drama in the pulpit are the story of the Prodigal Son, the Pharisee and the publican at prayer, Elijah confronting the prophets of Baal, and the tragic incident of Ananias and Sapphira. Drama will add new life to familiar stories.

Yet another approach is the dramatic monologue. This is also drama, but it is performed by one person. While not limited to biblical material, this kind of sermon generally depicts a biblical character, episode, story, or text. The biblical narrative is usually expanded. By the appropriate use of imagination, the missing details of an event, the conversation between characters, and the emotions and actions of the situation are added. This kind of preaching requires careful preparation, including the writing of a full manuscript. In addition to a manuscript, some preachers create a set and use costumes, lighting, and sound for dramatic impact.

This first-person preaching is highly dramatic, and thereby more interesting to many listeners. Real life is drama, and people are inherently interested in people. The "eye-witness" presentation also has the strong appeal of personal testimony.

Helpful examples of dramatic monologue preaching are to be found in Frederick B. Speakman, *The Salty Tang* and *Love Is Something You Do,* in G. Curtis Jones, *I Met a Man,* in J. Winston Pearce, *Paul and His Letters,* and in William L. Self, *The Saturday Night Special.*

It must be remembered that many third person sermons are highly dramatic. These sermons also imaginatively portray biblical scenes and events with vivid imagery. The regular monological sermon may also have the high interest appeal of personal testimony.

The most popular contemporary approach to preaching is the dialogue sermon. Today's world has embraced the dialogue technique. Since industry, government, and education use dialogue in seminar and conferences, it was inevitable that it would be applied to preaching. While the dialogue method is not new in preaching, it is being rediscovered and has many proponents. Reuel L. Howe believes that "the weakness of preaching stems from its wordiness and monological character."[6] He also insists that preaching can "have power when it is dialogical, when preacher and people become partners in the discernment and proclamation by word and action of the Word of God in response to the issues of our day."[7] Howe sees dialogue as "that address and response between persons in which there is a flow of meaning between them in spite of all the obstacles that normally would block the relationship."[8]

Thompson and Bennett have placed dialogue "within the experience of public worship."[9] They "define dialogue preaching to be an act within the context of public worship in which two or more persons engage in a verbal exchange as the sermon or message."[10]

Dialogue preaching generally falls into two categories: congregational dialogue and chancel dialogue. In congregational dialogue, the minister usually introduces a theme, and then he and the people share the message by question, comment, and evaluation. Some preachers introduce provocative topics and seek dialogue from the congregation. One pastor raised the question, "Is life really worth living?" in order to precipitate a discussion of the sermon theme, "What Makes Life Worth Living?" The pastor will usually summarize the discussion and apply it to life. Other dialogue sermons are freely written and shared by the dialogists. Excellent examples of this kind of dialogue preaching can be found in Thompson and Bennett, *Dialogue Preaching* and in Killinger, *Experimental Preaching* and *The 11 O'Clock News & Other Experimental Sermons.*

The other major category of dialogue preaching is chancel dialogue. Chancel dialogue involves two or more persons conversing with each other on a predetermined theme. These two persons may be ministers, or minister and layman, or minister and an authority in some field. One noted pastor and his minister of music often shared in chancel dialogue, occasionally combining sermon in word and sermon in song.

Thomas H. Conley has developed a unique form of chancel dialogue. His method and examples of that method are found in his book, *Two in the Pulpit.* In this instance, the two in the pulpit are really one—the preacher. The preacher alternately assumes two roles and has the characters engaging in a lively conversation.

The advantages of dialogue preaching are these: (1) it produces a high "interest level on the part of the congregation," (2) it "gets people involved in the communication of ideas," (3) it "affords opportunity for sharpening issues," (4) it "forces listeners to consider ideas which they might otherwise have blocked out of their minds," (5) and it has a "broadening effect . . . on both preacher and people."[11]

Some disadvantages are also inherent in this approach to the sermon. First, the dialogue sermon requires intensive preparation. More time will be required for the minister to do the general reading related to the specific topic. Otherwise he will not be able to anticipate questions and interpret comments. Moreover, since dialogue preaching is a new method to many congregations, some people will not participate; they will not talk back. This disadvantage may be overcome by teaching the method to the people and by getting them to learn by doing. Then, some listeners may feel that dialogue preaching is not real preaching.[12] Congregations do resist change. Reasonable people can be led to agree, however, that the wonderful "old wine" often needs "new wine skins."

Dialogue preaching may not be for every pastor and every congregation, but for those who are willing to venture, the dialogue approach and the other contemporary sermon approaches will offer a wholesome variety.

Regardless of the method, whether conventional or contemporary, one fact should be kept in mind:

Communicative preaching is dialogical and always has been. It is characterized by the preacher's concern for the attitudes, experiences, and needs of his people. In every aspect of his ministry he must listen to them and respond appropriately to their needs and feelings.[13]

NOTES

1. John Killinger, ed., *Experimental Preaching* (Nashville, Tenn.: Abingdon Press, 1973), p. 17.
2. Wilfred M. Bailey, *Awakened Worship* (Nashville, Tenn.: Abingdon Press, 1972), p. 126.
3. David H. C. Read, *Sent from God* (Nashville, Tenn.: Abingdon Press, 1974), pp. 111–12.
4. Killinger, pp. 111–15.
5. W. A. Poovey, *Cross Words* (Minneapolis: Augsburg Publishing House, 1967), p. 5.
6. Reuel L. Howe, *Partners in Preaching* (New York: Seabury Press, 1967), p. 5.
7. Ibid.
8. Reuel L. Howe, *The Miracle of Dialogue* (Greenwich, Ct.: Seabury Press, 1963), p. 37.
9. William D. Thompson and Gordon C. Bennett, *Dialogue Preaching* (Valley Forge, Penn.: Judson Press, 1969), p. 9.
10. Ibid.
11. Ibid., pp. 68–69.
12. Thomas H. Conley, *Two in the Pulpit* (Waco, Tex.: Word Books, 1973), pp. 12–13.
13. Thompson and Bennett, p. 9.

For Further Reading:
The Delivery of Sermons

Babcock, C. Merton. *The Harper Handbook of Communication Skills.* New York: Harper & Bros., 1957.

Baird, John E. *Preparing for the Platform and Pulpit.* Nashville, Tenn.: Abingdon Press, 1968.

Craig, William C. and Sokolowsky, R. R. *The Preacher's Voice.* Columbus, Ohio: The Wartburg Press, 1946.

Eisenson, Jon. *Voice and Diction: A Program for Improvement.* New York: Macmillan Co., 1974.

Gardner, Charles S. *Psychology and Preaching.* New York: Macmillan Co., 1919.

Harms, Paul. *Power from the Pulpit: Delivering the Good News.* St. Louis: Concordia Publishing House, 1977.

Kirkpatrick, Robert White. *The Creative Delivery of Sermons.* New York: Macmillan Co., 1944.

Macartney, Clarence Edward. *Preaching Without Notes.* New York: Abingdon-Cokesbury Press, 1946.

Mayer, Lyle V. *Fundamentals of Voice and Diction.* Dubuque, Iowa: Wm. C. Brown, 1968.

Stevenson, Dwight E. and Diehl, Charles F. *Reaching People from the Pulpit.* Grand Rapids, Mich.: Baker Book House, 1958.

Storrs, Richard S. *Conditions of Success in Preaching Without Notes: Three Lectures.* New York: Dodd & Mead, 1875.

Welsh, Clement. *Preaching in a New Key.* Philadelphia: United Church Press, 1974.

Part VIII

THE CONDUCT OF
PUBLIC WORSHIP

ONE of the historic functions of the Christian minister is to be a worship leader. Even the preaching comes in the context of worship. In the past some evangelical ministers have given little time to worship leadership. In fact, many of them have not really considered themselves as leaders of worship.

In the last decade, however, there has been a renewed interest in worship in the Christian church. Not only has there been a "liturgical" revival in more ritualistic groups, but also a new interest in worship in "free church" groups.

CHAPTER 34

Planning Worship

THE evangelical minister has discovered that his freedom does not relieve him of the responsibility of planning worship. Indeed, his freedom only heightens his responsibility, for liberty does not mean license, and informality does not mean formlessness. Even without fixed liturgies from other generations, he must plan and construct orders of worship. How can the pastor plan worship which has not only form and order but also variety and spontaneity? How can a leader of worship take the primary materials—the Scriptures, prayer, praise (hymns, anthems, instruments, etc.), sermon, and offering—and blend them into a satisfying worship experience? The answer to these questions is that there is no one way to arrange or to plan worship, but there are certain moods of worship and certain principles which will give guidance in planning.

In recent years, considerable thought has been given to certain moods, or elements, of worship that should be fulfilled in each worship period. Various writers suggest from three to eight of these moods. Five are here listed.

The first mood is generally called recognition. It may also be called adoration or vision. A service of worship should begin with a sense of God, a turning to God, a recognition of God. Various ways may be used to center attention on God. A prelude can create an atmosphere for worship; a call to worship, whether sung or spoken, asks the congregation to worship; an invocation, which seeks the blessing of God, recognizes God; the singing of the Doxology or Gloria Patri glorifies God—all of these may help the service to begin with a sense of God.

Praise of God is also an essential mood in worship. This praise is expressed primarily by hymns or other music. It may also be expressed by appropriate responsive readings or other Scripture readings. Moreover, praise can be and should be expressed in prayer.

After the praise of God which arises spontaneously from sensing his presence, perhaps the next mood of worship will be *confession.* For one to realize the presence of God is for him to be aware of his own unworthiness. This confession may be best expressed in prayer, in hymn or anthem, or by means of a period of silence where each worshiper may confess his own sin. Some congregations use a general prayer of confession which they pray in unison.

Another mood of worship is *illumination.* The heart of the worshiper is ready to receive new light, new guidance. This comes from the Scriptures and from the message. God speaks through his Word and through his messenger. The Holy Spirit gives illumination to the mind of the worshiper.

All the other moods are climaxed by *dedication.* To encounter God, to be moved in mind and heart, is to offer oneself to God. In the worship of most evangelical churches, the opportunity to express this new consecration and resolution is in the invitation. Here responses may be made. The offering can also be an outlet for dedication.

It is possible that several of these moods can be found in the same part of the service, that is, the prayers or the sermon. Moreover, since individual worshipers respond differently, it is difficult to determine just what mood will be created by a particular part of the service. The important consideration is that these moods be expressed in each order of worship.

After the pastor has in mind the moods which should characterize worship, what principles should guide the planning of the service? The basic qualities of good arrangement, which have been discussed earlier, apply to the planning of an order of service.

One quality of planning is unity. The service should be one. This does not mean that there will not be varied materials, elements, and moods. It does mean that the service will have a sense of oneness or wholeness. This unity may be derived from following a central theme, such as peace, thanksgiving, or grace. Many services are centered in one major theme. Because of a heterogeneous congregation, however, this thematic planning is not wise for most services. Generally, the single purpose, to worship God in spirit and truth, will provide sufficient unity. Though varied materials are used, they center in the general thought expressed in the Scriptures and the sermon. Even with diversity of material and mood, a dominant objective will provide unity.

Another quality of good planning is order. While unity has to do with the service as a whole, order has to do with the relation of the parts of the service to one another. The very desire to plan will generally bring a semblance of order to a service. To follow the different moods of worship will also give order to the service. The fact that "order of service" is the heading given to the parts of the worship service implies that order is essential.

A further quality of good planning is proportion. The various parts of the service should be characterized by balance. Each part of the service should be given the proportion of the worship time which its importance demands. If the entire service is to be approximately sixty minutes, then proportionate time should be given to the praise, the prayers, the Scriptures, the sermon, and the other parts of the service. The amount of time given to each part may vary Sunday by Sunday; but if one part of the service is out of proportion, every other part is affected.

Another quality of good planning is movement, or progress. The service should have a sense of forward movement. This is generally accomplished by a printed order of service with one part coming quickly after the part before. This movement is usually provided by the leader of worship who announces each part and gives the service a sense of continuing progress. A service that has a planned order from the call to worship to the invitation will usually be marked by progress.

Still another quality of worship is climax. Since the sermon, ideally conceived, is where God speaks to his people by and through the minister, the climax of the sermon is generally the climax of the service. In many "free-church" services, however, an even greater sense of climax is attained in the invitation where response is made to the truth presented in the sermon. Here the worshipers offer themselves to God in complete dedication.

These moods and principles of worship will help a pastor to plan in a tradition of freedom.

CHAPTER 35

The Sermon in Worship

AS the minister plans to lead worship, he must determine the place of the sermon in worship. Most of the discussion up to this point has dealt with the preparation and delivery of sermons. But the sermon usually comes in the context of a worship service. What is the proper relationship of the sermon in worship?

Two tendencies are to be observed in modern evangelical churches with respect to preaching and worship. One would make preaching primary and the other parts of the church service secondary, at best, nothing more than preparatory to the sermon. The other would give small consideration to the importance of the sermon, magnifying the other parts, which by way of distinction are called "elements of worship." Nonritualistic groups have failed to appreciate properly the spiritual values of orderly worship, of dignity and solemnity of movement, and of congregational participation in responses and otherwise. The service of worship has too often become a "preaching service" in which other elements are no more than an emotional barrage to soften up the congregation for the preacher's attack. On the other hand, the ritualists have tended to discount the sermon. The minister thinks of himself as priest only, not as prophet or evangelist. As the time allotted to the service of worship has been shortened, this subtraction has come from the sermon.

These tendencies will remain where there is no proper evaluation of the various elements of worship. It needs to be said that the sermon itself is an act of worship and should be thought of as an organic part of the service of worship. The following paragraph from Morgan Phelps Noyes's *Yale Lectures* is to the point:

On any theory, the sermon should be for the congregation a creative experience in which they know themselves to be in the presence of God. Therefore, the sermon cannot arrive at God at the end of an argument, or at the end of a meandering process not to be dignified by the name of argument, nor can references to God be arbitrarily thrust into the concluding paragraph of a sermon where they seem ill at ease and out of place, but the whole sermon must be lived in the presence of God whether the references to Him be explicit or implicit. Some continuity of thought between the service of worship and the sermon helps to band the two together into one bundle of life. This continuity should not be so pronounced as to become monotony. Worship moves through a variety of moods, and if every hymn and every prayer center too directly in the same thought, the service as a whole loses a richness which it may rightfully claim. And yet if the sermon deals with a large theme the worship of the hour will naturally voice aspirations, thanksgivings, and confessions which come within the same orbit. . . . If the sermon links the worshiper with his Christian heritage in the Bible and the church, if it keeps constantly in touch with "the timely and the timeless," if it lays hold on the worshiper so that as he listens he makes his response not to the preacher but to God whose Word finds the worshiper through the sermon, then legitimately it may be said that the sermon is not distinct from the church's act of worship but is a living part of that worship.[1]

But many sermons do not appear to be an integral part of the worship service. Indeed, the preacher may not give the impression of sharing in worship. If a sermon should be an act of worship, how can it be made so?

For a sermon to be an act of worship, the preacher must see himself as a leader of worship. He is not a master of ceremonies or a program expediter; he is a worship leader. One of the historic functions of the Christian minister is worship leadership. When the minister feels that he is a leader of worship, he projects a new spirit or atmosphere into the service.

Again, the minister must believe that the sermon is an act of worship. It should be, first of all, an act of worship for him. A sermon is an offering from the preacher to God. P. T. Forsyth said that the sermon is addressed to the people but offered to God. The sermon then is an act of worship before it is preached. When the minister comes to preach, he stands in God's stead and speaks for him.

Moreover, for a sermon to be an act of worship, it must be drawn from the Scriptures. If the preacher is to speak for God, he must go to where God has spoken. The preacher does not create his basic message; it has been given to him. His task is to interpret, to illustrate, to apply. One definition of preaching is, "Preaching is giving the Bible a voice." When a preacher confesses that he has nothing to preach, he is really confessing that he has stopped reading the Bible. Frank Cairns said in *The Prophet of the Heart:*

> The Christian preacher is one who stands in Christ's stead, and realizes that the function of his sermons is nothing else and less than to give the words Christ has given him to the people he has been called on to serve. It is to proclaim the Word of God, and it is that Word which inspires true worship.[2]

Again, for a sermon to be an act of worship it must be baptized in prayer. Often preachers read the apostles' declaration. "We will devote ourselves to prayer, and to the ministry of the word" (Acts 6:4) without seeing the vital relationship. Prayer and the ministry of the word belong together. When the minister comes before God and seeks his message, when he asks for the Holy Spirit to give him insight and power, then his preaching is an act of worship.

George Whitefield gives this dramatic account of his first serious Bible study:

> I began to read the Holy Scriptures on my knees, laying aside all other books, and praying over . . . every line and word. This proved meat indeed and drink indeed to my soul. . . . I thus got more true

knowledge in reading the book of God in one month than I could ever have acquired from all the writings of men.[3]

When preaching is immersed in a spirit of prayer, it becomes an act of worship.

Above all other things, for a sermon to be an act of worship there must be a dependence on the Holy Spirit. The real power of the preacher is the presence of the Spirit of God. Only he can truly teach; only he can freely convince; only he can bring regeneration. Often ministers do not have this power because they do not ask for it. The last prayer prayed before the preacher enters the pulpit should be a prayer for the Spirit of God. It is he who magnifies and intensifies our worship and changes a cold, dull service into a warm, moving one. The presence of the Spirit means a genuine encounter with God.

The sermon, then, should be a climactic act of worship. For in the preaching, God moves to us and speaks to us. Through the preacher, God's word is carried to his people.

NOTES

1. Morgan Phelps Noyes, *Preaching the Word of God* (New York: Charles Scribner's Sons, 1943), pp. 178–79.
2. Frank Cairns, *The Prophet of the Heart* (New York: Harper & Bros., 1935), p. 40.
3. Joseph Belcher, *George Whitefield: A Biography* (New York: American Tract Society, 1857), p. 32.

CHAPTER 36

Other Parts of the Worship Service

THE valuation of the sermon as an act of worship will accentuate at the same time the worship value of song, prayer, reading, and offering. The need is not more of one and less of the other but of fusing all into a harmonious, worshipful whole. This does not mean that the freedom, spontaneity, simplicity, and spirituality of New Testament worship should be abandoned. The failure of many worship services to satisfy people's souls is not that they are too simple or too free. The dissatisfaction is often caused, at least in part, by the coldness, lack of animation, lack of transition, and general slovenliness which in so many cases characterize worship. The preacher must pay far more attention to this than is common, both in the way of general cultivation and in preparation for each particular part of the worship service.

1. READING THE SCRIPTURES

1. In selecting the portion or portions of Scripture to be read, the pastor should choose those which are very devotional; for example, many of the Psalms, passages from the Pentateuch,

from Isaiah and other prophets, from the Gospels, Epistles, and Revelation. These will not only instruct but will inspire devout feeling. The particular kind of devotional passages selected, and the general tone of the sermon should harmonize. To read a sad passage and afterward preach a joyful sermon, or vice versa, would be inappropriate. Still, a general harmony is sufficient; great effort to find an exact correspondence is unnecessary and sometimes artificial.

But there are many cases in which the preacher wishes to read the text of his sermon. If this text is highly devotional in tone, it may be read as a part of the worship. If the preacher's text is sufficient in length, he may let it serve as the Scripture reading. Additional Scripture can be brought into the service by sharing a responsive reading from the hymnal. Good taste and devout feeling should govern the selection of Scripture to be read, and there should be an interesting variety without seeking after novelty.

2. To read well is a rare accomplishment. It is much more common to excel in singing or in public speaking. Good preachers are numerous compared with good readers. The requisites to good reading are several. First, one must have quickness of apprehension, understanding the meaning of whole sentences at a glance. One of the most common faults is to begin reading a sentence with an expression which is not appropriate to its end. The reader must always keep clearly in mind the entire context and read every sentence as part of a greater whole. This also shows the need of familiarity with what is read, and, if not with the language of the passage, at any rate with its subject matter. A second requisite is sensitivity, so as not only to understand but promptly and thoroughly to sympathize with the sentiment. Probably this is more often wanting than the former. There must also be great flexibility of voice to be able to express immediately and exactly every varying shade of feeling. And finally, public reading requires ample and careful practice. He who reads well must of course be a master of correct pronunciation and must have acquired a distinct and easy articulation. Beyond these, everything is included in what we call "expres-

sion"; and power of expression, so far as it is not a natural gift, must be acquired by disciplined practice. Each passage of Scripture should be read aloud in private at least twice before it is read in public. Some preachers in the course of their preparation will frequently memorize the passage; nevertheless, it should be read rather than recited. The latter tends to call attention to the preacher's memory and not to the meaning of what is read.

3. It was once a very common practice, and is still wisely done by some, to make explanatory remarks in connection with the reading. These should not be so numerous or extensive as to usurp the attention due the passage itself. If there has been thorough study of the passage, and if the preacher has taken pains to acquire skill in commentary, there may be brief, lively, and yet devout remarks that will make this part of public worship far more interesting and profitable. But random remarks, made without study and without skill, only interrupt the reading and sometimes interfere with its movement.

4. Highly important is that the worship service have adequate Scripture reading. Some "free church" services have only a verse or two of Scripture, and some evangelical churches are most unlike the New Testament church in this respect. The pastor has the responsibility to share the Bible with the congregation.

2. PRAISE

The Christian church received a rich legacy of musical praise from Judaism, as well as a wonderful heritage of exhortation and prayer in the Scriptures. For centuries, devout Jews gave expression to their worship of the living God by singing. This singing was often accompanied by musical instruments and was shared by the entire congregation. When the Christian church took form, praise was a part of its worship. It had a pattern of congregational singing, and the Psalter was its hymnbook. This was normal when Christians shared in synagogue worship. However, the psalms were used in distinctively Christian worship. The hymn used at the institution of the Lord's Supper—"After singing a hymn, they went out" (Mark 14:26)—probably was a psalm. And this practice continued.

The Christians not only sang psalms; they began immediately to develop hymns on Christian themes. Scholars feel that hymn fragments are found in the New Testament. The songs in Luke's Gospel, the songs of Zacharias, Mary, and Simeon—usually called the Benedictus, the Magnificat, and Nunc Dimittis—may have been used in the worship of the early church. The singing of the psalms and hymns was congregational. The congregation participated and gave voice to its praise. Some of the praise seemed to be spontaneous praise to the Lord Jesus Christ. Paul probably referred to this kind of praise when he urged the Ephesians to continue "singing and making melody with your heart to the Lord" (Eph. 5:19), and the Colossians to sing "with grace in your hearts to the Lord" (Col. 3:16, KJV).

As time passed, congregational singing almost ceased. Congregational participation also was lost. The Reformation not only recovered many practices of the New Testament and the early church, but it also gave the congregational hymn back to the people. Some believe that the Reformation reached its highest point of success when the New Testament pattern of congregational singing was so nearly restored.[1]

Congregational singing as it is known today did not develop until the eighteenth century. The hymns of Isaac Watts and John and Charles Wesley began this movement. The Wesleyan revival in England, the Great Awakening in America, the later evangelical revival in America, and the frontier revivals—all resulted in a tradition of congregations singing hymns and gospel songs. This practice developed a vast storehouse of evangelical music.

From this heritage of musical praise, many different types of praise have come into being. A knowledge of these types, both vocal and instrumental, will help worship leaders to give variety to praise in a given service. (1) The prelude is primarily an aid to worship. It calls attention to the fact that public worship is beginning, and it creates an attitude of expectancy in the worshiper as the beginning of the service approaches. (2) A call to worship reminds the worshiper that worship is beginning. Its first aim is to center attention upon God. A call to worship may be spoken or sung. A choral call to worship, such as "The Lord Is in His Holy Temple," not only calls the people to worship, but also is an act of praise itself. (3) Another kind of praise is the response. It is usually a response to prayer and may be a prayer continued. Though the response can serve as an aid to worship, it can also be an act of worship. In the New Testament, the people responded with the "Amen!" A choral amen is for the people. "Hear Our Prayer, O Lord" may express the heart's desire of the congregation. Congregations could sing such responses. (4) Another kind of praise is the solo and ensemble music, or "special music," as it is sometimes called. The choir, a small group, or a soloist may contribute the "extra" praise to the service. Such special praise can lift the congregation to an even higher level of worship. Often, the theme of such praise is similar to the theme of the sermon and creates an atmosphere for it. Also, the theme of this special praise may be related to the objective of the message and can prepare for its fulfillment. Care should be taken that the music by the choir or soloist is not performed for its own sake. Musical presentations offered to God and given for his glory stimulate worship. (5) The hymn is the kind of praise most frequently used. It may be a stately hymn or a gospel song; it may be objective or subjective; it may be addressed to God or to the people. But regardless of type, hymns comprise a large segment of each service. For the congregation to sing with the heart and understanding is in keeping with the spirit of the New Testament. Through the hymns, the congregation can voice its praise to God. This part of the worship belongs to the people and should not be minimized.

Since music in worship is important, some general advice about praise is offered for the worship leader. (1) Firsthand knowledge of the hymnal will be valuable to anyone who is responsible for planning worship and selecting hymns. Far too many congregations use only a limited number of hymns. The limit is not only in number, but also in the range of themes. A leader who has the regular task of selecting hymns should know the contents of the hymnbook. Most hymnals have a wide variety. A knowledge of the hymnal and other facets of praise will increase any worship leader's ability to help others in their worship of God. (2) Choose hymns which center in God—God, the Father; God, the Son; and God, the Holy Spirit. Select hymns which praise God for what he has done for man in Christ. Sing hymns which reveal God at work in his mighty redemptive mission. Some songs detract from a God-centered emphasis when they are addressed to man and not to God. It might not be good to eliminate all subjective songs addressed to humankind, but their use should be limited. Our praise should be addressed primarily to God. (3) Select hymns to meet the needs of various segments of the congregation. The average congregation has people of various educational, cultural, and age levels. Hymns around a topic or theme may be used, but a varied selection will probably contribute more to the people. One hymn or one special song might be the only part of the service which has meaning for a worshiper. Therefore, hymns chosen on different, yet related, topics may prove the most helpful to the majority of listeners. (4) The minister should participate in the praise. All the hymns or other acts of praise are also the minister's praise. Dean Brown of Yale once declared:

Sing yourself! Do it as a means of grace to your own soul. Do it as a bit of godly example to your people. The lazy, shiftless minister who announces a hymn and then goes back to his chair and sits down while the people stand up and sing it, as if praising God were no affair of his, ought to be cast out of the synagogue.[2]

3. PUBLIC PRAYER

The prayers form an important part of public worship. The one who leads a congregation in prayer, who undertakes to express what they feel, or ought to feel, before God, to voice their adoration, thanksgiving, confession, supplication, assumes a very heavy responsibility. It is a solemn thing for the minister to speak to the people for God; is it less important when he speaks to God for the people? Whatever preparation is possible for performing this duty should surely be most carefully made. And yet, while few now question the propriety of preparation, both general and special, for the work of preaching, many preachers still completely neglect to prepare themselves for the conduct of public prayer.

The general preparation for leading in public prayer consists chiefly in the following things: (1) The best preparation for public prayer is the regular habit of private prayer. If it is true that "the only way to learn to preach is to preach," it is still more emphatically true that the only way to learn to pray is to pray. And while some people do tolerate preaching for practice, most will condemn praying for practice. It is thus plain that no one will regularly pray well in public who does not pray often and devoutly in private. In every attempt to pray, under whatever circumstances, one should earnestly try to understand what he is doing. (2) Familiarity with Scripture, both as furnishing topics of prayer and in supplying the most appropriate language of prayer, will aid the preacher. The minister should be constantly storing in his memory the more directly devotional expressions found everywhere in the Bible, and especially in the Psalms and Prophets, the Gospels, Epistles, and Revelation. (3) Another aid in preparation will be the study of instructive examples of prayer. In the Bible there are found, besides the numerous single devotional expressions, various examples of complete prayers. These should be carefully studied, for instruction in the subject matter and the manner of praying. Some of the long-established liturgies are also very instructive. However sincerely some may oppose the imposition of any form of prayer, there is certainly much to be learned from studying carefully prepared forms of able and devout people. More modern works will also repay occasional examination.[3] The study of devotional works is also helpful. (4) The nature of public prayer should be clearly understood. Public prayer is more than private prayer. In private prayer, a Christian is under no special restraints. He is in conversation with his Lord and may follow his own moods. But in public prayer, the leader is doing more than offering a private prayer in public. He is attempting to offer a prayer for all the people. Public prayer is a corporate act; the one prayer is made in behalf of all those present. The leader

... is called to the delicate task of enlisting the minds, consciences, aspirations, and wills of a heterogeneous collection of people in one corporate act of dedication. He must speak for them ... and he must make it possible for them in their hearts to be at one with him as he addresses the Most High God in their behalf.[4]

The leader of prayer is faced with an awesome responsibility. His prayer must be more than a monologue to which the people listen. It must include the common petitions and desires of the people so that they actually share in it. In corporate prayer, the leader says the words, but the congregation prays. Public prayer is common prayer; the minister is to offer the prayers of the whole congregation.

This act of worship cannot be done in any careless, haphazard fashion. The conduct of corporate prayer is an art. The more knowledge a leader has of the task, the more likely he is to fulfill his important responsibility.

Corporate prayer can be expressed in a variety of ways. The leader of worship should be familiar with the different methods.

1. Extemporaneous or "free" prayer is the most commonly used method of praying in the free church tradition. This prayer is said as it comes to the person praying in the moment of delivery. He might have a general organization which he follows, but the objects of thanks, the sins confessed, the petitions, and the intercessions are those which come to the mind of the pastor as the prayer is offered.

Spontaneous prayer is the kind of prayer found in the New Testament and in the very early church. Every evangelical pastor or deacon should be able to lead a congregation in prayer when called upon to do so. The disadvantage of the extemporaneous method is that it sometimes lacks order, and the same elements and objects of prayer may be repeated service after service. Extemporaneous prayer is sometimes disorganized and irrelevant.

2. The corporate prayers can be prepared by the pastor. The minister decides what he will say in the different prayers in the service. He can prepare an outline, or he can write the prayer in detail. In common practice, few evangelical ministers write their prayers, and still fewer read them. But planned public prayer will generally be more intelligible and meaningful to the congregation.

3. Another method of public prayer is the collect. This kind of prayer is found in one of the historic liturgies. It can also be contemporary. A classic example is the beautiful invocation taken from the Gregorian Sacramentary:

> Almighty God, unto whom all hearts be open, all desires known, and from whom no secrets are hid, cleanse the thoughts of our hearts by the inspiration of thy Holy Spirit, that we may perfectly love thee, and worthily magnify thy holy name; through Christ our Lord. Amen.[5]

Many other usable collects are found in compilations of public prayer. The occasional use of a collect can offer some variety to the prayers of a worship service.

4. Another method of corporate prayer is the litany. In a litany, the minister offers a petition and the congregation responds. This type of prayer is usually printed in the order of service. Some groups engage in this kind of prayer only on special occasions such as the dedication of a sanctuary. Litanies could be used more often and would allow the congregation another avenue of participation in the service.

5. Still another way of praying is bidding prayer. This kind of prayer is guided meditation. The leader of worship asks the congregation to keep in mind one of the elements of prayer, or to pray for some specific object. For example, the leader might say, "Let us give thanks," or, "Let us pray for those who are sick." After each "bidding" to prayer, the leader allows time for the congregation to pray. This type of prayer lends itself to the evening service and to the prayer service.

6. Still another method of praying is the silent prayer. The pastor or worship leader calls upon the members of the congregation to pray silently. Most congregations appreciate sharing

in this kind of prayer. However, one caution should be observed. When the people are asked to engage in silent prayer, sufficient time should be allowed for them to pray. Some worship leaders call upon the congregation to pray and, then, do not give the members time.

Corporate prayer is not limited to one kind or method. Many types and methods of prayer are available to every worship leader.

Knowledge of certain qualities of public prayer will also assist the pastor in the leadership of such prayers.

One essential quality of corporate prayer is brevity. When people have their heads bowed and their eyes closed, it is difficult for them to maintain attention for a long time. Long prayers lose the congregation and are not effective. Remember that there are four or five prayers in most services. Each prayer, with the possible exception of the pastoral prayer, should be brief.

Order is a most important quality of public prayer. In corporate prayer, the elements and objects should not be mingled. For example, when the leader engages in thanks, he should include all the objects. He should not give thanks, offer petition, and return to giving thanks. In private prayer, a person praying may follow any order, but in public prayer, where many minds are involved, the leader should have a planned order.

Another necessary quality is concreteness. Many prayers suffer from vague generalities. The leader gives thanks "for all of our blessings," or he calls upon the Lord to "forgive us our sins." One who prays should specify the blessings and the sins. Since there are many in each category, different ones can be cited on successive Sundays until the whole range of thanks and sins have been mentioned in prayer.

Public prayer should be comprehensive. It should cover the range of major elements: adoration, thanksgiving, confession, petition, intercession, and dedication. A variety of objects under these elements should be expressed in the four or five prayers of a Sunday morning service. Of course, not all objects can be mentioned in one service, but they can be shared over a period of Sundays. This range of elements and objects should bring a wholesome variety to the prayers of a service.

Some practical advice might prove helpful to the leader of public prayer.

The prayer should be easily heard. It need not be loud. Just as God does not hear the worshiper for his lengthy speaking, neither does he hear him for his loud speaking. Yet, the prayer must be heard if it is to fulfill its purpose. The leader is offering a prayer for all of the people. If the people do not hear, they cannot participate. Sometimes when lay people and others are called upon to lead in prayer, the prayer is not heard. It is always better when the one leading in prayer faces the congregation. Therefore, the one leading in prayer should be on the platform. Prayer will be heard better if the one praying will lift up his head when he begins to speak. The leader of prayer should "bow" his heart, but lift up his head and his voice so that he can be heard.

Prayer is addressed to God and should be communication with him. It should not be talk about God which is directed to the people. There is a time to preach and a time to pray. When prayer leaves the direct address of the second person and drops into the third person, the leader is preaching and not praying. Occasionally, a listener feels that the pastor may be concluding the sermon in prayer and telling the people something he did not have the courage to say in the sermon. Those responsible for public prayer should not use it as an occasion to preach.

Since public prayer is addressed to God, it should not be used to make announcements to the people. Some leaders of worship, forgetting to make announcements at the proper time, incorporate them into prayer. When announcements are made or when other information is given to the congregation as a part of a prayer, then prayer ceases to be prayer.

The leader should let the congregation know that he is going to pray. He should not just slip into prayer. If he suddenly begins to pray, some worshipers will participate and some will not. Others will be embarrassed when they discover that they are not participating. A leader may give a common signal for prayer, such as the outstretched arm with palm down. Or he may simply say to the people, "Let us pray."

4. OFFERING

While the offering will take less time in the service than the areas just discussed, it is nonetheless an important part of worship. The offering should be seen not as a collection but an act of worship. Since the giving of money represents a combination of life, talent, and time being shared with God, it is a significant act of worship. The offering can be a time of real dedication as the worshiper first gives himself and then his means to God.

The worship leader may use a variety of methods for the offertory. As is customary in many services, he might have a prayer before the offering. He can also share a Scripture sentence before the offering and have a prayer of dedication after the offering. Then he could have the congregation sing the Doxology before the offering and have a prayer after. A few worship leaders have led a prayer of thanksgiving before the offering and a prayer of dedication after it.

While sermons on stewardship themes should be a regular part of preaching, the time before the offering is not the time for exhortations on giving. Stewardship sermons preached throughout the year will create a much better atmosphere toward giving. Announcements concerning giving and pleas for increased giving develop a bad mood before the offering.

A good mood or even a joyful mood should characterize the offering. The Scripture teaches that God loves a cheerful giver. If the worship leader can create a sense of dedication to God and show that the offering is an opportunity to express that dedication, then the offering can indeed be a time of celebration.

Just as the pastor participates in every act of worship, he should also participate in the offering. By being an example of regular giving, he can lead his people to give too.

5. PULPIT DECORUM

The worship leader should give careful attention to certain rules of pulpit decorum. (1) Each worship service should begin at the appointed hour. Punctuality is a virtue in every area, and worship is no exception. To begin a service late is an inconvenience to those worshipers who are present and only encourages continuing tardiness on the part of those who are habitually late. (2) A service should be kept in generally understood time limits. The "worship hour" should probably not be an hour and a half. By the careful planning of each part of the service, the leader will usually be able to control the length of the service. When there is some unusual gift of the Spirit in a service, the congregation will not be aware of time, and any lengthening of the service will not be noticed. (3) The manner of entering the church or the pulpit should be neither bold nor affectedly humble, neither careless nor sanctimonious. The preacher should be thinking of God's truth, of worshiping God, and be full of a desire to edify and save souls. (4) Also, two ministers should not talk together during the service. In case of any special services, such as ordinations, funerals, dedications, when several ministers are to take part, the details should be carefully arranged and thoroughly understood beforehand, so as to prevent awkwardness and unnecessary conference during the service. (5) A preacher should never exhibit irritation at inattention or misconduct in the audience. In the great majority of cases, public rebukes are better omitted. They often give offence, and the good they do might usually be accomplished in some other way. A kind but firm word in private is commonly much better. (6) The preacher's behavior in the pulpit should be natural and relaxed, but not too relaxed. He should never slouch or half-recline in the pulpit chair. His demeanor should express quiet dignity. (7) Finally, a preacher should guard his behavior immediately after a service. When a service or a sermon has made great emotional demands upon the preacher, he may tend to let down afterward. Some members of the congregation might not understand how the preacher who was so serious during the sermon can now be so lighthearted. In order not to give the false impression that his earlier dignity was not sincere, it will be necessary for the preacher to be conscious of the effect of his behavior after a service.

NOTES

1. Illion T. Jones, *A Historical Approach to Evangelical Worship* (New York: Abingdon Press, 1954), p. 258.
2. Charles Reynolds Brown, *The Art of Preaching* (New York: Macmillan Co., 1948), p. 207.
3. See Morgan Phelps Noyes, *Prayers for Services* (New York: Charles Scribner's Sons, 1947); see also S. F. Fox, *A Chain of Prayer Across the Ages* (New York: E. P. Dutton and Co., 1943).
4. Noyes, p. 180.
5. Noyes, p. 36.

For Further Reading:
The Conduct of Public Worship

Barry, James C. and Gulledge, Jack, comps. and eds. *Ideas for Effective Worship Services.* Nashville, Tenn.: Southern Baptist Convention Press, 1977.

Keir, Thomas H. *The Word in Worship.* London: Oxford University Press, 1962.

Knox, John. *The Integrity of Preaching.* New York: Abingdon Press, 1957.

Macleod, Donald. *Word and Sacrament.* Englewood Cliffs, N.J.: Prentice-Hall, 1960.

Palmer, Albert W. *The Art of Conducting Public Worship.* New York: Macmillan Co., 1940.

Randolph, David J. *God's Party.* Nashville, Tenn.: Abingdon Press, 1975.

Segler, Franklin M. *Christian Worship.* Nashville, Tenn.: Broadman Press, 1967.

White, James F. *Christian Worship in Transition.* Nashville, Tenn.: Abingdon Press, 1976.

——————. *New Forms of Worship.* Nashville, Tenn.: Abingdon Press, 1971.

Index